U-Boats Beyond Biscay

Other books by Bernard Edwards

Masters Next to God
They Sank the Red Dragon
The Fighting Tramps
The Grey Widow Maker
Blood and Bushido
SOS – Men Against the Sea
Salvo!
Attack and Sink
Dönitz and the Wolf Packs
Return of the Coffin Ships
Beware Raiders!
The Road to Russia
The Quiet Heroes
The Twilight of the U-boats
Beware the Grey Widow Maker
Death in the Doldrums
Japan's Blitzkrieg
War of the U-boats
Royal Navy Versus the Slave Traders
The Cruel Sea Retold
War Under the Red Ensign 1914-1918
The Wolf Packs Gather
Convoy Will Scatter

U-Boats Beyond Biscay

Dönitz Looks to New Horizons

Bernard Edwards

Pen & Sword
MARITIME

First published in Great Britain in 2017 by
PEN & SWORD MARITIME
An imprint of
Pen & Sword Books Ltd
47 Church Street
Barnsley
South Yorkshire
S70 2AS

ISBN 978 1 47389 6 055

A CIP catalogue record for this book is available from the British Library.

Printed and bound in Malta
by Gutenberg Press Ltd

Pen & Sword Books Ltd incorporates the Imprints of Pen & Sword Aviation, Pen & Sword Family History, Pen & Sword Maritime, Pen & Sword Military, Pen & Sword Discovery, Pen & Sword Politics, Pen & Sword Atlas, Pen & Sword Archaeology, Wharncliffe Local History, Wharncliffe True Crime, Wharncliffe Transport, Pen & Sword Select, Pen & Sword Military Classics, Leo Cooper, The Praetorian Press, Claymore Press, Remember When, Seaforth Publishing and Frontline Publishing.

For a complete list of Pen & Sword titles please contact
PEN & SWORD BOOKS LIMITED
47 Church Street, Barnsley, South Yorkshire, S70 2AS, England
E-mail: enquiries@pen-and-sword.co.uk
Website: www.pen-and-sword.co.uk

For those who voyage in deep waters

Now quietly falls the night whose crimson dawn
Will find us far from here. The unmarked ocean's ways
Will know our passing: morning's golden haze
Open to greet us, and the mellowed horn
Of kinder winds than these cold northern airs
Blow softer notes in welcome.

Michael Fitzgerald Page

Contents

Preface

A great deal has been written about the U-boats that stalked the North Atlantic convoy lanes, hunting in packs and preying on the merchantmen huddled together for mutual protection. Directed from Lorient in southern Brittany through the powerful transmitters of Norddeich Radio, they reaped a rich and continuous harvest and came within an ace of cutting the vital supply lines that kept the granaries and arsenals of Britain stocked.

It had not always been so. At the outbreak of war in September 1939 Admiral Dönitz had, at the most, thirty U-boats operational, and only six to eight of these would be at sea at any one time. Of necessity, their activities were restricted mainly to the North Sea and British coastal waters, and they rarely ventured past 12½° west. This changed when France fell in the summer of 1940 and a whole range of ports in the Bay of Biscay became available as bases. No longer did the U-boats have to make the hazardous 450-mile-long passage around the north of Scotland to enter the Atlantic. This meant more boats at sea more often, and Dönitz's grey wolves now ranged 1,000 miles deep into the Atlantic, while the Royal Navy was unable to supply escorts much beyond the Western Approaches. This was a recipe for disaster, and resulted in the U-boats sinking 500,000 tons of precious Allied shipping a month, every month.

With more boats at his disposal, Admiral Dönitz now looked over the far horizons, to the western Atlantic, the tree-lined coasts of Africa and the shallow waters of the Mediterranean, where Allied merchantmen sailed alone and unprotected. Here was another harvest to be gathered in, and it was a job for the long-range U-boats, the silent hunter killers, sometimes operating alone, on occasions with others, but always far from their bomb-proof concrete burrows on the coast of Biscay. This is their story.

CHAPTER ONE

Far Away Places

U-111 was a lone hunter, one of the shadowy outriders of Hitler's U-boat arm operating beyond the convoy routes. A Type IXB long-range boat, she was well equipped for the work in hand, having a top speed of 18½ knots on the surface and a cruising range of 12,000 miles at 10 knots. Her armament, too, was formidable: four bow and two stern torpedo tubes, a 105mm deck gun and, for defence against air attack, a quadruple-barrelled 20mm AA gun mounted abaft her conning tower. She was crewed by four officers, three chief petty officers, fourteen petty officers and thirty ratings, and carried one officer in training. In command was *Kapitänleutnant* Wilhelm Kleinschmidt.

Thirty-four-year-old Kleinschmidt had served seven years in German merchant ships before transferring to the *Kriegsmarine* in the early 1930s. Sailing first in motor torpedo boats and then as torpedo officer in light cruisers, he joined the U-boat arm in the spring of 1940 with a wealth of real sea-going experience behind him. After training, and one short war patrol in U-124 with Georg-Wilhelm Schulz, he was given command of the newly-commissioned U-111.

Kleinschmidt was described as being 'a most careful U-boat captain', and there seems to be no doubt that his service in merchant ships, where the safety of ship, cargo and crew is paramount, had a lasting influence on his approach to command. While he was a competent commander, he was not one to take those unnecessary risks which were really the stock-in-trade of a successful U-boat captain. Some said he was too old for the job, and they might well have been right. What is quite certain is that Kleinschmidt was sailing at a disadvantage in U-111, in that he had with him a largely inexperienced crew. His first lieutenant, 24-year-old *Leutnant-zur-See* Helmut Fuchs, had previously completed only one war cruise, and of U-111's petty officers and ratings only five had any experience of submarines before joining the boat. Coupled with this, Kleinschmidt had on board an officer in training for command, *Korvettenkapitän* Hans-Joachim Heinecke, who was his senior in rank. And to compound an already uncomfortable situation, U-111's junior watch officer, *Oberleutnant-zur-See* Friedrich-Wilhelm Rösing, happened to be the brother of the influential *Korvettenkapitän* Hans Rösing, formerly commanding officer of the 3rd U-boat Flotilla. There were too many watchful eyes at Kleinschmidt's back.

On his first war patrol in U-111, beginning in Wilhelmshaven on 5 May 1941, Kleinschmidt confounded his detractors by sinking two British merchantmen and damaging another in his first three weeks at sea. He opened his score with the 5,170-ton West Hartlepool steamer *Somersby*, sailing with the 28-ship convoy SC 30. The convoy ran into dense fog south of Iceland, and the *Somersby* straggled astern. Kleinschmidt put three torpedoes into her and she capsized and sank, taking her cargo of 8,000 tons of grain to the bottom with her. Secondly, Kleinschmidt torpedoed the 13,037-ton Eagle Oil tanker *San Felix* shortly after she dispersed from Convoy OB 322. The tanker was hit by one of two torpedoes fired by Kleinschmidt and was last seen with a heavy list disappearing into a rain squall. Being then in ballast, the *San Felix* did not sink, but she would spend the next five months in port under repair. Lastly, Kleinschmidt disposed of the 4,813-ton Whitby steamer *Barnby*, carrying 7,250 tons of bagged flour from St Johns, New Brunswick to Hull. She sank off Iceland on 22 May 1941. It is worthy of note that of the 131 crew members carried by these three ships, only three were lost. Such a low casualty rate may have been in part due to Wilhelm Kleinschmidt's entrenched regard for his fellow merchant seamen.

U-111 sailed from Lorient on her second patrol on 14 August 1941, with orders to cruise off Freetown, Sierra Leone, then a major convoy assembly port for Allied shipping. The indications were that this could be a prolonged voyage and Kleinschmidt, who had become engaged to be married while on leave, might have been excused if he faced it with a certain lack of enthusiasm.

When she left Lorient, U-111 was well prepared for a long voyage, every available space on board being packed with extra provisions, ammunition and spares. She carried eighteen torpedoes, six in the tubes, six in the bilges, two on the floor plates forward and four in the containers on the upper deck. In her fuel tanks were 160 tons of diesel.

The start of the voyage was not auspicious. Although the weather was fine at first, by sunset rain had set in, and under a heavy overcast sky the night that followed was dark and ominous. U-111 had not been many hours at sea when her patrol was almost brought to a sudden and premature end. She was saved by the eyes of an alert lookout, who spotted the track of a torpedo racing towards her. Kleinschmidt, equally alert, ordered the helm hard over, and the anonymous missile passed within a few feet of the U-boat and disappeared into the night. The torpedo may have come from a British submarine, or from another U-boat. Kleinschmidt would never know.

While crossing the Bay of Biscay U-111 was in notoriously dangerous waters, being within range of British reconnaissance aircraft based in the south of England and at Gibraltar. These planes, usually four-engined Sunderland flying boats, flew regular patrols over the Bay. They carried up to sixteen guns and a lethal assortment of bombs and depth charges, and were equipped with the new centimetric radar capable of picking up a surfaced U-boat at 7 miles.

Fortunately for U-111, no British aircraft were in evidence when she crossed Biscay, and thirty-six hours after leaving Lorient she had rounded Cape Finisterre and was heading south. She reached the vicinity of Freetown on the 22nd, where Kleinschmidt anticipated a busy time operating against ships northbound from West Africa and the Cape, but found only blue skies and an empty horizon.

After several frustrating days spent lying in wait, Kleinschmidt decided to move south of the Equator. There he found a similar lack of targets. Finally, after fourteen days at sea without sighting a single enemy ship, Lorient ordered him to try his luck further west, off the coast of Brazil.

At that time, Allied merchant ships sailing between the Cape of Good Hope and American ports were unescorted, following the old sailing ship route across the South Atlantic, passing between Fernando de Noronha Island and St Paul's Rocks, off the coast of Brazil. This was considered to be a safe route, as no U-boat had yet been known to venture into these waters; the only threat was from German surface raiders, and they were few in number. U-111 was about to put an end to this equable state of affairs.

On the afternoon of 10 September 1941, U-111 was cruising in the region of St Paul's Rocks, a group of fifteen small islets and rocks lying 500 miles off the Atlantic coast of Brazil. When Charles Darwin visited them in 1832 he found the sole inhabitants to be a colony of sea birds and a large species of crab that lived on the young of these birds. He noted that 'not a single plant or even a lichen could be found on the islands'. The rocky archipelago was also aptly described by Frank Worsley, first-trip apprentice in the wool clipper *Wairoa* in the early 1930s:

> Next morning at daybreak the 2nd Mate sent me aloft to look out for ships and St Paul's Rocks. It was a beautiful dawn, all mauve and silver. The South-East Trades were sleepily sighing to their death. We were sailing so slowly that it was three in the afternoon before we passed them, a mere ridge of rocks, black-based above the foaming surf with the upper parts white with guano. There was not a blade of vegetation on them. Clouds of boobies and noddies flew over the rocks and out towards us. It was fascinating to think that Pendo de San Pedro, to name them in accordance with their original Portuguese discoverer, though only the height of our main yard above the sea, were really the peaks of lofty mountains.

There could be no lonelier meeting place on earth than St Paul's Rocks.

*

For the motor vessel *Cingalese Prince* her voyage was turning into one to remember – or perhaps to be best forgotten. Sailing from the UK in late March 1941 with supplies for British troops in Greece, she had successfully run the gauntlet of German and Italian bombers in the Western Mediterranean, only to be caught with her anchor down and her hatches open in Piraeus harbour.

He 111s, ten of them flying nose to tail, had swooped down on the harbour just before midnight on 6 April, scattering their 500lb bombs amongst the crowded shipping. One of the unlucky recipients of three of their bombs was the ammunition carrier *Clan Fraser*, with 250 tons of TNT in her holds and another 100 tons in a barge tied up alongside. The explosion that followed can only be described as catastrophic. Thirteen merchant ships, sixty lighters and twenty-five motor sailing vessels were sunk, major damage was caused to port installations, and buildings as far away as 15 miles inland were shaken. Two other ships were badly damaged, one of which was the *Cingalese Prince.* Fortunately, there had been time to evacuate most of the ships' crews and people ashore before the *Clan Fraser* blew up, and there were few casualties.

The 8,474-ton *Cingalese Prince*, built on the Clyde in 1929 for Prince Line of London and commanded by Captain John Smith, reached Port Said under her own power, where temporary repairs were carried out. She then moved on to Bombay for further repairs, but was not ready to return to service until early August. Leaving Bombay, she made the circuit of the Indian ports, loading pig iron, manganese ore and an assortment of tea, jute and other produce. She returned to Bombay to complete loading, and when she sailed towards the end of August 1941 she had on board 11,156 tons of cargo for Liverpool.

In more normal times, the *Cingalese Prince* would have made the return voyage via the Suez Canal and the Mediterranean, reaching Liverpool within three weeks. The war had changed all that. Sailing the length of the Mediterranean, even in convoy, had become too risky, and all homeward bound ships were routed the long way round, via the Cape of Good Hope. Then, having rounded the Cape into the Atlantic, they steered a diagonal course across the South Atlantic to the coast of Brazil, and thence to Trinidad to await a convoy going north.

By this time the homeward passage would have stretched to thirty days, and there was much more to come. A week or so might be spent idling in Trinidad waiting for a convoy to form, then there was the long haul north under escort to New York or Halifax, Nova Scotia to join a transatlantic convoy. Given that even a so-called 'fast' convoy rarely exceeded 9 knots, a homeward passage from India often stretched to two months.

When on the night of 19 September the *Cingalese Prince* at last neared the coast of Brazil, she was over a month out of Bombay, all of which time, except for a brief call at Cape Town for bunkers, had been spent at sea. This had not caused any real hardship to Captain Smith and his crew, for the *Cingalese Prince* was used to sailing alone and on long passages. Furthermore, Smith drew comfort from the knowledge that in the little-frequented waters he was now entering no ship had been sunk by a U-boat since the outbreak of war. He did not, however, relish surrendering control of his ship when she came under the direction of the Royal Navy in Trinidad.

*

U-111 was still patiently playing the waiting game off St Paul's Rocks when, late in the afternoon of 10 September, smoke was sighted on the horizon to the north. Ever cautious, Wilhelm Kleinschmidt feared the smoke might herald the approach of a British armed merchant cruiser and he went to periscope depth to watch and wait.

The 5,719-ton Dutch motor vessel *Marken* was certainly no merchant cruiser – in fact, she was completely unarmed. Outward bound from the Bristol Channel to Calcutta with a military cargo, which included cased aircraft, the *Marken* had crossed the North Atlantic safely and was now southbound for the Cape. In fine weather she was putting the miles behind her at a steady 12 knots. Consequently, her master, Captain A. Kokké, who had been assured before leaving Trinidad that the area was clear of the enemy, was optimistically relaxed.

Kleinschmidt waited until the lone ship came within easy range, and having satisfied himself that she posed no danger, took careful aim and fired a spread of four torpedoes from his bow tubes. Two of the torpedoes missed their target but the others hit the *Marken* squarely amidships, blasting a huge hole in her engine room. The Dutch ship sank very quickly, giving her 37-man crew just enough time to lower their lifeboats and row clear.

Having watched his victim sink, Kleinschmidt brought U-111 back to the surface and approached the lifeboats. After questioning the survivors, he handed over some provisions, including chocolate, brandy and cigarettes, and gave them a course to steer for the land. Captain Kokké and his men, who were to spend the next eleven days adrift before being rescued by a passing Spanish merchantman, were suitably impressed by Kleinschmidt's small humanitarian gesture.

Having consigned the *Marken* to the bottom, U-111 continued her lonely vigil, criss-crossing the north-south trade route with monotonous regularity, and when darkness fell on 19 September she was lying stopped 250 miles to the south-east of St Paul's Rocks. Five weeks had gone by since sailing from Lorient, and Kleinschmidt was becoming increasingly aware that he was nearing the point of no return. Fuel and provisions were running low, and it would soon be time to head back across the Atlantic.

It was a very dark night, the wind was light, the sea calm, and only the muffled beat of U-111's diesels disturbed the silence. Kleinschmidt was in the conning tower and contemplating whether to go below to snatch a couple of hours sleep when, shortly before midnight, a dark shadow was seen approaching from the south. The *Cingalese Prince*, completely unaware that she was no longer alone on this silent ocean, was hurrying north for Trinidad.

It would have been easy for Kleinschmidt to wait until his unsuspecting victim came within easy range, but after his long vigil he had grown impatient. He fired too soon, aiming a three-torpedo spread at the *Cingalese Prince*, all of which missed. Another five hours were to pass before U-111 was able to manoeuvre into position to attack again, this time successfully

Chief Engineer Robert Wilson had been with the *Cingalese Prince* from the time she came out of Blythswood's yard on the Clyde in 1929. He had nursed her through her long voyages to South America and had grown to know intimately every inch of her, from stem to stern, from keel to weather deck. Yet when, at 0430 on the morning of 20 September 1941, he was rudely awakened from a deep sleep by U-111's torpedoes blowing the bottom out of his ship, he found himself completely disorientated. The cabin he had slept in for more years than he cared to remember had become an alien space. The beat of his beloved engine was stilled, and there was an eerie silence, broken only by the spine-chilling roar of water as it gushed into the bowels of the ship.

Dazed by sleep, Wilson groped around in the darkness, located his boiler suit, struggled into it, slipped on his lifejacket and, balancing himself against the increasing list of the ship, clawed his way out into the alleyway. He later recalled:

> Everything seemed to be deathly quiet, there was no vibration of the ship and no lights anywhere except for a few hand torches, and I surmised that she had been hit in the engine room. I ran along the alleyway and opened the door [to the engine room]. There was complete darkness down below, except for the noise of rushing water. Even then I did not know just where the ship had been hit but learned afterwards that both torpedoes had struck on the

starboard side in Nos 5 and 6 holds. The starboard propeller shaft tunnel was badly damaged and the rush of water was reaching the engine room through the watertight door, the inrush must have been so great that no time was available to shut the door.

The watertight doors between the engine room and the propeller shaft tunnels were normally kept open at sea to allow periodic inspection of the shafts and their bearings by the engineers on watch. Only in dangerous waters would the doors be kept closed, and in this case the *Cingalese Prince* was assumed to be in a safe area. Now, with those doors wide open, she was a doomed ship.

Recovering from the initial shock of the torpedoing, Wilson's next concern was for his men:

> I endeavoured to find out how many of the staff could be accounted for, the affair having occurred shortly after the change of watches. In the messroom I saw all three of them, the 8 to 12 watch were by then all turned out and getting dressed by the light of torches in the alleyway, so that was all six accounted for. I saw the engineer officer who was in charge of the watch at the time of the torpedoing but he was some distance away from me and apparently did not hear my query as to whether the other two on watch with him had happened to get out of the engine room. Neither could anybody else give me any information of them, and in addition to them I had not seen either of the two electricians.

It was by then apparent to Chief Engineer Wilson that the ship could not stay afloat for much longer. She had come upright again as she sank lower, which helped to normalize the situation, but the after deck was already awash and she was going down by the stern. No order had yet come from the bridge to abandon ship, but by now it was obvious to all that the boat deck was the best place to be.

When he reached the boat deck, Wilson found nothing but chaos. The *Cingalese Prince* carried four full-sized lifeboats, all of which were kept swung out at sea ready to launch. This operation, in the experienced hands of Chief Officer John Gray and Second Officer Jowett, should have been relatively straightforward. However, the night was black, and with the ship so obviously sinking, panic had broken out amongst the Malay and Indian crew.

Launching a ship's lifeboat in the 1940s, even in good weather and with the ship upright, was never easy. The average shipowner of the day did not take kindly to ships' boats being lowered without good cause, and most crews had had little practice in handling them. The most frequent cause of disaster was when one of the falls ran away while lowering, causing the boat to up-end, tipping its occupants into the sea below. Not surprisingly, in view of a panicking crew, this is what happened to the *Cingalese Prince's* lifeboats, not once but twice.

Wilson was on his way to his allotted boat on the port side of the deck when he heard the unmistakeable sound of a boat fall running out of control:

> Looking around, I saw the boat hanging in a vertical position by the forward falls and a lot of men must have been spilled out into the water. It appears that the after falls had been slacked away before the belly bands had been cast adrift and when they had been cut the boat just took charge. An effort was made to slack off the after falls but this could not be done quickly enough. I discovered that a similar accident had happened to the forward boat on the starboard side. The remaining after starboard boat was being lowered by the Second Officer and there were about twenty men in it. By this time the forward weather deck was not very far off being awash and it was quite clear that she was about done for and I had to act quickly.

The boat was now nearing the water, and Wilson's only means of boarding lay down the lifelines slung between the davits, but as the davits were swung out he could not reach the ropes. Then, at the last moment, his luck changed for the better. The sinking ship gave a lurch to port and one of the lifelines came within his reach:

> I grabbed this and slid down into the boat which was then waterborne and only about 10 feet below me. The after falls were adrift but there was some unrecognizable person trying to get the forward falls adrift. The patent releasing gear didn't work – perhaps there was still a certain amount of way on the ship which was keeping

too much strain on the falls for it to work. There did not appear to be more than eight men, all natives, in the boat and while the man trying to get the forward falls adrift was still busy on them, I endeavoured to induce some of the natives to get the lashings off one or two of the oars, but without exception they still appeared too dazed to do a thing. None of us had a knife but I managed to get one of the lashings off. Then I happened to look forward and saw the man who had been busy on the boat falls disappearing, and a further glance showed me that the ship was going down stern first and at the same time heeling over towards our boat. I distinctly saw the funnel coming down towards me and decided it was time I got out of the boat, and did so.

Wilson dived overboard and was immediately dragged down by the suction as the *Cingalese Prince* took her last plunge. Luckily, he was clear of the ship and the tangle of ropes swirling around the lifeboat, which had now capsized, and when the sinking ship finally released its hold on him, buoyed up by his lifejacket, he shot back to the surface.

When he had cleared his lungs, Wilson looked around in desperation for some means of support. Then came another miracle. Only a few yards away, clearly visible in the darkness, was one of the ship's large wooden life-rafts. Wilson swam towards it and pulled himself aboard, joining several other survivors. As he lay exhausted on the raft he heard plaintive cries for help from the darkness all around. There were men out there drowning, but the few already on board the raft were too weak to paddle in search of them. It was only by pure chance that Second Officer Jowett and the ship's carpenter were picked up a while later. Both were suffering from severe exposure.

What remained of the night was long and uncomfortable. A head count revealed that there were sixteen men on the raft. Six were Europeans: Chief Engineer Wilson, Second Officer Jowett, the carpenter and three naval gunners; the remaining ten were Malay sailors and Indian engine room greasers. With the exception of Jowett, who had been about to go on watch, they had been sleeping soundly when the ship was torpedoed, and as the night was warm, they wore the minimum of clothing. Now they were wet, cold and in shock. Miserable and lost on an empty ocean, they settled down to wait out what was left of the night.

When, at about 0600 hours, daylight finally came and the night gradually gave way to a warm tropical day, their spirits rose with the sun. And when a long dark shape emerged silently from the morning mist, hopes of an early rescue soared, only to be cruelly dashed when their 'rescuer' was seen to be a rust-streaked submarine. Kleinschmidt had come to identify his victim.

Knowing what was coming, Wilson slipped off his lifejacket, on which was stencilled 'CHIEF ENGINEER' in bold white letters. He was aware that the U-boats had orders to, whenever possible, take prisoner either the master or chief engineer, or both, of any ship sunk; this was all part of Hitler's policy of creating a shortage of senior officers in Allied merchant ships. Clad only in a white boiler suit Wilson was anonymous, and he answered truthfully the questions regarding the ship and her cargo put to him by Kleinschmidt. Adrift on a raft in the middle of the ocean with his ship on the bottom and a machine gun trained on him, the engineer saw no point in lying. He later reported:

> He then circled round but some little while later came close to us again and told us there was another raft with a few survivors on some distance away. I asked him if there was a rescue ship in the vicinity. He answered that he could not use his wireless but the first 'free' ship he saw he would give them our position. I assumed he meant 'neutral'. The Commander was quite young – middle 20s I should think – and a number of his crew who were congregated around the conning tower had some among them who could not have been more than sixteen to seventeen years of age. The Commander asked me if we had plenty of 'pwowisions', also if we would like some chocolate, cigarettes and a bottle of brandy. A tin containing the cigarettes and chocolate was then handed over, also a bottle of French cognac; the chocolate was also of French make. At the time these articles were being handed across to us, at least two of his crew were taking cine-Kodak pictures of us on the raft. The Commander then told us to make our way towards the West, circled around again, then submerged.

When the submarine had gone, three smaller life-rafts were seen drifting nearby, but they were devoid of life. Second Officer Jowett, being the only deck officer present, now took charge. Paddles were broken out, and after a great deal of effort, largely by the six Europeans, the other rafts were rounded up and made fast to the bigger raft. The survivors were then distributed amongst the four rafts.

With the sun up and drying out their wet clothing, Wilson and Jowett were able to turn their minds to what lay ahead. Jowett, being the ship's navigator, had taken sun sights only twelve hours before the *Cingalese Prince* was torpedoed, and he was aware of their position. He calculated that the nearest land, St Paul's Rocks, lay roughly 250 miles to the north-west, while the coast of Brazil was 800 miles to the west. St Paul's Rocks, uninhabited and waterless, were out of the question. The rafts had no means of propulsion other than paddles, and even if they were able to rig makeshift sails, they were in the Doldrums and there was hardly any wind, so they could not go north. Their only real hope lay with the current, which in that area flowed steadily west at an average of 20 miles a day. Jowett's conclusion was to put themselves at the mercy of the prevailing current, which would carry them towards the coast. It would be at least forty days before they saw land, but there was also the distinct possibility that they would drift into the track of ships sailing between North and South America. Taking stock of their resources, the survivors found that the rafts contained enough food and water to last about thirty days, if used sparingly. After that, their fate lay in the lap of the gods.

Chief Engineer Wilson recorded:

> We settled down to make the best of it. The days were very hot with a burning sun, but the nights were quite chilly . . . Everybody was stiff and cold when daybreak came. Fortunately for us, the weather kept fine all the time and a gentle breeze blew steadily, in more or less the direction we wanted to go . . .
>
> [Later] By this time, the tenth day on the raft, some of the natives were showing signs of having just about had enough of it and one confessed to having been drinking salt water, in spite of the strictest warnings . . . Some painful cases of sunburn were also showing up now, myself among them. The left side of my face just under the eye,

the back of my neck, legs and feet, were badly blistered and swollen.

The passing days were marked by cutting a notch in a plank of the main raft for every twenty-four hours, and on the evening of the eleventh day, when Jowett estimated they must be approaching the north-south shipping lane, hopes of an early rescue were high. Wilson wrote:

> We all settled down as usual, wondering no doubt if the following day would be the one for our rescue. I had been sure in my own mind right from the beginning that we would be picked up. About 1 a.m. of the twelfth day, the lights of a steamer were sighted.

The rescuer proved to be the Spanish ship *Castillo Montjuich*, northbound for the Cape Verde Islands. In answer to the flares burned by the men on the rafts, she lowered a boat, and soon all sixteen men of the *Cingalese Prince* were taken on board and given a hot meal, their first for twelve days. Six days later, they were landed at St Vincent in the Cape Verde Islands.

Only two other men, one officer and one seaman, survived the sinking of the *Cingalese Prince*. They were found by sloops of the Royal Navy sent out to search for survivors. Captain John Smith and fifty-six others lost their lives.

U-111 by this time had reached the limit of her endurance. She still had nine unused torpedoes on board, but her fuel tanks were running low, with just enough diesel left to get her back to Biscay. Kleinschmidt radioed Lorient for advice and was ordered to return east to rendezvous with U-68 and hand over his remaining torpedoes.

CHAPTER TWO

The Road to the Cape

U-68 was then some 2,000 miles further north and maintaining a lonely, and so far pointless, vigil off the Canary Islands. The Type IXC was on her second war patrol, having sailed from Lorient nine days earlier, and had still to claim her first Allied ship. This failure to make any significant contribution to the war had noticeably affected morale on board the boat, a state of affairs which her present monotonous cruising up and down on the same stretch of empty sea was doing nothing to improve.

In command of U-68 was 36-year-old *Korvettenkapitän* Karl-Friedrich Merten, who had commissioned the boat in Kiel seven months earlier. Merten was new to the U-boats but had served ten years in the surface ships of the German Navy, as gunnery officer in the cruiser *Königsberg*, in command of the escort vessel F-7 and then as Cadet Training Officer in the old coal-burning battleship *Schleswig-Holstein*. He had served the *Kriegsmarine* well in these various roles, but it was in the U-boat arm that Merten found his true vocation. By the time he made the change he might, like Wilhelm Kleinschmidt, have been considered too old for the cut-and-thrust world of the U-boats, but he soon proved that his extensive sea-going experience more than made up for his mature years. Those under his command saw him as patient, careful, and unwilling to take unnecessary risks, a good man to sail under.

U-68's first war patrol had proved to be a disappointing start to her career. Soon after emerging into the Atlantic for the first time in July 1941 she had joined a group of other boats in an attack on a British convoy. The Gibraltar-bound OG 69 had sailed from the Bristol Channel on 20 July and consisted of seventeen merchantmen, a mixture of ships bound for the Cape and beyond, and small short-sea traders with cargoes for Lisbon and Gibraltar. They were escorted by an exceptionally heavy force of nine corvettes and four armed trawlers.

OG 69 was first sighted by a long-range Focke-Wulf Condor based at Bordeaux-Merignac on the morning of the 25th·

However, due to a serious error in navigation, which may well have been brought about by the Condor being under attack (it was later shot down), what was meant to be a coordinated operation turned chaotic. The position of the convoy given by the German aircraft, some 420 miles west of Land's End, proved to be wildly in error. OG 69 was in fact 200 miles further south, off Biscay.

By late afternoon on the 25th, *Kontra-Admiral* Dönitz, C-in-C U-boats, had assembled a pack of ten submarines, including the two Italians *Barbarigo* and *Calvi*, which he ordered to form a patrol line and sweep south. When, by 2100 hours, no contact had been made, the patrol line was disbanded and instructed to spread out and hunt independently. It was not until the next morning, when the convoy was again sighted from the air, that it was realized that the boats had been searching in the wrong place.

The sun was setting on the 26th when, by a combination of luck and diligent quartering, U-68 stumbled on the convoy to the north-west of Cape Finisterre. Merten at once reported the sighting to Lorient, only to be given the onerous duty of shadowing the convoy at a discreet distance, sending beacon signals for the other boats of the pack to home in on. This meant more excruciating idleness, hardly the reward Merten had expected for his vigilance. However, later that night, between 1930 and 2040 hours, U-68 was joined by U-79, U-371 and U-561, and they were sent in to attack.

Wolfgang Kaufmann in U-79 was first to strike, realizing as he drew near that the merchant ships had an almost impenetrable screen of escorts around them. Approaching cautiously, he closed the convoy and fired at random, using a spread of four torpedoes from his bow tubes, then turning short about to fire his stern tube. The wake of this shoal of torpedoes was seen, and within minutes a corvette was bearing down on U-79, intent on ramming.

As he dived deep, Kaufmann glimpsed a tall column of fire through his periscope and heard several loud explosions. On the basis of this he claimed to have sunk three ships and damaged one other. In fact, Kaufmann's random shoot had found only one target, the small Swansea-registered collier *Kellwyn*, carrying a cargo of coke for Lisbon. If the attack had come twenty-four hours later the *Kellwyn* would have already left the convoy. As it was,

Kaufmann's torpedo ripped her bottom open and she sank in minutes, taking with her Captain Alexander McLean, ten of his crew and three naval gunners. Nine survivors were picked up by the trawler *St Nectan*.

The other U-boats in the pack were now arriving: Ernst Bauer's U-126, Rolf Mützelburg's U-203, Hans-Dietrich von Tiesenhausen's U-331, Robert Bartells in U-561, Herwig Collmann in U-562 and Reinhard Suhren with U-564. The two Italian boats ordered in failed to make contact. However, by the morning of the 28th Dönitz had eight U-boats circling the perimeter of OG 69, and despite the tight defensive screen, when night fell slaughter followed.

Rolf Mützelburg in U-203 took the lion's share, sinking the 2,475-ton *Hawkinge* and the two short-sea traders *Lapland* and *Norita*. Robert Bartells sank the 1,884-ton *Wrotham*, while Ernst Bauer claimed the 1,335-ton *Erato* and the Norwegian-flag *Ingar I*. The latter, just a fraction over 1,300 tons and registered in Bergen, had escaped from Norway when the Germans invaded in the spring of 1940. Under the command of Captain Lorentz Tvedt, she had a total crew of nineteen, and carried a cargo of 1,670 tons of coal, coke and general for Gibraltar. When the U-boats attacked, Tvedt was on the bridge of the *Ingar I* with Second Mate Olav Ringsjø, and both men witnessed the sinking of the *Erato*, which was leading their column. Two minutes later, they saw a torpedo tracking towards them on the starboard bow. Tvedt was unable to take avoiding action as there were other ships close on either beam, but he did have time to get all crew on deck and to the far side of the ship before the torpedo struck. This action saved many lives.

The torpedo, fired by Ernst Bauer in U-126, exploded in the *Ingar I*'s starboard coal bunker, causing major damage. Both lifeboats on that side were smashed, also the motor lifeboat stowed on top of No.3 hatch. The ship then took such a heavy list to starboard that it was impossible to lower the port boats. From then on it was every man for himself, the only way out being over the rail and into the sea. Captain Tvedt, who stayed on the bridge to throw the ship's code books over the side, was pulled down by the ship when she sank, but when he surfaced again was able to find sanctuary on a wooden hatch cover. Second Mate Ringsjø did likewise, and Second Engineer Emanuel Høiland found the wooden top of the wheelhouse. Despite the chaos, only three of the Norwegian ship's crew lost their lives.

While the others were choosing their targets, U-68 had been obliged to keep her distance, still under orders to send position reports. She may have been forgotten by Lorient, but to Karl-Friedrich Merten watching from his conning tower the omission seemed poor reward for the U-boat that had been first to find the convoy. It was not until midnight that he was given permission to join the attack, and then, with OG 69's escort force fully on the alert, U-68 walked into a wall of fire.

It was a dark night with no moon, and Merten approached the convoy on the surface. Unfortunately for him, U-68 was immediately detected by the escort, and the corvette HMS *Rhododendron* came racing to meet her. Seeing the danger, Merten cleared the conning tower and made an emergency dive, but the boat was hardly below the surface before *Rhododendron*'s depth charges came crashing down.

The corvette dropped four patterns of six charges each, and twenty-four times the U-boat felt the concussion of a giant hand slamming against her hull. Eventually, twisting and turning, she escaped, but not until she had incurred significant damage. She limped into Lorient four days later, where she would remain for seven weeks under repair. Merten claimed to have sunk *Rhododendron*, but the truth was that, other than locating the convoy, U-68's involvement with OG 69 was minimal and very nearly ended in disaster.

Despite its heavy escort, Convoy OG 69 had received a severe roughing up at the hands of the U-boats, losing seven ships totalling 11,503 tons gross, but nothing like the savaging Admiral Dönitz claimed in his War Diary:

> The great convoy battle of the last few days can be considered as concluded (30.7). This was the first case of successful operation between Intercept Service, air reconnaissance and U-boats. Air reconnaissance, sent in on a report by the Intercept Service, detected the enemy continually through 5 days and was able to guide the boats by means of reports of position and beacon signals. All the boats operating against the convoy were inexperienced boats on their first or second enemy operation.

The following reported:

U-79 – 3 vessels sunk (17,000 GRT) 2 vessels torpedoed.
U-126 – 4 vessels (19,000 GRT).
U-68 – 1 corvette.
U-203 – 5 vessels (31,000 GRT).
U-561 – 1 freighter, 1 large tanker (16,000 GRT).
U-371 – 15,000 GRT.

19 ships approximately 108,000 GRT and 2 escort vessels from this convoy were torpedoed or sunk.

*

U-68 sailed from Lorient on her third war patrol on 11 September, and nine days later she was to the south of the Canaries once more patiently searching the ocean for targets for her torpedoes. The mind-numbing boredom of her previous patrol was repeating itself.

Early in the morning of 21 September Günther Hessler, in U-107, also on her third war patrol, was 380 miles south-west of Las Palmas when smoke was sighted on the horizon to the south. By mid-morning the masts and funnels of a small convoy were recognizable and Hessler signalled Lorient with news of his discovery. His radio transmission was brief, but not brief enough. An alert radio officer aboard the Liverpool-registered *Dunelmia*, bringing up the rear of Convoy SL 87, was listening on the same wavelength and immediately took D/F bearings. Hessler's cover was blown.

SL 87 had sailed from Freetown seventeen days earlier, and had inched northwards at a painfully slow crawl. The convoy consisted of just twelve ships, the usual mixture of ex-Mediterranean traders and deep-sea tramps, ranging from the 2-year-old Norwegian *Fana* of 1,375 tons, with her paintwork still unsullied, to the Liverpool-registered *Niceto de Larrinaga*, 5,591 tons and a veteran of the 1914–18 war. They were all down to their marks – some even discreetly over – and carried a huge bounty from the fertile shores of West Africa: phosphates, palm oil, cocoa beans, copper, groundnuts. Nothing of great value – although one ship did carry a small quantity of bullion – but all vital ingredients required to keep Britain at war.

The vessels were sailing in five columns abreast, led by the Commodore's ship, the 4,975-ton *John Holt*, commanded by

Captain Cecil Hime. She was a regular West African trader built by Cammel Lairds at Birkenhead, and had accommodation for twelve passengers. Many ships on the West African run had this extra accommodation, which catered for the movement of minor colonial officials, planters and shipping companies' shore personnel between the UK and the coast. There was nothing luxurious: clean, comfortable cabins and no frills, but the fares were comparatively cheap. On this occasion, only five of the *John Holt*'s passenger cabins were occupied, leaving ample space for the convoy commodore, Captain A. MacRae DSC, RD, RNR, and his staff of seven. It was MacRae's unenviable task to maintain order amongst the merchant ships, and also to liaise with the Senior Officer Escort.

On the *John Holt*'s starboard beam, sailing at the head of Column 4, was the 5,302-ton London steamer *Silverbelle*, under the command of Captain Hilon Rowe, who had been appointed Vice Commodore for the passage. It would be Rowe's duty to take over control of the merchant ships should anything happen to the *John Holt*.

SL 87's escort force, ships of the 40th Escort Group based at Londonderry, was led by Commander Ronald Keymer RN (Rtd) in the ex-US Coastguard cutter HMS *Gorleston*, with the Shoreham-class sloop *Bideford*, the Flower-class corvette *Gardenia*, another ex-Coastguard cutter HMS *Lulworth* and the Free French minesweeper *Commandant Duboc*. Forty-year-old Commander Keymer had retired from the Navy in 1934 but had been recalled on the outbreak of war in 1939.

At first sight this seems an exceptionally strong escort for twelve nondescript merchantmen loaded with West African produce, but in fact not one of Keymer's ships was really up to the task on hand. The two Coastguard cutters, on loan to the Royal Navy under Lease Lend, were of 1,500 tons displacement and armed with a single 5-inch gun and two depth charge racks. Built in 1929, they had had no combat experience under the American flag, the only claim to fame of either being that in her previous life *Gorleston* had acted as radio guard ship for Amelia Earhart when she made her ill-fated bid to fly around the world in 1937. The *Commandant Duboc*, the only escort capable of more than 16 knots, was an unknown quantity. A French minesweeper seized by the Royal Navy at Dunkirk, she displaced just 647 tons and was manned entirely by Free French personnel. Her twin diesel engines were reputed to give her a top speed of 20 knots and she was armed with a single 4-inch gun, two depth charge throwers and a roll-off rack at the stern. Three of Keymer's ships, *Bideford*, *Gorleston* and *Lulworth*, were fitted with radar, but two of these sets were out of action for the entire passage north due to lack of spare parts. *Bideford* had the only serviceable radar, and she and *Gardenia* were the only two ships with any substantial experience in convoy escort work. None of SL 87's escorts had worked together as a team before, and to further handicap them they had encountered a shortage of oil fuel in Freetown.

Freetown, once a safe haven for the slave traders of the eighteenth century, has the largest deep-water harbour on the West African coast, and following the virtual closure of the Mediterranean to merchant shipping in June 1940, it became a major convoy assembly port and bunkering station. However, the huge increase in traffic soon led to occasions when coal, oil and fresh water were all in short supply. The resultant delays were frequent and chaotic. The Anti-Submarine Warfare Division's report on the problems encountered by SL 87's escort makes disturbing reading:

> By 20th September, GORLESTON realized that she could only reach Londonderry without refuelling if she played a completely passive part in any attacks on the Convoy, while LULWORTH estimated that at the present consumption she would arrive in the U.K. with only 74 tons of fuel remaining. BIDEFORD, who anticipated distiller trouble which eventually took place, necessitating her being supplied with fresh water from LULWORTH under way, would also have been unable to play more than a passive role if fuel was to be conserved . . . GARDENIA, who had been unable to complete with fuel prior to leaving Freetown, reported that it would be difficult even to reach the Azores should it be necessary to zig-zag on route.

It was perhaps just as well that those under the protection of the 40th Escort Group were blissfully ignorant of the shortcomings of their guardians.

SL 87's fate was sealed on the morning of the 21st, when the galley stoves being stoked for breakfast added to the dark cloud of smoke over the convoy already created by the tall funnels of the merchantmen. It was a fine, clear morning with a calm sea, a gentle breeze and a horizon as sharp as a whetted knife.

The significance of the elongated black cloud hanging low down on the horizon was not lost on *Korvettenkapitän* Günther Hessler, who was examining it through powerful binoculars from the conning tower of U-107. He had found the enemy at last.

SL 87 was then on a course of 350° and making 8 knots, aiming to pass midway between Madeira and the Azores. None of the merchant ships had been long away from home waters, two months at the most, but there was hardly a man in them not feeling the strain of the voyage. The West African run was a punishing experience, especially for those who were new to the trade. The organization in port, if there was any, was habitually poor, and it fell to the ship's officers to supervise all cargo handling, often using untrained labour rounded up from the nearest village. The hours worked were impossibly long, the heat and humidity overpowering. And always threatening were the dreadful diseases the jungle harboured: blackwater fever, malaria, yellow fever, cholera, and a host of other infections. It was rare that a ship escaped the coast without at least one death on board from the miasmas of West Africa. Now there was an added danger to be faced, another eight days steaming through waters thick with U-boats.

For Hessler the discovery of this convoy promised to be yet another bonus to add to the extraordinary run of luck that he and U-107 had been enjoying. U-107 and her crew were still basking in the glory of their previous sortie into the Atlantic which was on record as being 'the most successful patrol of the entire war against Allied shipping to date'. In a little over three months at sea she had sunk fourteen ships, totalling nearly 87,000 tons gross. It was a voyage that elevated her commander, 31-year-old Günther Hessler, into the exalted ranks of Karl Dönitz's 'aces'.

Hessler had joined the much-diminished German Navy as an 18-year-old cadet in 1927, serving first in the torpedo boats and then in cruisers, seemingly condemned to a mediocre career. Then, in 1937, he married Admiral Karl Dönitz's only daughter and his fortunes changed. He transferred to the U-boat arm in the spring of 1940 with the rank of *kapitänleutnant* and, six months later, although he had no previous experience in submarines, was given command of U-107. His second patrol in her earned him the Knight's Cross and promotion to *korvettenkapitän*. It has always been strongly denied that Hessler's marriage had any effect on his subsequent career, but suspicions will always remain.

SL 87 was 400 miles north of the Cape Verde Islands when Hessler first sighted its collection of masts and funnels. He reported the convoy's position, course and speed to Lorient, and Dönitz then ordered all other boats in the immediate area to report in. The response was not encouraging, the signal being answered by only three boats, Günther Müller-Stockheim's U-67, Karl-Friedrich Merten's U-68 and Werner Winter's U-103.

Meanwhile, dusk settled uneasily on SL 87. Commander Keymer and Commodore Macrae had conferred on the significance of the D/F bearings obtained by the *Dunelmia* earlier in the day and agreed on the strong possibility that the U-boats were closing on them. Despite his fuel problems, Keymer decided to increase speed and take *Gorleston* ahead to sweep for the enemy. He planned to return at dawn in the hope of surprising any U-boats stalking on the surface. The remaining escorts then closed in around the convoy, with *Gardenia* leading, *Lulworth* covering the port beam and *Bideford* to starboard. *Commandant Duboc* was astern, keeping visibility distance. The weather was good, but on the side of the U-boats, the wind light and variable, the sea a flat calm and visibility up to 6 miles. There was no moon.

Nearest to the convoy was U-68, but it would be some hours before Merten could intercept. Meanwhile, U-107 was ordered to shadow the ships and report in at frequent intervals. This passive role was not to Hessler's liking, and during the course of the morning he closed in on the convoy and fired a spread of four torpedoes from his bow tubes. They all missed. Then, to add to Hessler's rising frustration, U-107's diesels began to give trouble and he was forced to retire to a safe distance to carry out repairs.

It must be said that SL 87 had been given fair warning of the danger from U-boats. The first indication came at 2258 hours on the 21st, when the Admiralty signalled that there was a U-boat in the area west of the Canary Islands, within 250 miles of 28°N 21°W. *Lulworth* received this signal and passed it on to *Gardenia* for transmission to *Bideford*. *Lulworth* then closed the *John Holt* and passed to message to Commodore Macrae, who later commented, '*Lulworth* made a signal re D/F reports from the Admiralty but as it was in a form incomprehensible to me, I thought this action in flashing a light was very unnecessary and dangerous.'

The sun was going down when U-68 closed in on the convoy. At 2100 hours Merten reported that he was in position, but it was not until 0200 on the morning of the 22nd that he was ready to attack. He then appears to have fired several spreads of torpedoes, claiming hits on at least two ships. In fact, most of Merten's torpedoes missed their targets, only one hit being scored, and that on the 14-year-old motor vessel *Silverbelle*.

The 5,302-ton *Silverbelle*, owned by Silver Line of London, was a typical product of the North East Coast shipyards, blunt in the bow, with a box-like hull and cavernous holds capable of carrying a prodigious amount of dry cargo of any nature. On this occasion, under the command of Captain Hilon Rowe, she was on passage from Durban and Freetown with 6,000 tons of phosphates and produce, including copper, cocoa beans and palm oil, for Liverpool. She also had on board five passengers, including Captain Jack Lavis, who had survived the sinking of his ship *Vulcain* off West Africa by U-38. Lavis had spent some months as a guest of the Vichy French authorities in French Guinea, before being repatriated to Freetown. Now, his nightmare was beginning all over again.

The torpedoing of the *Silverbelle* prompted a flurry of activity that achieved nothing other than making a bad situation worse. The *Niceto de Larrinaga*, sailing on the *Silverbelle*'s starboard quarter in Column 5, lit up the night sky by firing two distress rockets, while the ship directly astern, the *St Clair II*, broke radio silence to broadcast an SOS. SL 87's position was thus revealed to all U-boats in the area. And if that did not suffice, the escorts joined in with a brilliant display of starshell. The pyrotechnics were such that they were seen by HMS *Gorleston*, 50 miles ahead of the convoy and conducting her futile search for lurking U-boats. Commander Keymer at once altered course to return and increased to maximum speed.

Gorleston had the convoy in sight at 0447 on the 23rd, and Keymer was astonished to find that the merchant ships had been left completely undefended. *Lulworth, Bideford, Gardenia* and *Commandant Duboc* were all clustered round the damaged *Silverbelle*, which was straggling well astern of the other ships. Keymer detailed the Free French ship to stand by the *Silverbelle*, and ordered the other escorts to return to the convoy at once.

The *Silverbelle* had been hit in her engine room, but remained afloat. An inspection was made of the damage, and it was established that although the steamer's main engine was out of action, she was in no immediate danger of sinking. In view of her valuable cargo, it was decided to attempt a tow to Las Palmas, the nearest port where repairs might be affected.

Lulworth and *Bideford* rejoined the convoy at dawn, reporting they had lost contact with *Gardenia* along the way. Knowing the corvette to be short of fuel, Commander Keymer became concerned for her safety and decided to look for her, setting course for the *Silverbelle*, now drifting 40 miles astern. The crippled ship came in sight at 0922, and as *Gorleston* approached her, Asdic signals indicated the presence of a submerged U-boat. Keymer ran in at high speed, zig-zagging and dropping depth charges.

Both *Gardenia* and *Commandant Duboc* were standing by the *Silverbelle* but had made no move to take her in tow. Keymer ordered *Gardenia* to return to the convoy at full speed, and then decided to attempt the salvage himself. This was a strange decision, for as Senior Officer Escort Keymer's place was with the convoy. However, by 1300, *Gorleston* had *Silverbelle* in tow and was making for Las Palmas at 5 knots, with *Commandant Duboc* escorting.

In hindsight, it is impossible to say why Commander Keymer decided at this critical moment to desert his convoy and take in tow a damaged merchantman. His decision left SL 87 protected only by the two sloops *Lulworth* and *Bideford*, with Lieutenant Commander Gwinner in *Lulworth* being the senior officer. Then, to further exacerbate an already precarious situation, as darkness approached, Gwinner, as Keymer had done before, concluded that the U-boats were lying in wait ahead of the convoy. At 2015 he took *Lulworth* and *Bideford* to the north to search for the enemy. *Gardenia* had then not yet arrived back on station, so the ten ships of SL 87 were again left completely undefended. It was an open invitation to the U-boats to move in and fill the vacuum. Contrary to Gwinner's assessment, four of them, Müller-Stockheim's U-67, Merten's U-68, Winter's U-103 and Hessler's U-107, were stealthily keeping pace with the convoy, waiting the opportunity to strike.

By 2100 Werner Winter had manoeuvred U-103 into a favourable position off SL 87's starboard wing column, and at 2152 he fired a spread of four torpedoes at the tightly bunched merchantmen. The 5,003-ton Elder Dempster motor vessel *Edward Blyden*, lead ship of the starboard column, was the first to be hit. Lookouts on her bridge saw the track of one of Winter's torpedoes approaching from the quarter, but there was no time to take avoiding action. The torpedo slammed into the *Edward Blyden*'s after hold and exploded with a muffled roar. The ship sheered wildly to port, and Captain Exley ordered the wheel hard to starboard to bring her back on course. In doing so, he inadvertently ran into Winter's second torpedo, which took the ship squarely amidships under her bridge. The *Edward Blyden* shuddered to a halt, settling rapidly by the stern.

A brief assessment of the damage was enough to convince Captain Exley that his ship could not be saved, and he gave the order to abandon. The sea being calm and the wind light, three lifeboats, carrying all fifty-one crew and twelve passengers, had no difficulty in clearing the ship. Last man to board the boats was the Fifth Engineer, who had been in his bunk with a fever and a temperature of 105°.

The *Edward Blyden* and her valuable cargo slipped beneath the waves at 2204, just twelve minutes after the first torpedo struck. The only casualty was a lady passenger who complained that water in the lifeboat had ruined her best pair of shoes. This same lady, a report states, had been taking the air on the boat deck with a gentleman passenger, and the couple were so absorbed with one another that they were completely unaware of the first torpedo striking. Furthermore, they had watched the second torpedo as it tracked towards the ship, believing it to be a cavorting porpoise. Such is the magic of a warm, star-studded night off the coast of West Africa.

Directly astern of the *Edward Blyden* was the Liverpool tramp *Niceto de Larrinaga*, commanded by Captain Frederick Milnes, who was on the bridge at the time. He saw the flash of the torpedo striking the ship ahead and immediately altered course to port to avoid running into her. Six minutes later, as Milnes was bringing his ship back on course, one of U-103's bow salvo slammed into her hull directly below the bridge. The navigation bridge was demolished, and the Third Officer, who was in the starboard wing, was blown overboard.

Almost instantaneously, a second torpedo hit the *Niceto de Larrinaga* on her starboard quarter. The exploding torpedo set off the ship's 4-inch gun magazine, and the combined blast literally blew her stern off. She sank in eight minutes, with the loss of two of her crew.

Having fired his bow tubes, Winter brought U-103 round in a tight circle and followed up with a spread of two from his stern tubes. He later claimed to have seen and heard a total of five explosions and to have observed 'a freighter of about 7,000 tons capsize and sink, two freighters totalling some 11,000 tons sink by the stern, a torpedo explosion on another ship of about 5,000 tons and a large blue/green explosion on the rear ship.'

Lulworth and *Bideford,* who were then 4 miles ahead of the convoy, heard the exploding torpedoes and saw the distress rockets soaring skywards. They immediately reversed course and raced back at full speed. Needless to say, the enemy had long gone when they arrived on the scene, and the only useful purpose they could serve was to pick up the survivors. While they were so engaged, *Gardenia* finally caught up with the convoy and joined in the rescue work. By 2300 all survivors were on board, and it was only then that the three escorts made any coordinated effort to seek out the U-boats. Too late, the stable door was at last slammed shut.

The remainder of the night passed quietly, allowing the convoy a brief space in which to recover from the turmoil of the previous twenty-four hours. Then, early in the afternoon of the 23rd, the Admiralty signalled that a U-boat had been detected following the convoy. The wolves were gathering again, as evidenced by an entry in Dönitz's War Diary for the day, which read: 'U-67 established contact with the convoy at 1400 and sent continuous contact messages which later were also picked up by U-107.'

CHAPTER THREE

Island Rendezvous

SL 87 was saved from complete annihilation by the failure of the U-boats to follow up their advantage, a failure that stemmed from a mistaken belief by all four U-boat commanders that the convoy had been destroyed. The misapprehension was taken up by Admiral Dönitz in Lorient who, basing his findings on reports from the U-boats, made the following entry in his War Diary for the day:

> Operations on this convoy may be considered to be at an end. Four boats attacked and the following ships were sunk;
> 5 ships, 42,000 grt – sunk.
> 4 ships, 24,000 grt – sunk.
> 2 ships, 12,000 grt – damaged.
>
> With the exception of the small steamer observed by U-107 then, the entire convoy was wiped out.

Within hours of this entry being made, Lorient received urgent signals from Hessler in U-67 and Merten in U-68 requesting that they be allowed to return to base without delay. Hessler pleaded a sick man on board, while Merten, despite having hit and damaged only one ship – the *Silverbelle* – had used up all his torpedoes under deck and was running short on fuel. Given that the two U-boats had been only nine and twelve days at sea respectively, Dönitz was reluctant to accede to their requests.

In the case of U-67, the sick man was one of Hessler's wireless operators who had contracted VD while on his last run ashore in Lorient. In most ships this would have been of no great account, VD being an occupational hazard for seamen since time immemorial. However, in the close confines of an operational submarine any man with a highly contagious disease was a serious threat to health and morale. Hessler wanted him landed as soon as possible.

Lorient responded with a plan unlikely to please either U-boat commander. A rendezvous was being arranged in Tarafal Bay in the Cape Verde Islands, where U-67 and U-68 would meet up with the then homeward bound U-111. Kleinschmidt's boat had been forty days at sea, but through lack of opportunity still had most of her torpedoes left on board. She was to transfer some of these and hand over any spare diesel to U-68, while at the same time U-68's doctor was to treat Hessler's sick man. If the patient required hospitalization he was to be transferred to U-111 and brought home.

The Cape Verde Islands, which lie deep in the Atlantic some 330 miles off the coast of Senegal, consist of ten islands and five small islets. All were uninhabited when first discovered in 1460; they were later colonized by the Portuguese with African slaves. In the heyday of sail they became a convenient provisioning station for the windjammers, but with the advent of steam they faded back into obscurity. The westernmost of the group, Ilha de Santo Antão, was in the 1940s still little populated, and on its southern coast the lonely Tarafal Bay was an ideal spot for a clandestine rendezvous. The North Atlantic Memoir, the Bradshaw's Guide of the sailing ship men, describes the bay concisely:

> The watering place of Tarafal Bay is one of the most con-
> venient for the purpose amongst the Cape Verde Islands.
> The bay is spacious and has a black sandy bottom. Vessels
> anchor in 20 fathoms at three quarters of a cable's length
> [150 yards] from the shore, sheltered from the north-east
> and south winds and sea; and when the wind comes to
> the westward of south or north there is always, from the
> extreme high land, a calm in the bay, the wind never blow-
> ing home, but only occasioning a swell to set in.

Tarafal Bay had changed little over the years since that was written, and in 1941 afforded an ideal meeting place for U-boats oper-
ating against the Freetown convoys. The Portuguese authorities in the islands appeared to be turning a blind eye to the blatant misuse of their waters, at the same time professing strict neutrality. The situation had not gone unnoticed in Britain, and in March 1941 Winston Churchill wrote to the Admiralty:

> The whole question of the Cape Verde islands being used
> as a German U-boat fuelling base must now be reviewed
> with a view to action being taken. I shall be glad to hear
> from you on all these points.

Portugal was Britain's oldest ally, the association between the two countries dating back to the Anglo-Portuguese Alliance of 1373, sealed by the marriage of Philippa, daughter of John of Gaunt, Duke of Lancaster, to King John of Portugal in 1387. However, when war came in 1939, Portugal, although sympathetic to Britain's cause, remained strictly neutral. After France fell in 1940 and the survival of Britain was in question, it became obvious that the Portuguese were reconsidering their position. Nevertheless, they continued to trade with both sides in the conflict, their main export being tungsten, which is widely used in the manufacture of weapons.

As to the question of espionage the Portuguese were equally unbiased. The port of Lisbon was a hotbed of intrigue, crawling with spies and agents of every nation, most of them hostile to the Allies. A similar situation prevailed in Oporto, as recounted by Chief Officer Jack Stow of the British motor vessel *Starling*, which had entered Oporto to land the survivors from a sunken Swedish ship:

> We arrived safely in Oporto with the rescued crew. At this time Portugal was of course neutral, and when we were ashore we rubbed shoulders with Germans and all other nationalities. We were not allowed to wear any uniform or badge showing who we were. I recall being in a night-club and someone pointed out a table where one of the leading Nazis in the city was sitting. Later we sailed up the River Douro in our ship's dinghy and picnicked on the private estate of the German Ambassador. Needless to say, he did not know that a bunch of British sailors were on his grounds.

In the months that followed Churchill's directive, the capture of the Enigma machines from the German weather ships and U-110 enabled the code breakers at Bletchley Park, for the first time, to read most traffic between Lorient and the U-boats in the Atlantic. This included the signal from Admiral Dönitz to U-67, U-68 and U-111 concerning the rendezvous in the Cape Verde Islands. An indiscreet reference in plain language to Tarafal Bay by Wilhelm Kleinschmidt completed the picture.

The opportunity for the Royal Navy to intervene was too good to pass up. Coincidentally, the River-class submarine HMS *Clyde*, which had been stationed in Freetown providing anti-submarine practice for convoy escorts, had been ordered to patrol off the Canaries and had arrived off Tenerife on 24 September. She was well placed to take action, and when intelligence was received of the U-boat rendezvous she headed for Tarafal Bay at her best speed of 17½ knots.

The *Clyde*, a 2,206-ton ocean-going submarine, commanded by 38-year-old Commander David Ingram DSC, RN, had distinguished herself as a formidable attacker early in the war. While patrolling off the west coast of Norway in May 1940 she sighted what appeared to be a German supply ship of about 8,000 tons. Believing he was challenging a defenceless merchantman, Ingram gave chase on the surface. Much to his surprise and consternation, however, as *Clyde* began to overhaul the enemy ship she ran into a hail of heavy gunfire. The 'defenceless merchantman' was, in fact, the commerce raider *Widder*, ex-*Neumark* of the Hamburg America Line. Manned by the German Navy and armed with six 150mm guns and an array of torpedo tubes, the *Widder* was then just eight hours out from Kiel and about to embark on her first raiding sortie in the North Atlantic.

A fierce gun battle lasting for over an hour followed, with *Clyde* using her single 4-inch to good effect against the enemy's vastly superior armament. No hits were scored by either side, but the British submarine put up such a withering fire that the *Widder* broke off the action and escaped under cover of a convenient rain squall. It was a clear victory for HMS *Clyde,* and a very inauspicious start to the German raider's maiden voyage.

Five weeks later, the British attempt to drive the Germans out of Norway ended in failure and eventual evacuation. At that time, HMS *Clyde* was patrolling off Trondheim on the lookout for German naval ships. Cruising on the surface in the half-light of dusk, she sighted the battleship *Gneisenau* accompanied by the heavy cruiser *Admiral Hipper*. The two enemy ships, who mounted a huge number of big guns between them, were on their way out into the Atlantic to begin operations against Allied shipping.

Under the cover of darkness, Ingram moved in to attack, firing a full bow salvo of six torpedoes at the *Gneisenau* from 4,000yds. Three minutes later, one explosion was heard, and Ingram, anticipating the retribution to come, immediately went deep. Depth charges rained down after him, but although one salvo of eight charges exploded close to the *Clyde*, she escaped with no more than a few broken gauge glasses. It was later learned that one of Ingram's torpedoes had blown a large hole in the *Gneisenau*'s bows, putting her out of action for six months.

Following these two incidents, neither the *Widder* nor the *Gneisenau* had much success in the Atlantic, and it could be said that HMS *Clyde*'s aggressive treatment of the two German raiders played a significant part in saving many Allied merchant ships. In recognition of his outstanding initiative, David Ingram was promoted to full commander.

The logic of sending to Tarafal Bay a single submarine instead of surface ships was questionable, but it may be that *Clyde* was all that was available at the time. Certainly, Commander David Ingram, tired of patrolling the empty waters south of the Equator, welcomed the diversion. And so, as September 1941 came to a close, four submarines, three German and one British, were converging on the remote bay.

The German plan called for U-68 and U-111 to meet in Tarafal Bay on 27 September to transfer torpedoes. They were to put to sea again that night to await the arrival of U-67 off Tarafal next morning, and then arrange the treatment or transfer of Hessler's sick wireless operator. U-68 was first to arrive, entering Tarafal soon after sunrise on the 27th submerged to periscope depth. U-111 followed an hour or so later, also proceeding cautiously at periscope depth. When they had identified each other, the two German boats surfaced. Merten then anchored U-68 about 200yds off the beach, and Kleinschmidt secured U-111 alongside her.

The day was fine and warm, with little wind, but the long Atlantic swell was making itself felt in the bay, and the handling of the one-and-a-half-ton torpedoes from one submarine to the other was not going to be easy. And that they were being watched soon became apparent. An eyewitness in U-111 stated that a small boat put out from the shore containing a 'very dark-skinned man'. The man boarded and asked if they were Americans. When this was denied, he left, but returned later with a sealed envelope, which he handed over to Kleinschmidt. It is not known what the envelope contained, but it is certain that the Portuguese had no intention of interfering with the U-boats, although the transfer operation that followed was closely monitored by a group of soldiers on the beach. In line with Portugal's strict neutrality, they made no move to intervene.

Even in a sheltered harbour the transfer of live torpedoes is a difficult, time-consuming operation. In this case, without the assistance of a shore crane and with the boats rolling in the swell, it was doubly difficult. The first two hours were occupied in rigging a derrick, and after the four torpedoes from U-111's deck containers had been sent across, Kleinschmidt called a halt. He decided that bringing torpedoes up from inside U-111's hull would take too long and would be too dangerous. Furthermore, he wished to keep some torpedoes on board in case he met up with enemy ships on the run home.

It had been a long hard day, and by the time the sun went down on Tarafal Bay the crews of both U-boats were exhausted. As the rendezvous with U-67 was not scheduled until the following evening, the temptation to overnight in the sheltered waters of the bay was strong. However, as neither Kleinschmidt nor Merten was happy with the prospect of being caught with no room to manoeuvre, they decided to put to sea during the night. But first there was time to relax and socialize. The night was warm and tranquil, and under a black velvet sky sprinkled with a myriad twinkling stars the two captains dined together, while their crews mingled and yarned on deck. For a brief while the war receded into the far background. No one dreamed that it might still be out there in the darkness, waiting for them.

And it was. While the German U-boat men rested and reminisced, 7 miles offshore the gently heaving ocean suddenly erupted in a welter of foam, and with a loud and ominous hissing a long grey shape emerged from the depths like a disturbed whale breaking surface. HM Submarine *Clyde* was ready to go to war.

Clyde had arrived off Tarafal Bay during the afternoon while the German U-boat crews were fully occupied in the transfer of torpedoes. Commander David Ingram verified his position when 20 miles off West Point, but was unable to see deep into the bay at that distance. Unwilling to risk being seen approaching, he went to periscope depth to await the coming of darkness.

Five hours later, when he surfaced again, Ingram found that, although the moon was up, he could see nothing of the land. It was only when he moved in closer that he realized that the bay was covered by a dense, low-lying mist. It was still clear to seaward, however, and *Clyde* must have been visible in silhouette against the lighter horizon. Without radar, which was then only at its earliest experimental stage in British ships, it would have been suicidal to attempt to enter the bay. Ingram decided to stay offshore until the visibility in the bay improved, hopefully when the moon went down.

Remaining on the surface, Ingram began to cruise up and down between the two headlands of Tarafal Bay, reducing speed to little more than a drift. It seemed like a ridiculous anti-climax to the mad dash *Clyde* had made to cut off the U-boats, but was very necessary. The moon went down at thirty minutes past midnight, and the darkness was complete. Ingram now approached to within 3 miles of the entrance to the bay, and then came to a halt bow-on to the shore.

The low-lying mist had now cleared and Tarafal Bay appeared to be completely empty. The only sign of life came from a few flickering lights on the high land behind the beach, which Ingram took to be oil lamps in fishermen's cottages. Using binoculars, he scanned the bay but could see nothing remotely resembling the U-boats he had been told to expect. Likewise, an underwater search by hydrophone revealed that nothing was on the move. The British commander began to question the validity of the information passed to him by the Admiralty. Had he been sent on a wild goose chase?

As the night wore on, the wind and sea rose, the sky became heavily overcast and by the early hours of the 28th Ingram was finding it very difficult to hold *Clyde* in position. The light which should have been showing on Tarafal's West Point was unlit, and there was no other means of checking the big submarine's distance from the shallow water inshore. The time for decisions was fast approaching.

At about 0400, with no movement detected, Ingram decided to enter the bay. He moved in slowly and cautiously, but before *Clyde* had progressed more than a few yards, hydrophone effect was reported on the starboard bow, drawing aft. Something was coming out of Tarafal Bay.

Whatever it was had no lights showing, but there was every likelihood that it was a dimly-lit fishing boat moving out to sea to cast her nets at daylight. Ingram stopped and waited, straining his eyes to catch a glimpse of the unknown craft. Then, when the hydrophone operator reported the engine beat of the target to be 224 revolutions, obviously the high-revving diesels of a submarine, Ingram knew he was facing the enemy. And at that crucial moment the sky cleared and *Clyde*'s lookouts reported a U-boat off South Point heading out to sea. Karl-Friedrich Merten's U-68 was leaving Tarafal, oblivious to the danger waiting outside.

Ingram immediately rang for full speed and brought *Clyde* hard round to starboard to line up his bow tubes on the U-boat. The British submarine was only halfway round on to her new heading when there was a shout from one of her lookouts, who had seen another U-boat close on the port beam. U-111 was about to slip past while Ingram was preoccupied with U-68.

HMS *Clyde* had inadvertently put herself in a very vulnerable position, with a U-boat on either side of her, and one of them, U-111, well placed to use her bow tubes or ram. Ingram was forced to break off his attack on U-68 and turn to face the new and more immediate threat.

Fortunately for him, Wilhelm Kleinschmidt had been caught equally unawares. U-111 had left Tarafal Bay ahead of U-68 and she was on slow speed waiting for the other boat to catch up. It was the intention of both U-boat commanders to gain sea room before daylight, then to submerge and await the arrival of U-67.

In the conning tower of U-111 were Kleinschmidt, the watch officer *Oberleutnant* Friedrich Rösing and a boatswain's mate 2nd Class. It was reported that they had sighted a 'shadow', which they thought must be a patrolling Portuguese destroyer. As they moved closer, the 'shadow' turned out to be a large submarine, estimated to be of about 1,800 tons. She was painted with light grey camouflage, described by the boatswain's mate as 'snow-white'. As there were very few Axis submarines of this size in service, and certainly none with Mediterranean-style paintwork, she could only be British.

Clyde was too close to U-111 to use her torpedoes or her deck gun, so Ingram increased speed with the intention of ramming, bringing the submarine round to port under full helm. And as she heeled over, the raucous blare of a klaxon echoed across the water, followed by the thunderous roar of escaping air indicating that the U-boat had opened her main vents and was crash-diving.

Clyde was within yards of U-111 when she disappeared under-water, Kleinschmidt taking an incredible risk to escape. He passed under *Clyde*'s keel with only inches to spare, Ingram reporting that looking down he could see the wash of the U-boat's conning tower on one side and the threshing of her propellers on the other. It was a very near miss, and could have ended in disaster for both submarines. Later reports say that Kleinschmidt's action came in for severe criticism by some of his senior petty officers, who claimed that he had panicked when he ordered the crash-dive, risking the lives of all on board U-111. They may have been right, but under the circumstances prevailing it is difficult to see what else Kleinschmidt could have done. Fortunately, his gamble paid off.

With U-111 apparently out of the fight, Ingram returned to the attack on U-68, which in the flurry of activity had been lost sight of. The darkness was now impenetrable, and with the wind and sea still rising, it seemed that *Clyde*'s mission was at an end. Then a dimmed signal lamp was seen flashing to the west. Merten in U-68 was trying to re-establish contact with U-111, and in doing so had inadvertently given away his own position. He was obviously unaware of the presence of the British submarine.

Ingram immediately altered course to put the U-boat ahead, and increased speed to close the range. At 1,400yds he fired three torpedoes from his bow tubes. Merten evidently saw the wake of the torpedoes speeding towards him and took violent evading action, turning through 180° and heading back into Tarafal Bay. *Clyde*'s torpedoes missed.

Following the fleeing U-boat, Ingram fired his three remaining torpedoes in a fan, but Merten was zig-zagging wildly and all three missiles sped past U-68 into the dark void of the bay. Ingram's last sight of the enemy boat was of her conning tower disappearing underwater.

It was now imperative that Ingram dive to reload his empty bow tubes. While *Clyde* was below, at eighteen and twenty minutes after the bow tubes had been fired, two 'moderately distant' explosions were heard. It is believed that this was two of the torpedoes aimed at U-68 exploding on the beach at Tarafal.

The following is an extract from a report by the Admiralty's Naval Intelligence Division on the action:

> Having reloaded torpedo tubes and not having established contact, 'Clyde' surfaced at 0215.
>
> At 0315, with two hours of darkness left, a charge was necessary, and was started. At 0330 'Clyde' was four miles west of the position in which the first encounter took place, steering 280° at 10 knots, charging.

The sky was overcast and the night had become pitch dark; there was a strong wind blowing and some sea.

A streak of white foam was seen broad on the starboard bow and the wheel was put hard to starboard towards. A few seconds later the conning tower of a U-boat was sighted and her course was estimated to be similar and parallel; it was evident that she had only just surfaced. Interrogation of survivors of 'U-111' established the fact that this U-boat was 'U-67', whom 'U-111' was to have met on the next night. 'Clyde's' telegraphs were put to full speed ahead and gun action ordered. As the ship began to swing to starboard it was seen that the U-boat was on a much more converging course than had been first estimated and that she was turning towards 'Clyde' and closing very rapidly.

It immediately became obvious to 'Clyde's' captain that he could never get round in time to ram the U-boat and that he would be rammed amidships himself unless he could dive fast enough. The wheel was put amidships, the gun's crew and all hands were ordered below, and the captain was about to press the Klaxons, when he realized that a collision could not be avoided and that his ship would stand a better chance on the surface with the engines kept at full speed.

'U-67' struck 'Clyde' right aft on No.7 torpedo tube. Her sloping bow rode up slightly, but she very quickly went ahead again and passed under 'Clyde's' stern. As she did so, her main vents were heard to open and she was soon lost to sight.

'Clyde's' captain subsequently greatly regretted having previously ordered his gun's crew and Lewis gunners below, as it was not possible to get them closed up again in time to open fire before the U-boat disappeared.

Five minutes later, after it had been ascertained that the damage sustained was not serious, 'Clyde' dived to endeavour to regain contact. She continued to patrol submerged and to sweep for U-boats for the next eight hours; she steered to seaward in the hope that they would be doing the same thing and might surface to proceed away on their engines.

The damage sustained by *Clyde* was too slight to be of any consequence, but U-67 had been hard hit. Shortly after the incident Müller-Stockheim sent the following brief signal to Lorient: RAMMED A BRITISH SUBMARINE WHILE TAKING AVOIDING ACTION.

In a subsequent signal, presumably after assessing the damage to his boat, Müller-Stockheim reported that U-67's bow was twisted and that the caps of her forward torpedo tubes had been buckled. From then on U-67's usefulness as a fighting unit was severely restricted and, not surprisingly, Dönitz ordered Müller-Stockheim to return to port. Later, after all three U-boats had reported in, U-67 and U-68 were ordered to rendezvous off the coast of French Morocco, where U-67 was to transfer most of her remaining torpedoes, and as much diesel oil as she could safely spare, to U-68. Furthermore, as U-67 was returning to Lorient, it would no longer be necessary for her to transfer her sick man to U-111, as at first planned.

Having received reports of the Tarafal Bay action, Admiral Dönitz suspected that the Enigma codes might have been compromised, but he could not be sure of this. He wrote in his war diary on 28 September 1941:

> The most likely explanation is that our cipher has been compromised, or that there has been some other breach of security. It is highly unlikely that an English submarine would just happen to turn up in such an isolated area.

The Admiral was correct in his latter supposition, and his concern led to an investigation into the Tarafal Bay incident by *Kontra-Admiral* Erhard Maertens, head of the German Naval Communications Service. In his subsequent report to Dönitz, Maertens described the German Naval Enigma as 'the most secure system for enciphering messages in the world'. He concluded that, 'The acute disquiet about the compromise of our secret operation cannot be justified. Our cipher does not appear to have been broken.'

Grudgingly, Dönitz accepted Admiral Maerten's findings, but he still could not accept that the appearance of HMS *Clyde* in Tarafal Bay at the same time as his U-boats was accidental. He speculated that the British had developed a new very long range radar, or perhaps that they were tracking the U-boats with some ultra accurate system of radio direction finding. Drastic measures were called for, resulting in changes in the Enigma code which temporarily put a stop to Bletchley Park's decrypting. These adjustments were in vain, however, since within a week the British decoders had found another way in and were busy reading the U-boat radio traffic again.

HMS *Clyde*, meanwhile, had continued to search for the U-boats for the remainder of the night and into next morning. Ingram assumed they would be moving out to sea as fast as possible and would not surface until they thought they were safe. Remaining at periscope depth, he watched and listened. At 1100 on the 28th, having made no contact, he surfaced and broke radio silence to report to the Admiralty.

As U-67 and U-68 headed east for the African coast to make their transfer, Kleinschmidt was taking U-111 to the north again following a report that a 9,000-ton British ship damaged by torpedo was drifting 400 miles west of Las Palmas. This must have been the *Silverbelle*, torpedoed by U-68 in Convoy SL 87 six days earlier.

*

While the waters off the coast of West Africa were in a frenzy of activity, it was business as usual for the anti-submarine trawler *Lady Shirley*, based in Gibraltar. The daily grind of anti-submarine patrols was as boring as it was unproductive, and when orders were received to go deep sea they promised a welcome break from the routine.

Built in 1937 for Jutland Amalgamated Trawlers of Hull, the *Lady Shirley* was a typical East Coast trawler, the like of which could often be seen in the halcyon days of peace trailing smoke through Icelandic waters attempting to satisfy the insatiable demand for fish in Britain. Her builders had talked confidently of 12½ knots, but she would never make more than 10, and that with a fair wind. She did, however, have a huge bunker capacity, capable of sustaining her coal-burning boilers on long voyages away from home.

When war came along in 1939, and the Admiralty found itself woefully short of small ships for escort and patrol work, the *Lady Shirley*, along with many of her kind, found herself summarily drafted into the Royal Navy. Without more ado, her fishing gear was ripped out, her fish hold was converted to mess decks, a Mark VI 4-inch was mounted on her forecastle and a brace of machine guns abaft her bridge house. To complete her transformation into a man-of-war, the once-humble fishing boat was fitted with Asdic and a rack of depth charges on her after deck. In place of the flat-cap-wearing skipper of her other life came Lieutenant Commander Arthur Callaway RANR.

Tall, blue-eyed, and wearing a full black beard, Arthur Henry Callaway was a commanding figure in all respects. Born in the quiet, tree-lined suburb of Woollahra in Sydney, Australia in 1906, he was educated at Bondi Superior Public School and trained as an accountant. On the outbreak of war he was managing director of the Hygienic Feather Mills, engaged in the manufacture of upmarket bedding. Despite this mundane occupation, he was also a keen member of the Royal Australian Naval Reserve, which he had joined soon after leaving school. In 1940 he was seconded to the Royal Navy and given command of HMT *Lady Shirley.*

Lieutenant Commander Callaway had received his sailing orders by hand, a wise precaution, given the proliferation of German spies in Gibraltar. *Lady Shirley*, in company with her sister-trawler *Erin*, was to play nursemaid to the ocean boarding vessel HMS *Maron*, escorting her to her patrol area off the Canary Islands.

In September 1940 Hitler contacted the Spanish ruler General Franco requesting the use of naval bases in the Canaries. Franco was prepared to agree, but only in return for an inordinate amount of weapons and equipment for his army, plus sovereignty over part of French North Africa. Hitler refused the General's demands, which was just as well, for the presence of German naval bases in the Atlantic islands would have been disastrous for British shipping. However, Spain did agree to allow German supply ships access to the islands, and for most of 1941, and into 1942, two German merchantmen, the *Charlotte Schliemann* and the *Corrientes*, were based in Las Palmas supplying diesel oil and provisions to U-boats. These ships, it was later revealed, were being supplied with oil by American tankers.

The Standard Oil Company of America had close links with the German chemical giant I.G. Farben, and in 1940 Standard Oil put all its tankers under the Panamanian flag; it was under the cover of this foreign flag that oil was being carried to the Canary

Islands. Much of this fuel was used to top up the tanks of the *Charlotte Schliemann* and *Corrienties*, the rest being transferred to German tankers running the blockade to Hamburg. Standard Oil, and therefore the United States of America, were helping to keep Hitler's U-boats at sea.

With the Second World War now old history, the *Deutsches U-Boot Museum* has put it on record that:

> The neutrality declared by Spain and Portugal has been underlined in Standing Orders and other directives of the BdU [*Befehlshaber der U-boote* or C-in-C U-boats] explicitly at the outbreak of war. Notwithstanding, in the case of Spain, there were clear expectations for logistic support in Spanish ports of U-boat operations given the special relations to the country after the massive support of France during the Spanish Civil War 1936–1939. Therefore, already before the war certain negotiations had started, which eventually led to the establishment of a restricted system of depots with fuel and rations in the ports of Ferrol, Vigo and Cadiz, however, considerable concerns with regard to the re-supply of these depots remained. To enable the support capacities envisaged in Spain during the early years of the war it was agreed to station German merchant vessels as supply ships in these three Spanish ports, a similar arrangement was agreed later at Las Palmas at the Canary Islands. The BdU took these supply facilities clearly into account for its operational planning of U-boat employments. In the case of Portugal no plans by the BdU became known yet with regard to the supply of U-boats in the country and its overseas territories.

And so it fell to HMS *Maron*, an ex-Blue Funnel Line steamer of 6,487 tons armed with two 6-inch guns, to keep watch on the tanker traffic around the Canaries. Admiralty Intelligence had warned that nine or more U-boats were known to be in the vicinity of the islands and, ignorant of the American involvement, had ordered *Maron* to intercept and board any Spanish tankers found in the area.

The three naval ships left Gibraltar on the afternoon of 25 September, and once clear of the Straits took up an inverted 'V' formation, steaming at 9 knots, with *Maron* in the middle, *Erin*

2,000yds off on her port bow and *Lady Shirley* a similar distance on her starboard bow. The weather was fine and warm, the ocean quiet, so for the trawlers at least it promised to be an untaxing voyage, a welcome five or six days away from the stifling bureaucracy of Gibraltar's naval establishment.

Nearing the Canary Islands, Lieutenant Commander Callaway received orders for *Lady Shirley* and *Erin* to leave *Maron* to her own devices and steam at full speed to meet the British tanker *La Carriere*, then inbound to Gibraltar with a full cargo of fuel oil from the Caribbean. *La Carriere* was then 400 miles to the west of Gran Canaria and averaging just over 10 knots.

That evening, just as the trawlers were about to make their farewells to HMS *Maron*, Callaway received another signal from Gibraltar countermanding the first. *Erin* was to remain with *Maron*, while *Lady Shirley* was to mount a patrol around the island of Tenerife, remaining out of sight of the land. It had been reported that three enemy tankers, one German and two Italian, were about to leave the port of Tenerife, where they had been taking advantage of Spanish neutrality. *Lady Shirley* was to intercept and, if possible, sink the enemy ships. It was a tall order for the little trawler, but Callaway and his men welcomed the challenge.

CHAPTER FOUR

West of Africa

Some 400 miles west-south-west of the Canaries, the fight to save the *Silverbelle*, torpedoed in Convoy SL 87, had finally ended in defeat. *Silverbelle*, listing heavily but showing no immediate signs of sinking, had initially been taken in tow by HMS *Gorleston*, with the corvette *Gardenia* and the Free French sloop *Commandant Duboc* screening. The intention was to tow the crippled merchant-man towards Las Palmas to rendezvous with a salvage tug. The four vessels were then 40 miles astern of the convoy, which had been left with only the sloop *Bideford* and the cutter *Lulworth* escorting. Several U-boats were believed to be still in the vicinity of the convoy, and the situation was obviously fraught with danger. However, the Senior Officer Escort, Commander Keymer in *Gorleston*, for some unexplained reason still seemed to think that his first priority lay in saving the *Silverbelle*.

In the course of the afternoon of the 22nd *Gardenia* signalled that she was running low on fuel, and she was ordered to rejoin the convoy. Then, as dusk was falling, Captain Rowe, who was still on board the *Silverbelle* with all his crew, signalled that his after engine room bulkhead was under severe strain and might well collapse during the night. As a precaution against this eventuality, he requested that most of his crew be taken off. He and a few volunteers would remain on board to attend to the tow.

In retrospect, this appears to have been a perfectly sensible suggestion, but Commander Keymer took it as meaning that Rowe wished to abandon his ship. Rowe, in turn, perceived this as an accusation of cowardice, and the flurry of signals between the two captains that followed became more and more acrimonious. Eventually, Rowe said he would keep his men on board and wait out the night. By this time Keymer had become worried for the safety of his own ship should the *Silverbelle* sink without warning, and he cast off the tow, leaving the engine-less merchantman adrift.

By now the Admiralty had become seriously concerned for the safety of the convoy, which was then protected by only two escorts, and at 0137 on the morning of the 23rd Commander Keymer received a signal from the C-in-C Western Approaches ordering *Gorleston* to return to SL 87. The *Commandant Duboc* was left to look after the *Silverbelle.*

There were huge sighs of relief in the ranks of SL 87 when, just on sunset, HMS *Gorleston* finally rejoined the convoy. Commander Keymer resumed control and ordered the eight remaining merchantmen to close up into four columns abreast, while the escorts took station around them. HMS *Bideford*, having the only serviceable radar, took the lead, positioning herself 1,300yds on the port bow of the convoy. *Lulworth* covered the starboard side, while *Gorleston* was on the port quarter. The fourth escort, the corvette *Gardenia*, her fuel tanks dangerously low, was out of sight ahead, on her way to the Azores to refuel. Given that at least four U-boats were known to be within striking distance, SL 87's defensive screen was hardly adequate. The only thing in the convoy's favour was that, as night fell, the weather deteriorated noticeably, the wind strengthening from the south-east, accompanied by passing rain squalls.

The complete darkness – there was no moon – and the keening of the wind in the rigging served to increase the air of nervous anticipation spreading through the convoy. This intensified when, at 2145, *Bideford*'s radar picked up a small but strong echo on the starboard bow at 4 miles. *Gorleston* at once increased speed and pulled ahead to investigate. The anti-climax came ten minutes later, when the target was identified as *Gardenia* crossing ahead on her way to the Azores. Having used up a great deal of fuel he could ill afford to waste, Keymer took *Gorleston* back to her station astern.

Leading the starboard wing column of SL 87 was the 3,753-ton steamer *St Clair II*, labouring under a heavy load of palm kernels for the Lever Brothers' refinery at Bromborough on the Mersey. Built as the *Saint Clair* for *Compagnie Generale Transatlantique* of Nantes, she had been seized when France collapsed in the summer of 1940 and handed over to the Ministry of War Transport. The Ministry, in turn, put her under the management of the United Africa Company. In command was Captain Harry Readman, who headed a British crew of forty-four.

Pacing the starboard wind of his bridge, stopping from time to time to peer into the darkness, Readman had good cause to feel uncomfortable. Being lead ship of the outside column, the *St Clair II* was in a dangerously vulnerable position. The British captain would have been even more on edge had he known that hidden in the night to starboard was U-67, her tubes loaded and biding her time.

Günther Müller-Stockheim, conscious that his choice of targets was dwindling by the hour, had brought U-67 closer in on the starboard side of the convoy, where only the radar-less *Lulworth* stood guard. Perhaps loath to expose his boat even to the slightest danger, Müller-Stockheim appears to have fired a full broadside from his bow tubes at random. Three out of the four torpedoes missed completely, carrying on through the convoy to eventually sink harmlessly in deep water. The fourth torpedo was the lucky one, hitting the *St Clair II* amidships. Captain Philips, on the bridge of the *Lafian*, another of United Africa's ships, astern and to port of the *St Clair II*, was witness to the sudden end of the ex-French steamer. Philips wrote in his report:

> She soon disappeared, in fact they did not have time to lower any boats, and had to jump for it. They were later picked up by one of the escort vessels, but there were 13 missing when a roll call was taken.

The *St Clair II*, weighed down by a cargo far in excess of her gross tonnage, broke her back and foundered by the stern within five minutes of being hit. With a superb display of seamanship, Captain Harry Readman and his crew successfully launched three lifeboats, but such was the suction created by the ship when she went down that all three boats capsized, throwing their occupants into the sea. Fortunately for them, *Gorleston* and *Lulworth* came to their rescue promptly, but even so thirteen men lost their lives. They were all Cardiff men, from the youngest, 17-year-old Assistant Steward Peter Livingstone on his first voyage, to the oldest, Donkeyman Henry Barker, fifty-six years old and with a lifetime of hard seafaring behind him. The capital city of Wales would soon be in mourning.

The convoy reacted quickly to this new attack, Commodore Macrae signalling for an emergency turn to port to put the U-boat astern and give the escorts clear water to carry out a search.

Gorleston, *Lulworth* and *Bideford*, using starshell and Asdic, spent the next thirty-five minutes searching the area, but nothing was seen or heard.

Three hours passed, and all was quiet, but those keeping watch on the bridges of the seven surviving merchantmen were all too aware that the U-boats were still out there in the darkness, watching and waiting. Commander Keymer, for some reason not easy to explain, decided that any further attack would come from the port side, and arranged his small force accordingly. Convoy speed was increased to 8½ knots, the absolute maximum attainable by most of the merchantmen.

Two more hours dragged by, and by 0430, with the dawn only an hour away, there was a growing hope that the enemy might have abandoned the attack. It was a forlorn hope, for U-107 had by now completed her engine repairs and was returning to the fray. Then, at 0630, with the sky in the east beginning to pale, and contrary to Commander Keymer's prediction, Günther Hessler came in from the starboard side and emptied his bow tubes into the tight formation of slow-moving ships.

The Commodore's ship, *John Holt*, now leading the starboard wing column, was the first to be hit. One of Commodore Macrae's signallers saw the torpedo streaking towards the ship, but his warning shout came too late for avoiding action to be taken. The torpedo went home just aft of the *John Holt*'s bridge, blowing a great hole in her hull plates. She began to go down at once. Captain Hime gave the order to abandon ship, and the boats were lowered away. Of the *John Holt*'s total complement of sixty-nine, only one man, a naval gunner, was lost. The others, including Commodore Macrae and his staff, were picked up by HMS *Gorleston*.

As the *John Holt*'s boats were hitting the water, Günther Hessler's second torpedo found its mark in the next ship in line, the 3,790-ton Elder Dempster motor vessel *Dixcove*, then leading column 2. Mortally hit, she went to her last resting place with her throaty air whistle sounding her death knell. Tight discipline ensured that her lifeboats were lowered promptly, and forty-five of her crew and six passengers were later rescued by the British steamer *Ashby* and the Norwegian *Fana*. Two men, Third Engineer John Morrison and Carpenter John Day, had been killed by the exploding torpedo.

United Africa's 4,876-ton *Lafian* fell victim to another of Hessler's torpedoes. The British ship, sagging under a massive

7,662-ton load of West African produce, began to founder at once. Captain Philips later reported:

> When I reached the bridge after we were hit my Chief Officer, Mr Croft, asked if he could lower the lifeboats. I could feel the ship was doomed as she was filling up and taking a list to starboard. I of course agreed and then went forward to the sailors' and firemens' quarters to make sure that none had slept through it. I found no one and returned amidships where all the officers and crew were assembled, all accounted for. We lowered the boats and while the men were filling them an apparition in white flew past me. This latter turned out to be the 2nd Officer going for his trousers.
>
> According to the best traditions and customs I was the last man to leave the ship. Shortly after the two boats got clear of the *Lafian* she turned over and slowly sank.

Captain Evan Llewellyn Philips, a dour Cardigan man not normally given to flippancy, showed snatches of wry humour in his report. His approach to a life or death situation was a typical example of how the average British merchant captain reacted to the many dangers facing him in time of war.

Three ships going down so quickly, one after the other, proved to be the last straw for those few remaining afloat, namely the British ships *Ashby* and *Dunedin*, the Norwegian-flag *Fana* and the Greek steamer *Rios*. With only one escort, the sloop *Bideford*, actively defending them, they scattered away from the danger, each prepared to take their chances alone. It was not until full daylight, when *Gorleston* and *Lulworth*, who had been busy astern picking up survivors, returned that the remnants of the convoy were reformed into some sort of order. By this time the U-boats, their torpedoes expended, had moved away.

Throughout this, the fourth attack in forty-eight hours on SL 87, the sloop *Bideford* had been the only escort present. As might be expected, she had been reduced to running in circles and firing star shell at fleeting shadows, while the U-boats took their pick of the helpless merchantmen. All this time, *Gorleston* and *Lulworth* were still astern looking for survivors from the torpedoed ships. Commander Keymer, the Senior Officer Escort, later laid some of the blame for his failure to protect the convoy on the merchant ships themselves. To quote from his report to the Admiralty: 'Except for the Norwegian FANA, who showed praiseworthy initiative, there appeared little ability or willingness to assist, and *Gorleston* was forced to join in the rescue work.' On examination, this seems an unfair accusation, since the ships of SL 87 were all very heavily loaded and slow to manoeuvre. For most of them, to stop to pick up survivors would have been suicidal, and in any case they were under orders from the convoy Commodore to maintain station. The only ship amongst them remotely suited to the role of rescue ship was the 1,375-ton *Fana*, and she did what she could.

*

When daylight came on the 23rd, the *Silverbelle*, a credit to the Sunderland shipyard that built her, was over 150 miles astern of SL 87 and still very much afloat. It was then decided that the *Commandant Duboc* should take her in tow and attempt to reach the Canaries, or at the very least, to rendezvous with the salvage tug said to be on the way from Las Palmas. It was late that afternoon before a towline was connected, and the two ships began their long crawl to the north. Perversely, the commander of the French sloop, perhaps taking his cue from Commander Keymer, then decided it would too dangerous to tow at night. Now the salvage operation became a pointless exercise, in fact a ridiculous farce, the tow being cast off at nightfall, then much of the following day being spent in re-connecting. Consequently, over the next six days the *Silverbelle* made little progress towards her destination.

Aboard the *Silverbelle*, the time had not been wasted. Working day and night, Captain Rowe and his crew had succeeded in jettisoning a considerable amount of her cargo in order to lighten the ship. Unfortunately, all their efforts proved to be wasted. On the 28th, the promised salvage tug having failed to turn up, *Commandant Duboc* announced she was running short of fuel and would have to return to Freetown. Captain Rowe, being confident that his ship would stay afloat for at least another week, was reluctant to abandon her. He was only persuaded to leave by the promise that he would be able to return with a salvage tug sent from Freetown to pick up the tow.

Before leaving the *Silverbelle*, Rowe succeeded in unshipping her Bofors gun, lowering it into a lifeboat and rowing it across to the *Commandant Duboc*. This was at a time when the 40mm

Bofors, which fired at the rate of 120 rounds per minute, was new to merchant ships, and consequently, in Rowe's opinion, would be needed elsewhere. Misguided or not, Rowe's achievement in salvaging a gun weighing nearly two tons was a commendable feat. Ironically, when the Bofors was landed in Freetown, instead of being congratulated on his achievement, Rowe was rebuked for losing two spanners belonging to the gun.

Captain Hilon Rowe, determined to the end, tried to persuade the authorities in Freetown to fly him back to the *Silverbelle* in one of the Sunderland flying boats stationed in the port, but this was deemed impossible. He left Freetown again in the *Commandant Duboc* on 4 October, hoping to find his ship and bring her in, but in spite of an extensive search, the *Silverbelle* could not be found.

*

The Anti-Submarine Warfare Division of the Naval Staff was scathing in its criticism of the defence of SL 87:

> The fact that seven out of eleven ships were sunk with no retaliation against the enemy is to be deplored. The escort was a strong one for a convoy of this size . . . It is clear that the efforts of the escorts were poorly coordinated. Four attacks took place and on only one occasion were the escorts in station on the convoy. Diversion of the escort vessels for purposes of transmitting W/T messages, towing the disabled *Silverbelle*, carrying out dusk sweeps and picking up survivors of torpedoed ships was responsible for this. It was particularly unfortunate that the S.O. of the Escort spent so much time out of touch with his group . . . There appears to have been an excessive use of R/T and this may, perhaps, have simplified the enemy's task of keeping in touch with the convoy. *Cdt. Duboc* reported that, whilst she was standing by *Silverbelle*, R/T was heard from corvettes forming up with the next convoy off Freetown, over 1,200 miles away.
>
> The general inference to be drawn from this analysis is that the escort vessels were not sufficiently alive to the vital necessity of prosecuting the most vigorous possible search for the attacking U-boat, immediately after the attack has developed.

Admiral Dönitz, on the other hand, and not without good cause, was well satisfied with the outcome. An entry in his War Diary for 24 September reads:

> The convoy west of Africa was attacked by U-67 and U-107 during the night.
>
> U-67 sank a freighter of 7000 GRT, but was beaten off and had various engine troubles.
>
> U-107 reported having sunk a tanker of 13,000 GRT and possibly sank 2 ships of 8000 likewise 5000 GRT. A small steamer escaped with the escort (4 destroyers, 3 escort vessels.)
>
> Operations on this convoy may therefore be considered at an end. Four boats attacked and altogether the following ships were sunk:
>
> 5 ships – 42,000 GRT – sunk for certain.
> 4 ships – 24,000 GRT – possibly sunk.
> 2 ships – 12,000 GRT – damaged.
>
> With the exception of the small steamer observed by U-107 then, the entire convoy was wiped out.

Dönitz's assessment of the outcome of the attack on SL 87 may have been an exaggeration, but it must be deplored that seven ships and nearly 40,000 tons of valuable cargo went to the bottom. Mercifully, only eighteen lives were lost, this being largely due to the calm weather and the determined, however misguided, rescue efforts of Commander Keymer and his ships.

*

Captain Cecil Hime survived the sinking of the *John Holt*, and after a short spell of survivor's leave, returned to sea. In March 1943, as was fitting, he took command of the new *John Holt*, a smart 5,000-tonner built by Cammell Laird of Birkenhead. A year later, in March 1944, Hime and his command were in the familiar waters of the Gulf of Guinea, bound for Douala in the French Cameroons with a cargo of cement.

It was an idyllic West African night, the sea like a millpond, the horizon endless and a half-moon climbing in a black velvet sky against a background of twinkling stars. It was a night for dreams to be dreamed. The *John Holt* was 60 miles south of the entrance to the Opobo River and making a comfortable 12 knots. There were no other ships in sight.

All dreams that may have been dreamt were rudely shattered when, at thirteen minutes past nine, a torpedo slammed into the *John Holt*'s starboard side in the vicinity of her forepeak. Her forward hatch covers and tarpaulins were blown off, and a wide crack appeared in the deck between Nos.1 and 2 hatches. Then, hard on the heels of the first, a second explosion ripped open the British ship's hull directly under her No.1 hatch. With her forward holds wide open to the sea, the *John Holt* immediately began to go down by the head. *Oberleutnant* Gerhard Seehausen, patrolling Nigerian waters in U-66 in the hope of meeting up with unescorted Allied ships, had struck gold.

Captain Hime was on the bridge within seconds, and quickly grasping the hopelessness of the situation, ordered the ship to be abandoned. Although, the *John Holt*'s foredeck was under water within three or four minutes, her total complement of ninety-five, which included four passengers and forty Sierra Leonean stevedores, cleared the ship in good order in four boats and three rafts. As soon as they were clear of the sinking ship, Seehausen brought U-66 to the surface, and before he was able to hide, Captain Hime found himself prisoner aboard the U-boat along with one of his passengers, Stanton Elliot, a shipping agent for the John Holt Company. The rest of the survivors were later picked up by a passing ship.

U-66 continued to hunt in the Gulf of Guinea, and sixteen days later sank the palm oil tanker *Matardian*, but thereafter Seehausen's luck deserted him, and he decided to move north. Here the horizon was equally empty of Allied merchantmen, but the US Navy was present in abundance. On 1 May U-66 was in the region of the Cape Verde Islands when she was picked up by the radar of the escort carrier, USS *Block Island*. The carrier's aircraft immediately took off and gave chase, as did *Block Island*'s accompanying destroyer, *USS Buckley.*

The chase was prolonged, but the Americans refused to give up, and five days later, in the early hours of 6 May, *Buckley* caught U-66 on the surface. A fierce exchange of gunfire and torpedoes ensued, the fight ending with the destroyer ramming the U-boat.

With U-66 impaled on *Buckley*'s bows, a party of Germans, some of them armed, climbed on to the destroyer's forecastle head.

It is not clear whether these men were intent on taking over the American ship, or whether they were surrendering, but they were vigorously repulsed and a number were killed or wounded.

Gerhard Seehausen eventually managed to free his boat from the destroyer's bows, and backed away. He then attempted to escape on the surface, but *Buckley* opened fire with her 3-inch guns. In desperation, Seehausen fought back by ramming the American destroyer. *Buckley*'s starboard propeller was damaged in the collision, but she continued to pound the U-boat. U-66 was last seen running away with smoke and flames coming from her open conning tower and foredeck hatches. She sank shortly afterwards, scuttled by her own crew. USS *Buckley* picked up thirty-six survivors from the water, but *Oberleutnant* Gerhard Seehausen was not amongst them. Neither were Captain Cecil Hime or Stanton Elliot. They died with the enemy who had imprisoned them.

*

Unable to locate the abandoned *Silverbelle* again, Captain Hilon Rowe carried on with the *Commandant Duboc* to Gibraltar, where he was landed to await a passage home. The French minesweeper, on the other hand, was given no respite. After refuelling and taking on stores, she was assigned to the northbound convoy HG 75 as rescue ship. This would involve her bringing up the rear of the convoy to pick up survivors from any ships sunk during the passage.

Convoy HG 75 consisted of sixteen nondescript merchantmen, tramps mostly, the majority of which were loaded down to their gunwales with Spanish iron ore. In times of peace this would have been regarded as a dirty and unwelcome cargo, but in wartime, with the blast furnaces of Britain working overtime, it was like gold dust. Evidently this is how the Admiralty saw it, for HG 75 had an escort of no fewer than fourteen warships. Led by the legendary Tribal-class HMS *Cossack* were five destroyers, a sloop, six corvettes, a CAM ship (merchantman with a catapult-launched fighter aircraft) and the minesweeper/rescue ship *Commandant Duboc*.

The heavily escorted convoy sailed from Gibraltar at about 1600 on 22 October, and then, perversely, spent several hours forming up in Algeciras Bay in full view of the multitude of binocular-equipped Spanish and German agents known to be watching from the shore. Captain Paul Drouin, a wireless operator in the *Commandant Duboc* at the time, remarked, 'You could almost hear the telephone lines humming, the message being quickly passed on by visual signals or radio between agents amazed at having such a target in full view.'

Captain Drouin was not mistaken. As, with darkness setting in, HG 75 finally left the bay and set course to the west, Lorient was already setting up an ambush. Six U-boats of a group code-named *Breslau* were on station in the western approaches to the Straits of Gibraltar: U-206 (Herbert Opitz), U-563 (Klaus Bargesten) and U-564 (Reinhard Suhren) were off Cape Trafalgar, while U-71 (Walter Flaschenberg), U-83 (Hans-Werner Kraus) and U-204 (Walter Kell) were in the vicinity of Cape Spartel, on the African side. Four Italian submarines were further out in the Atlantic and closing in. Fortunately, and unknown to Admiral Dönitz, Bletchley Park had been reading his signals to the U-boats.

Once clear of the land, HG 75 steaming in six columns abreast set course to the west at 9 knots. Forewarned of the danger ahead, the destroyers *Cossack*, *Legion* and *Vidette* were scouting in the van, while the other escorts formed a tight ring around the convoy. Bringing up the rear as appointed rescue ship, *Commandant Duboc* put on a brave face, carrying out wide sweeps from side to side. Since the French minesweeper had neither Asdic nor Sonar, this was rather a pointless exercise, but it was hoped that her mere presence would deter any shadowing U-boats. Captain Drouin described the atmosphere prevailing:

> Soon, at about midnight, we could make out Cape Spartel a few miles away – the night being very bright not good for us. An hour later the first alarm sounded, but it was a false one which nevertheless made us send up a few flares. The 'berlogue' [bugle call to stand down] sounded shortly afterwards. From then on it was difficult to sleep soundly . . . we were all – or nearly all – aware of being under threat; we were not anxious as much as realistic, taking account of how vulnerable we were defending these fine merchantmen entrusted to us.

The next day, 23 October, was fine and warm and passed without incident. The convoy routing called for the ships to steam out into the Atlantic as far as 10 degrees west, and then alter course to the north. Aircraft from Gibraltar reinforced the escort throughout the daylight hours, keeping the U-boats at bay. Herbert Opitz in U-206 reported to Lorient, 'Kept under water by aircraft'. This fortunate state of affairs lasted until the sun went down, but under the cover of darkness the *Breslau* boats closed in.

At 2306, U-563 was on the surface on the starboard beam of the convoy and creeping up on the leading ships, when a look-out in the corvette *Carnation* spotted her. *Carnation* immediately increased to full speed and turned to ram. Quick to react, Klaus Bargesten hit the klaxon, cleared the conning tower and dived. The corvette followed U-563 down with salvo of five depth charges set to 50ft. At the same time, she fired a flare to alert the other escorts.

Carnation was joined by HMS *Bluebell*, and the two corvettes began stalking U-563 by Asdic. *Bluebell* obtained a solid echo and attacked with depth charges, but with no positive result other than a great deal of disturbed water. The echo was lost and the corvettes returned to their stations.

It was first blow to the U-boats when, half an hour later, U-563 returned to the attack torpedoing the destroyer *Cossack*, which was then covering the port quarter of the convoy. HMS *Legion* raced in to help *Cossack*, but the torpedoed ship's bows had been blown off, and she was burning so fiercely that *Legion* was unable to approach her. It was left to the *Commandant Duboc* to pick up survivors. Captain Drouin wrote:

> One by one we picked up 5 men on a raft; the sea was covered in oil . . . flames coming from the burning 'Cossack' gave the feeling of Dante's *Inferno*. We rescued 16 men, one an officer, from a second raft. They were exhausted, paralysed by the cold, poisoned by the oil. We had to take hold of them and hoist them aboard; in some cases we had to get into the water ourselves to help them to take hold. The Captain of the 'Cossack', together with some of his crew, hadn't wanted to leave the ship and had stood on the poop deck, hoping the fire wouldn't reach that far.

HMS *Cossack* was later taken in tow by a tug sent from Gibraltar, but she eventually sank on the morning of the 27th.

The flaming bonfire following the torpedoing of the *Cossack* was the signal for a night of horror to come. When the burning wreck of the *Cossack* had drifted astern out of sight, at first an uneasy calm settled over the convoy. Nobody doubted that the U-boats were still out there in the darkness, awaiting the opportunity to strike. And they came again in that darkest hour before the dawn, when Reinhard Suhren in U-564 penetrated the escort screen and fired a spread of five torpedoes. Two of these missed, but the red rockets soaring up into the night sky minutes later told a grim story.

First to be hit was the 1,352-ton, Glasgow-registered *Alhama*, on passage from Almeria to Barrow with 2,000 tons of onions, wine and cork. Fortunately for her crew, she sank slowly and reluctantly. Ellerman Wilson's 2,176-ton *Ariosto*, part-loaded with ore and topped off with cork, also made a dignified exit. The third of this unfortunate trio was another Glasgow ship, the 3,670-ton *Carsbreck*, carrying 6,000 tons of iron ore from Almeria to Belfast. Short on reserve buoyancy, she went down with a rush, taking most of her crew with her. The *Commandant Duboc* once again had the grim task of picking up the human debris. Captain Drouin later wrote:

> We stopped where the first rockets had gone up, and found 2 ship's boats from the first victim, which had not gone down too fast, the oarsmen, with precision as if in training, come alongside with oars shipped; the bosun stood at the bow and completed the manoeuvre. The second boat then came alongside; the captain, at the tiller, came aboard last – there were 34 men in all . . . With regret we cast off the 2 boats from the 'Alhama', and the 'Duboc' sped towards the little flashes of light bobbing on the surface over to the North-West, 3000 metres away. The 'Duboc' was all alone and the convoy ships were off to the north; dawn was approaching – a few gleams of pink between two layers of grey and black cloud over a flat, joyless sea.
>
> We came to the little lights – the cargo boat had rapidly broken in two and had gone down in 30 seconds. These twinkling little lights fixed to the life jackets could fortunately be spotted from quite a long way off in good weather. The lifeboat was lowered; it was a lot harder than with the 'Cossack' because all the survivors were badly shocked, many of them wounded, clinging to floating

debris. There were shouts, calls – veritable yelling, when the terror of not having been 'spotted' gave them that extra awful strength to shout out to show where they were.

Working tirelessly throughout what remained of the night, the *Commandant Duboc* picked up another fifty-six men, and when full daylight came, including those already saved from HMS *Cossack*, she had a total of seventy-seven survivors on board.

The battle for Convoy HG 75 lasted for another six days and became an unequal contest. The *Breslau* Group U-boats were joined by a number of Italian submarines, while overhead German long-range Focke-Wulf Condors circled constantly out of gun range, looking for an opportunity to swoop down on any merchantman straggling behind the others. The mêlée finally drew to a close in the early hours of 29 September, in the northern reaches of the Bay of Biscay, when the U-boats, having expended all their torpedoes, returned to their bases. HG 75 had lost a destroyer and four valuable merchantmen and their cargoes, while the CAM ship *Ariguani* sustained serious damage. In return, the attackers lost U-204 and the Italian submarine *Gallileo Ferraris*. It had been a hard-fought battle, one in which the *Commandant Duboc*, a small, lightly-armed minesweeper with no Asdic, had played a vital part.

CHAPTER FIVE

Lady Shirley and the U-boat

The peak of Tenerife's 12,000ft-high Mount Teide was just visible on the horizon when, at first light on the 28th the armed trawler *Lady Shirley* left *Maron* and *Erin* and surged ahead to begin her wait for the enemy tankers believed to be about to leave harbour.

In ancient times the Canary Islands were said to be mountain peaks of the lost continent of Atlantis rearing up out of the sea. Greek mythology had them as the paradisiacal home of the daughters of Hesperides, who guarded the 'golden apples' sought after by Hercules. Mythology turned to reality when in 1312 the Genoese navigator Lanzarotto Matocello accidentally discovered the islands while searching for the fabled Rio de Oro, along which it was said all the gold of Africa flowed. Christopher Columbus used the Canaries as stepping stones to America, but by the nineteenth century they had become little more than a convenient provisioning base for the windjammers taking advantage of the North-East Trade winds. When the steamers came along, Las Palmas and Tenerife gained some importance as coaling, and later oiling, stations, but it was not until the outbreak of the Second World War that the archipelago became of any strategic value.

General Franco, Spain's dictator, received considerable support from Germany in the Spanish Civil War of 1936–9, but when the Second World War broke out he was reluctant to throw in his lot with either side. At first he declared Spain to be a non-belligerent, then later adopted total neutrality. This led Hitler, who saw the Spanish-controlled Canaries as an ideal base for refuelling and resupplying his U-boats, to plan a takeover of the islands. The proposed invasion was vetoed by his Naval Staff, who argued that although the Canaries might be easily taken, Germany's limited surface fleet would not be able to hold them against the might of the Royal Navy. Furthermore, the Admirals pointed out that any U-boat base established on the Atlantic islands would have to be supplied by sea, which again was a virtual impossibility given the overwhelming superiority of Britain's navy. The idea was quietly dropped.

At about 0900 on 28 September, the *Lady Shirley* was south of Tenerife when Lieutenant Commander Callaway received yet another signal from Gibraltar countermanding his earlier orders. News had reached the Rock that the *Commandant Duboc* had abandoned the *Silverbelle* and headed south for Freetown with Captain Rowe and his crew. Callaway was assured that when last seen the *Silverbelle* was still afloat, and that a salvage tug was on the way from Las Palmas to take her in tow. It would be *Lady Shirley's* responsibility to escort the tug and her tow back to Gran Canaria.

When the trawler arrived at the position given on the morning of the 29th, the *Silverbelle* was nowhere to be seen. Callaway searched for her throughout the daylight, but with no success. He was then ordered to resume his watch off Tenerife for the enemy tankers. Meanwhile, the inevitable outburst of wireless traffic accompanying the attempt to salvage the *Silverbelle* had not gone unnoticed by German Intelligence. All U-boats in the vicinity had been warned to keep a lookout for the ship under tow and, if possible, to finish the work begun by U-68.

At the time, U-111 was making her way north to Lorient, and as the position given for the *Silverbelle* was on her proposed route, Wilhelm Kleinschmidt decided to investigate. He was still smarting from his humiliating flight from Tarafal Bay, and having been at sea for seven weeks and crossed the Atlantic twice with only two enemy ships sunk, he desperately needed to add to his score. There would be no military band to welcome U-111's return to Lorient, no medals handed out, but if he could find this '9,000-ton' abandoned ship and send her and her cargo to the bottom it would help to compensate for what had been a disappointing voyage.

U-111 reached the position given by Lorient on the morning of 2 October, and for the next thirty-six hours cruised up and down looking for the torpedoed ship, which was obviously the *Silverbelle*. During the night of the 3rd a 'dim shadow' was sighted, but for reasons unknown, Kleinschmidt failed to investigate. Had he done so, U-111's second war patrol might have come to a very different conclusion.

Sunrise on Saturday 4 October brought with it the promise of another fine, warm day. The sky was a cloudless blue, the sea mirror-calm and visibility unlimited. HM Trawler *Lady Shirley* was on economical speed and a westerly course, with only the lazy thump of her idling engine disturbing the quiet of the morning.

Temporary Sub Lieutenant Frederick French RNR had the watch on the bridge, and lulled by the tranquillity of the opening day, was leaning against the forward rail contemplating the antics of a small shoal of porpoises cavorting off the port bow. Twenty-four-year-old French, the *Lady Shirley*'s First Lieutenant, tall and gangling with a neat beard, was described as 'an alert and determined officer'. He had joined the trawler after service in an armed merchant cruiser.

The shrilling whistle of the bridge voice pipe jerked Sub Lieutenant French out his reverie and he shot into the wheelhouse. The lookout in the trawler's crow's nest was reporting a suspicious object, possibly a ship's funnel, on the starboard bow. French slid down the ladder to the deck, ran forward and climbed the mast to see for himself.

There was a shimmering haze on the horizon, and even using his binoculars, French was undecided. It could be a ship hull-down – on the other hand, it could be the conning tower of a submarine. The object disappeared as he was studying it, but it had been substantial enough while visible. French clambered down the rigging, ran for the wheelhouse and called Lieutenant Commander Callaway, who joined him on the bridge within seconds.

Callaway listened to his Number One's breathless explanation while sweeping the horizon to starboard with his binoculars. There was nothing to be seen, not even disturbed water, but for two men to have reported an object there had to be something there. Callaway altered course on to the bearing indicated by French and rang for full emergency speed. When, a few minutes later, Asdic operator Seaman Norman Mitchell reported a firm echo right ahead at extreme range, Callaway hit the alarm bells.

As the calm of the morning was shattered by the strident clanging of the alarm bells, the *Lady Shirley* immediately became a warship again. Whereas earlier only a handful of men had been in evidence, swabbing down and polishing brass, the decks were now suddenly alive with running men pulling on lifejackets and steel helmets. Sub Lieutenant Waller, the ship's navigator, found his off-watch lie-in rudely interrupted. He later wrote:

> I had kept the middle watch and on this occasion my ship-mates had not called me for breakfast, this did not happen if a particularly good breakfast was on. I therefore

fell out of my bunk, grabbed my life-belt and tin hat and rushed to my action station. My sub action station was aft at the depth charges. The ship was very quickly at full sub action stations. Lieutenant Boucant was on the bridge as Asdic Control Officer with the Captain, Sub Lieutenant French was on the 4-inch gun platform, the Coxswain HSD Ldg. Seaman Mackrill had taken over the Asdic and Seaman Mitchell had joined his friend Ken Hibbs at the 0.5 in. Seaman Sydney Halcrow was at the depth charge rails.

Twenty-one-year-old Allan Waller, although born far inland, like Lieutenant Commander Callaway had always had an insatiable love of the sea and ships. As a young boy growing up in Croydon he had spent all his school holidays amongst fishermen on the Suffolk coast, and he joined the RNVR as a signalman rating in 1938. On the outbreak of war a year later, he had been commissioned for service in anti-submarine trawlers.

Waller's war did not begin well: his first ship, HMT *Amethyst*, under the command of Temporary Lieutenant the Hon W.K. Rous, hit a mine in the Thames Estuary in November 1940 and went down in ten minutes. There were no casualties, but when the survivors were landed at Southend they were thought to be from a sunken German ship and were promptly arrested. Recovered from this ordeal, Waller served for a short while in the Flower-class corvette *Primula*, only to lose her when she was severely damaged in a collision while escorting a convoy. He then joined the anti-submarine trawler *Tourmaline*, and in January 1941 was mentioned in despatches for 'courage and skill' during an encounter with German E-boats in the North Sea. Two weeks later, he was wounded when the *Tourmaline* was bombed and sunk by enemy aircraft off the North Foreland. In the space of a few short months young Allan Waller had faced the brutal realities of war and earned himself the nickname the 'Jonah of Parkeston Quay', Harwich then being his home port.

The 'object' sighted by the *Lady Shirley* was Wilhelm Kleinschmidt's U-111, still searching for the abandoned *Silverbelle*. On such a fine, clear day, even in this apparently empty ocean, it would have been wise for Kleinschmidt to go to periscope depth for the first hours of daylight, but instead he chose to remain on the surface, and so eventually brought about his own downfall. It was later said by some of U-111's crew that the trawler had been spotted 10 miles off, and that Kleinschmidt had mistakenly identified her as the derelict ship he was looking for. Even when closer and viewing the approaching *Lady Shirley* through the periscope, Kleinschmidt persisted in the belief that he had a 5,000-ton derelict in his sights, and at a distance of 3 to 4 miles off. His hydrophone operator questioned his commander's estimate, saying the echo he was getting was from only 500 metres away. This Kleinschmidt dismissed as wildly inaccurate. Those in the control room with him later said they assumed that either something was very wrong with the U-boat's periscope, or that Kleinschmidt's judgement was clouded and he was clinging to the belief that he had found the *Silverbelle*. On the other hand, it may have been that what Kleinschmidt saw was a distorted image of the anti-submarine trawler, her silhouette being greatly enlarged by refraction caused by the early morning haze on the horizon, a common occurrence in those latitudes.

It beggars belief that Wilhelm Kleinschmidt, a naval officer with seven years sea service, could have made such a mistake, yet there was no evidence that there was anything wrong with U-111's periscope. It may be that when Kleinschmidt executed the high-risk manoeuvre off Tarafal Bay by diving under HMS *Clyde,* with just inches to spare, U-111's periscope did make contact with the British submarine's keel, although no damage was logged.

All this time, the *Lady Shirley* was bearing down on U-111 at an unprecedented 12 knots, with her bow-wave foaming and every rivet in her hull in danger of popping. The distance recorder on the bridge for her Asdic was out of action, and a stopwatch was being used to time the echo, a system perfected by Callaway's insistence that every possible eventuality be covered by frequent practice drills while at sea.

The range was shortening rapidly, beginning at 1,800yds when the first Asdic contact was made, dropping to 1,200, 800 and then 600yds. The bearing of the target remaining steady.

In U-111's control room the threshing of *Lady Shirley*'s propeller could be heard growing louder as the seconds passed. Kleinschmidt appeared to be mesmerized, like a rabbit caught in the headlights of an approaching car. Those around him were so disturbed by his actions that they were on the point of mutiny.

Sub Lieutenant Waller, aft at the *Lady Shirley*'s depth charge rails, takes up the story:

> The firing bell rang and the first charge was dropped from the rails; at the second ring, the depth charge throwers were fired and simultaneously another charge from the rails, finally a third charge from the rails, this was a standard charge pattern. The charges were set to explode at different depths, the theory being to have the submarine in the pattern with depth charges exploding all around it.

Waller's first and third charges were set to explode at 350ft, the second and fourth at 150ft, and those from the throwers at 250ft. Certainly, any U-boat unfortunate enough to be caught in this lethal trap consisting of six charges, each containing 290lbs of Amatol, would be bound to take a severe hammering; and if any of the charges exploded within 20ft of the submarine, her pressure hull would probably have been split open. However, it seems that when the attack came U-111 was still shallow, no more than 40ft below the surface. Her lighting, usually the first thing to go, did not even flicker, but there was a report of water entering her engine compartment. In any event, *Kapitänleutnant* Kleinschmidt seems to have panicked, and he gave the order to surface.

While the starboard throwers were being reloaded, Sub Lieutenant Waller went round to the port side of the deck, where Seaman Halcrow was in charge, to see if all was well. As the two men talked, they saw the bow of a submarine break the surface some 400yds astern in the turbulence caused by the depth charges. The bow was followed by a periscope, then a conning tower, as U-111 reared out of the sea. Waller was astonished by the sheer size of the U-boat – 'fully twice the size of our little ship', he later said. And he was not wrong. While the *Lady Shirley* tipped the scales at just 472 tons loaded, the Type IXB displaced 1,034 tons and was 90ft longer than the trawler. Furthermore, compared with *Lady Shirley*'s 10 knots, the U-boat had a top speed on the surface of 18 knots. Kleinschmidt could easily have run away on the surface, but he did not.

With the surfacing of the U-boat, the nature of the fight changed completely. What had been a straightforward anti-submarine action fought with depth charges, Asdic and hydrophones, had suddenly become a surface confrontation between equals. Again, thanks to Lieutenant Commander Callaway's regular drills, the transformation was carried out smoothly, with officers and men changing roles with practised ease.

As ship's navigator, Allan Waller's place was at Callaway's side on the bridge, while Ian Boucant took charge of the after deck. Seaman Sydney Halcrow followed Waller to take over the Hotchkiss in the starboard wing of the bridge. The port machine gun was taken by Seaman Billy Windsor.

When Waller reached the bridge, the *Lady Shirley* was already heeling over under full helm as Callaway brought her short round to put the surfaced U-boat ahead. When she was broadside-on, the twin .50 Vickers on the poop had a clear field and opened up, sweeping U-111's deck and conning tower with short bursts. The duel had begun.

Callaway steadied the trawler on an interception course, and she surged forward, her pistons hammering out a mad tattoo as Chief Engineman George Wyatt spun the steam control valve fully open. The range was already down to 500yds and dropping fast. Up in the trawler's bows the 4-inch was loaded and ready to fire, its crew as tense as bowstrings. Sub Lieutenant French slashed down with his hand: 'Fire!'

The long-barrelled gun thundered and recoiled and the first shell went whistling across the intervening water to land 40yds short of U-111. It was a near-miss that did no more than drench the U-boat with spray, but it tested the range. The smoking breech of the trawler's 4-inch was swung back ready to take the next round when the twin-20mm abaft of the submarine's conning tower opened up and the *Lady Shirley*'s foredeck was sprayed with tracer. Seaman Leslie Pizzey, the 4-inch gunlayer, was hit in the stomach and fell to the deck mortally wounded. Sub Lieutenant French immediately took his place at the sights, and the gun continued with rapid fire, hurling semi-armour piercing and shrapnel at the enemy submarine.

The barrels of the *Lady Shirley*'s bridge-mounted Hotchkiss guns were running hot, concentrating their fire on the men milling around the 105mm gun on U-111's foredeck. This, in turn, drew fire from the U-boat's 20mm guns, and a long-range duel developed. The contest was hopelessly unequal: the trawler's .303 Hotchkiss guns, relics of an earlier war, had a calibre similar to that of a British infantry rifle and were no match for the modern

German armament. Their twin-barrelled Flak 30 was pumping out 240 rounds a minute of what was said to be the most destructive 20mm shell in existence. The rattle of gunfire was incessant and deafening and, adding to the noise and confusion, a steam pipe on the trawler's deck had been punctured and was filling the air with clouds of scalding steam. The word bedlam comes to mind.

Aboard U-111, now stopped and drifting, the situation was even more chaotic. The *Lady Shirley*'s machine guns had made the submarine's open decks untenable, and she had received two hits from the trawler's 4-inch, one striking at the base of the conning tower, the second exploding inside the tower with devastating results. Wilhelm Kleinschmidt, *Oberleutnant* Rösing and *Leutnant* Fuchs had been killed, as had the five ratings who were in the tower with them. On the foredeck, the 105mm gun was manned and shells were being passed out through the jagged hole in the base of the conning tower, but when the first round was fired the gun blew up. U-111's main armament was out of the fight, and the men manning it were being mowed down by the unrelenting fire of the *Lady Shirley*'s Hotchkiss guns.

This was warfare at its most basic, reminiscent of the close-quarters gun battles of Nelson's day. The two antagonists were barely 200yds apart, trading shot for shot, and it was now that the chaos prevailing on board U-111 became plainly evident.

Sub Lieutenant Waller later wrote:

> We could not understand why the U-boat had not opened fire with its big gun. We could see several members of this gun's crew scattered around it and we had soon killed or wounded most of them without suffering a single shell in reply. It was mystifying. But we took a real hammering from their conning tower cannon. Our bridge was riddled . . . I had been quietly working out the ship's position and the Captain told me to take it down to the wireless cabin.
>
> The wireless cabin was behind the wheelhouse, but when I tried to leave the bridge by the back door I found it obstructed by one of our two signalmen, who had been hit in the thigh by a cannon shell – one of the Army corporals was trying to patch him up. I dashed back to the bridge, got through the front window and slid down the ladder at the front. There was a fresh stream of fire from

the U-boat as I went down and I felt a shell narrowly miss me. I reached the wireless cabin to find Sparks there all ready to send, but coolly leaning out of the scuttle taking photos. I gave him the signal and he whipped it off straight away.

On his way back to the bridge Waller again ran the gauntlet of enemy shot, and when he reached the bridge he found that the Hotchkiss guns in either wing had fallen silent. Both gunners, Seaman Billy Windsor and Seaman Sidney Halcrow, were down with leg wounds. Halcrow, who was obviously in great pain, pleaded with Waller to reload his gun so that he could fight back. Waller ordered the wounded man to go below, but he refused to leave his post. Incensed by the bloody scene around him, Waller slammed a magazine into the Hotchkiss and was about to empty it in the direction of the U-boat when he saw that her crew were abandoning ship. He held his fire.

While carnage engulfed the U-boat's upper deck, below in her engine room *Oberleutnant* Günter Wulff had been engaged in a desperate struggle to restart the diesels. A ragged cheer went up when at last both motors fired up. The euphoria was short-lived; the fast-revving engines worked up to 500 revs per minute, then coughed and stopped, filling the engine space with dense black smoke. Wulff now had no alternative but to evacuate the engine room. There is no clear evidence as to what had caused the diesels to backfire, but it seems possible that the water that leaked into the engine spaces during depth charging may have been to blame. Whatever the cause, U-111's last chance to escape had gone.

Korvettenkapitän Heinecke, who had been lending a hand in the engine room, went forward to the conning tower to report and there found total devastation. Kleinschmidt's lifeless body was lying at the foot of the conning tower hatch, while the shattered remains of the other occupants of the tower were scattered amongst the smoking wreckage. As the senior surviving officer it then fell to Heinecke to take command of U-111.

The engine-less U-boat, now noticeably down by the stern, was obviously beyond saving, and it remained only for Heinecke to surrender without sacrificing any more lives. He ordered the remaining crew to don lifejackets and abandon ship. The shell-shocked men needed no urging.

Allan Waller described the finish:

> The end for the U-boat came very quickly, her bow rose
> up and she just slipped away at which all her crew in the
> water gave three cheers. But I was sure we had sunk her
> rather than some of her crew opening seacocks. Our depth
> charges had forced her to the surface; they must have split
> her aft, as she never got her stern out of the water. Besides,
> she had taken at least nine direct hits from our 4-inch; she
> was finished all right. The time was now 1027. The action
> had lasted just 23 minutes from start to finish.

The U-boat's demise was hastened by her Chief Engineer,
Günther Wulff, who without waiting for orders had opened the
main vents. She began her final dive. Her career had been brief
and not very successful. In her only two war patrols she spent a
total of 116 days at sea, sank only four Allied ships and damaged
one other.

When it became plain that the U-boat had no fight left in her,
Lieutenant Commander Callaway ordered his guns to cease fire.
Sub Lieutenant Waller, who had anticipated the order, remarked,
'We were treated to the extraordinary sight of the U-boat's crew
all abandoning ship. They jumped into the sea, groups of them,
all keeping together in perfect drill, until there seemed to be hundreds of them in the water waving their arms and shouting.'

In choosing to fight the *Lady Shirley* on the surface Kleinschmidt
had gambled and lost heavily. A U-boat was designed to fight by
stealth, to creep up submerged on an unsuspecting enemy, torpedo him and then run away. She was not up to a surface fight,
gun to gun, as some had found to their cost when attempting to
sink merchant ships with their deck guns. Although the 4-inch
British merchant ships carried was usually old and outdated, with
an experienced naval gunlayer, backed by a gun's crew of merchant seamen, largely untrained but enthusiastic in the defence of
their ship, the outcome was often uncertain.

In the case of U-111 there were contributory factors which
may have helped to bring about her loss. Kleinschmidt himself
was by training a merchant seaman and had been less than a year
in U-boats, while *Oberleutnant* Rösing and the first lieutenant,
Helmut Fuchs, were also new to submarines. The only really experienced officer on board was the Engineer Officer *Oberleutnant*

(*Ing*) Günther Wulff, and he will have had little say in the operation of the boat.

Of U-111's petty officers only five had served in U-boats prior to joining, and only two of these would have been considered experienced by U-boat standards of the day, while the loyalty of some of them was in question. The captain of the twin 20mm gun, a boatswain's mate, 1st Class, was considered a persistent trouble maker and was stated to have refused to man his gun when the U-boat first surfaced, presumably because he saw the situation as hopeless. Another ex-merchant service man with many years experience at sea, he was said to have often expressed his doubts about the way the war was going for Germany. Such pessimism has no place in a fighting ship at sea.

U-111's ratings were of similar ilk. Some were conscripts to the U-boat service, and very few had much in the way of sea-going experience prior to joining the boat. It was said that their morale quickly collapsed when they were faced with the critical situation that developed.

The fact that U-111 had extra men on board, a total complement of fifty-two as opposed to the normal forty-three, did nothing to help matters. Overcrowding in any submarine is bad for morale, and as U-111 had been on a prolonged voyage, it must have had an effect. It was also reported that Wilhelm Kleinschmidt was not particularly well respected by his crew. Added to this, the presence on board of the commanding-officer-in-training, *Korvettenkapitän* Heinecke, who by all accounts was a rather objectionable character, will have tended to undermine Kleinschmidt's authority.

Lady Shirley, on the other hand, although only a minimally armed 10-knot trawler, was a highly efficient fighting ship. Her commander and officers were keen reservists, and the majority of her ratings were men hardened by the rigours of Icelandic fishing waters. She carried out a full set of drills every day, no matter where she was, and practised her gunnery whenever possible. U-111 had chosen to challenge the wrong ship, and had paid the price.

CHAPTER SIX

Return to Harbour

The enormity of what he was about to undertake dawned on Lieutenant Commander Arthur Callaway as he leaned over the fore end of his blood-spattered bridge and counted the men in the water. He stopped at forty, with the uncomfortable realization that his own crew would be hopelessly outnumbered by the prisoners they were preparing to take on board. The Germans may have suffered the trauma of losing their submarine, but they were still very fit young men, who by nature of their calling would be quick to take advantage of any weakness shown; and with the *Lady Shirley* four days' steaming from Gibraltar they would have plenty of time to make mischief. Callaway was tempted to ring for full speed, sheer away and leave the Germans to their fate – and there were those who might have said he would have been fully justified in doing so – but these men had surrendered, and he felt duty bound to save them.

The *Lady Shirley* was not well endowed with small arms; she could muster only half a dozen rifles and four revolvers. These were broken out, and armed men lined the rails of the trawler to await their prisoners. Fortunately, the weather was still benign; there was no wind and the sea was mirror-calm, disturbed only by a long, undulating swell. A scrambling net was thrown over the side, and Callaway swung the engine room telegraph to full astern to take the way off the ship. As he did so, he was conscious that he was putting his small command in a very vulnerable position. Stopped and rolling in the swell, the *Lady Shirley* was a sitting duck for any other U-boat that might be lurking at periscope depth, watching and waiting for the opportunity to strike. It would take only one torpedo to rip the bottom out of her.

Unknown to Lieutenant Commander Callaway, perhaps just as well, his fears were fully justified. It was later claimed that another U-boat was submerged nearby and watching the rescue operation; she did not intervene for fear of harming U-111's survivors, but was said to have surfaced later and reported the incident to

Lorient. The presence of this U-boat has never been confirmed, nor has her identity been established, but given that a number of German and Italian boats were known to be in the area at the time, it does seem likely that the *Lady Shirley* was being observed.

The survivors were hauled in over the trawler's rail one at a time. Some wore Davis escape apparatus, others just lifebelts, and most were in shorts, bare-chested and showing healthy sun tans, acquired no doubt over long days spent in tropical waters. At first, because of their dark skins, they were thought to be Italians, and it was only when they spoke that their true nationality was revealed. Contrary to expectations, they showed no signs of giving trouble and seemed grateful to their captors for being rescued. Some of them, on reaching the deck of the trawler, appeared to be amazed that this lightly armed, insignificant little ship had beaten them.

The only prisoner to show any belligerence was *Korvettenkapitän* Heinecke, the officer in training who had assumed command of U-111 in her final moments. Heinecke had a serious head wound, but as soon as he stepped aboard he began protesting at his treatment. He was still protesting when he was led away to have his wound dressed. The only other officer to survive, *Oberleutnant (Ing)* Günther Wulff, was willing, if not eager, to cooperate. He had studied at Birmingham University before the war and spoke fluent English. In the days to come he would prove to be a valuable liaison between Callaway and the prisoners.

While the rescue was in progress, two men who were obviously in trouble were seen drifting away from the trawler. Callaway went after them as soon as the others were aboard, and when they were pulled from the water one, 21-year-old *Matrose* (Seaman) Hans Rüskens, was found to have lost a leg, shot off below the knee, and was unconscious. The other man, who was unharmed, had kept Rüskens afloat.

When the sheer numbers of Germans being unceremoniously hauled over the ship's side rail became plainly evident, it was realized that the gunfight between *Lady Shirley* and U-111 had been merely the prelude to Lieutenant Commander Callaway's troubles. Wilhelm Kleinschmidt had gone down with his command, as had seven others, and two were injured, one very severely; but forty-three tough and very fit young Germans had, in effect, invaded the *Lady Shirley*. To watch over them for the next four days at sea all Callaway could muster were twenty-eight able-bodied men.

Seaman Gunlayer Leslie Pizzey had died at his post, the Hotchkiss gunners, Halcrow and Windsor, were both injured, though not seriously, and Signalman Warbrick, who had been hit by a cannon shell, had a broken thigh. Of the others, most would be fully occupied in manning the ship and her weapons. Furthermore, Gibraltar was 1,000 miles away, the trawler was running short on coal and her only lifeboat had been shot to pieces. The fight was not yet over.

The wounded were fortunate in that *Lady Shirley's* First Lieutenant, Ian Boucant, had spent three years in medical school before deciding that life as a solicitor would be more to his liking. As a very able assistant in ministering to the wounded Boucant had Corporal H.J. Fittall of the Royal Engineers, a passenger in the trawler and a very competent first aider. Between them they were able to deal with most of the injuries, except those of Hans Rüskens. They could do little for him other than keep him warm and comfortable.

The injured men, including *Korvettenkapitän* Heinecke, were put in the officers' cabins, while the other prisoners were locked into the *Lady Shirley's* tiny wardroom, the only really secure accommodation on the ship. It was a tight squeeze for forty-one men, and they would have an uncomfortable passage, but there was no other alternative. When the prisoners were inside, the wardroom hatch was secured from the outside and one of the Hotchkiss guns was set up on the after end of the bridge covering the hatch. The officer of the watch on the bridge was armed with a revolver and hand grenades, and an armed patrol was set up on deck. As an added precaution, Callaway posted a sentry in the empty fish tanks directly below the wardroom in case the prisoners attempted to break out through the deck of their prison.

Then, with the *Lady Shirley* once more under way and on course for Gibraltar, it was time to see to her wounds. She was pockmarked with bullet and cannon shell holes, several small fires had been started on deck and, more seriously, one of the depth charges on the rack had been holed by a cannon shell. This was tackled first, the lethal canister being carefully manhandled to the ship's side and dumped overboard. Then the fires were extinguished, debris cleared from the deck and the blood mopped up.

With the prisoners secured, Lieutenant Commander Callaway had the sad duty of committing the body of Seaman Gunlayer

Leslie Pizzey to the deep. Sub Lieutenant Allan Waller described the ceremony:

> The Captain took the service using my prayer book. Len Pizzey was then gently lowered into the sea in a canvas shroud weighed down with fire bars and covered with a White Ensign, the ship being stopped. This was a very sad moment for us all. He had been a very popular member of the crew. In civil life he had been a cinema projectionist in Southend. He was always cheerful and in addition to being our gunner was the chief organizer of our sports and similar activities. Ironically, and tragically, he should not have been aboard for that trip. He had broken an ankle while playing football and had been taken to hospital. He was so keen to get back to the Lady Shirley and not be drafted to another trawler on recovery, that when he heard our cook was ill he pleaded with the doctors to let him come back to us as cook. They agreed and he came back to us with his ankle in plaster.

Matrose Hans Rüskens, who had lost a leg, was still unconscious, and as the *Lady Shirley*'s first aid box contained only the basics for treating simple wounds, there was little that could be done for him. He died that evening without regaining consciousness. Callaway was unwilling to stop the ship at night for a funeral, so this was postponed until the next morning. Shortly after sunrise on 5 October, the *Lady Shirley* was hove to and, while flying fish and porpoise cavorted around her, young Hans Rüskens, wrapped in an anonymous black flag – there was no German ensign on board – was committed to the deep. Six of the prisoners were allowed on deck to witness the burial, and afterwards, through Günther Wulff, they expressed their gratitude to Lieutenant Commander Callaway for the respect shown to their fallen comrade.

The dead having been committed to the deep, Callaway had to address the needs of the living. At the best of times, the *Lady Shirley* carried just enough provisions to feed her small crew for the short periods she was at sea, and having sailed from Gibraltar seven days earlier her stock was already low. Now, with her complement more than doubled, strict rationing was necessary. It would be corned beef and ship's biscuits for crew and prisoners alike, and what fresh water was left would be used for drinking and cooking only. For washing, there was always the sea. Here again, the services of Günther Wulff proved invaluable. Once he had explained the situation to his fellow prisoners, there was no trouble.

And so the homeward passage to Gibraltar began with food and water rationed and the crew of the trawler outnumbered by their captives. It was a situation fraught with all sorts of danger, and Lieutenant Commander Callaway had good cause to be apprehensive. He sent a brief signal to Gibraltar asking for guidance, but there was no answer. Thereafter he kept radio silence; too many unfriendly ears might be listening.

Anxious to anticipate any breakout by his prisoners, in addition to the guard beneath the wardroom, Callaway posted four men armed with rifles and grenades on deck day and night. The Germans were allowed on deck in small groups for exercise during the day, and most seemed content with their lot. Stoker Ian McCready, a passable German speaker, engaged them in conversation and reported to Callaway that their morale had been shaken by the ease with which an apparently impotent little trawler had been able to outgun and sink their large and powerful submarine. In the course of these conversations McCready learned the reason for U-111's 105mm deck gun's failure to fight back. In the rush to get the gun into action its crew had made the classic mistake of forgetting to remove the watertight tampion from the muzzle. The first shell fired split the barrel, and the 105mm was out of the fight.

It also came to McCready's ear that Boatswain's Mate Gerhard Hartig, an ardent Nazi, had made an attempt to organize a breakout by the prisoners but had found only a small handful of sympathizers. It could well have been that if the wounded *Korvettenkapitän* Heinecke had not been isolated from the others, the outcome might have been different. Even so, it was necessary for the *Lady Shirley*'s crew to be constantly on their guard, and sleep was at a premium, especially for her officers. They had lost their cabins and the wardroom, and had to bed down wherever they could. Lieutenant Commander Callaway had the use of his bunk, but the settee in his small cabin was occupied by the wounded signalman Warbrick.

Two days out from Gibraltar, *Lady Shirley* was steaming parallel to the coast of French Morocco and on full alert. It was known that for some months German troops had been manoeuvring across the border in Spanish Morocco with the object of frightening the French authorities into allowing them to set up a naval base on the Atlantic coast. This would enable German U-boats to bar access to the Straits of Gibraltar, with disastrous consequences for Allied shipping. Given that the French were still smarting at the destruction of their Mediterranean fleet at Mers-el-Kebir by the Royal Navy three months earlier, it could be that the proposed base was already a reality. It was therefore with considerable relief that Callaway received a signal from Gibraltar during the day to the effect that the destroyer HMS *Lance* was on her way to meet the *Lady Shirley.*

The rendezvous was kept before dark on the 7th, the 36-knot L-class destroyer appearing over the horizon as the sun was setting. With her eight quick-firing 4-inch guns and racks of depth charges poised for launching, she was a comforting sight as she closed in to ride shotgun on the battered trawler. Her doctor was sent across to look after the wounded, and the two ships set course for Gibraltar.

The *Lady Shirley* and her escort reached Gibraltar at daybreak on 8 October, and the trawler steamed into the harbour to the cheers of men lining the rails of the other ships in port. The news of her amazing victory had gone ahead of her. A flashing lamp on the signal station instructed the trawler to berth alongside the receiving ship HMS *Cormorant* to land her prisoners. The 1870s-vintage *Cormorant,* once an *Osprey*-class sloop of the Pacific Fleet, was a sad looking, mastless hulk moored to a pontoon in a forgotten corner of the harbour. In her day she had been used by the press gang to house new 'recruits', and so had secure accommodation.

Sub Lieutenant Allan Waller recalled their arrival:

> The Vice-Admiral Commanding North Atlantic, Sir George Frederick Basset Edward-Collins, and his chief of staff, Captain G.A.B. Hawkins, boarded the ship accompanied by Surgeon Commander Button, who was in charge of the Dockyard Medical Centre. On the mole were ambulances, medical staff and what appeared to be half the Army stationed in Gib. The Surgeon Commander could speak German and told the wounded prisoners they were going to hospital. In the meantime our casualties had been landed and were on their way to the Military Hospital. The Germans

could not believe they were at Gib and it was still very British. Propaganda had informed them that Gib had long since fallen. The Admiral and his Chief of Staff spoke to the Captain and the rest of us and asked many questions.

When the preliminaries were over, the Army boarded and the *Lady Shirley*'s prisoners were escorted ashore. The sheer size of the armed party brought smiles to the faces of the men who had stood guard over the Germans for 1,000 miles with so little in the way of deterrents. There was now really no need for such a show of force; the prisoners were subdued and a little incredulous at the strictly correct way in which they were being treated. Callaway and his officers shook hands with *Oberleutnant* Wulff and thanked him for his cooperation, which had done much to defuse what could have been a very dangerous four days. This display of apparent friendship was viewed by the Army escort with amazement bordering on disgust. They were not to know of that bond of mutual respect that exists between seamen, friend or foe.

Having landed her prisoners, *Lady Shirley* proceeded further into the harbour to the anti-submarine trawler base, cheered all the way by the other ships. When she was safely moored and her company could at last relax, a cable was brought aboard from Prime Minister Winston Churchill offering his sincere congratulations to Callaway and his men. Later would come the medals – and there were many.

Lieutenant Commander Arthur Callaway received the immediate award of the Distinguished Service Order – 'for daring and skill in a brilliant action against a U-boat in which the enemy was sunk and surrendered to HM trawler *Lady Shirley*'. Callaway's first lieutenant, Ian Boucant, and his navigator, Frederick French, were awarded the Distinguished Service Cross, while chief engineer George Wyatt was Mentioned in Despatches. Seaman Sydney Halcrow, the wounded Hotchkiss gunner, received the Conspicuous Gallantry Medal with the citation, 'so badly wounded that he was ordered to go below, but stood to his gun until the action was over, when he fainted'. Of the others, there were DSMs for Leading Seaman William Mackrill, Seaman George Bussey, Seaman Albert Milne, Seaman William Windsor, Seaman Ian McCready and Seaman Andrew McInneney. Four other Mentioned in Despatches were awarded, including a posthumous mention for Seaman Gunner Leslie Pizzey. For a man killed at his post in battle this seems a poor reward, but at the time only a Mention in Despatches, the Victoria Cross and the George Cross qualified for posthumous award. Corporal H.J. Fittall of the Corps of Royal Engineers, who helped to care for the wounded, was also Mentioned in Despatches, which would entitle him to wear the Atlantic Star, a rare honour for a land-based Army man.

The loss of U-111 was largely due to a number of poor decisions made by Wilhelm Kleinschmidt and negligence on the part of her gun's crew in failing to clear the muzzle of the 105mm before firing, which led to the destruction of the gun. However, in the end it was the tight discipline and superior training of *Lady Shirley's* officers and men that won the day against a vastly more powerful enemy. The action was a clear demonstration of the way Britain was fighting the war at sea.

*

While Callaway and his men squared up their ship and looked forward to a spell of well-earned local leave, the long-range U-boats were again active in the south. Ernst Bauer in U-126, still smarting from his lack of success against Convoy HG 70 in mid-August, when he sank only the 40-year-old Yugoslav tramp *Sud*, had sailed out of Lorient again, desperate for a quick victory. His orders were to operate against convoys bound north and south from Freetown which at the time were sailing at frequent intervals. Yet on the run south Bauer found nothing worthy of his torpedoes.

Forty-eight hours after U-126 sailed out of the Loire into the Bay of Biscay, the 4,926-ton Cardiff steamer *Nailsea Manor* left Belfast Lough, down to her summer marks with supplies for British troops fighting in the Western Desert. In her holds she carried 5,000 tons of military stores: guns, armoured cars, lorries, rations and a large consignment of Army mail. Packed into every other conceivable space was 1,000 tons of ammunition. Up on deck, on top of her hatches, were lashed the four sections of a 450-ton tank landing craft. This huge unwieldy deck cargo overhung both sides of the ship and reached as high as the wheelhouse windows. The heavily laden steamer closely resembled a floating warehouse.

Nailsea Manor, under the command of Captain John Hewitt, joined Convoy OS 7 after clearing Belfast, where she had loaded her deck cargo. Freetown-bound OS 7 consisted of forty-four merchant ships escorted by three sloops and two corvettes of the Royal Navy. It being known that U-boats were active around the islands off West Africa, this seems hardly an adequate escort for such a large convoy. As for the *Nailsea Manor*, deep-loaded and with deck cargo as high as her bridge, the real enemy to be feared was meteorological, not that she was a stranger to foul weather. On her previous voyage, while homeward bound in convoy across the North Atlantic, she had collided with another ship in dense fog and sustained serious damage. While returning westwards for emergency repairs, she had run headlong into a roaring Atlantic storm which would be long remembered. Many years later, John Slader, then a young apprentice, wrote:

> It was the worst weather I had experienced. We rolled on our beam ends; there were occasions when my heart missed a beat as I wondered whether she would stay there . . . The waves were curling over the bow as the north-westerly with great gusts of spray flew across the bridge. Visibility was down to 300 yards, the wind increasing from force 9 strong gale to force 10 storm: for'ard she was white with broken seas overall, the alleyways amidships deep in water.

It was with considerable relief, then, that Captain Hewitt now took his ship south towards kindlier seas. The North Atlantic was in summer mood, and by the time they reached the latitude of Gibraltar the sighs of relief aboard the Cardiff ship were plainly audible. From then on, at least until they reached the Cape, the weather should be set fair.

Not unexpectedly, however, the *Nailsea Manor*'s bad luck had followed in her wake. On 1 October OS 7 was passing between Madeira and the Canary Islands, running before a dying north-easterly trade wind, and soon to enter the calms of the Doldrums. Then, with little warning, the wind swung round to the south-west and began to blow gale force.

Within the hour the *Nailsea Manor* was pitching heavily in rough seas, and her deck cargo was in danger of breaking adrift. Hewitt was eventually forced to reduce speed and then heave to while the lashings on the sections of landing craft were tightened up. Two other ships, the *Ger-y-Bryn* and the *Hazelside*, both similarly loaded, were obliged to do the same. The corvette HMS *Violet* was detached to stand by the troubled ships, while the rest of the convoy carried on to the south.

The three ships were hove to for twenty-four hours while their crews worked feverishly to secure their deck cargoes, conscious all the while that at any time an enemy torpedo might put a sudden end to their efforts. While they worked, their escorting corvette circled endlessly around them, its Asdics probing the depths for lurking U-boats.

Finally, on the morning of the 2nd, the three stragglers were ready to get under way again, by which time their convoy was more than 200 miles ahead. The sea was still rough, but the wind had gone back round to the north-east and was blowing force 5–6.

U-126 had been a late arrival off Convoy SL 87, too late in fact to join in the attack. Commander Keymer's escort force was by then thoroughly on the alert, and try as he might, Ernst Bauer could not penetrate the screen. After several abortive attempts he gave up and moved closer to the African coast. There he narrowly missed the main bulk of OS 7, but at dusk on 9 October he stumbled on HMS *Violet* and her three charges, then 250 miles north-east of the Cape Verde Islands. Hurrying after the little convoy, Bauer settled down to shadow them.

The night was dark and humid, with the fresh north-easter heaping up white horses that glinted with ghostly phosphorescence in the fitful light of a half moon. At 0230 on the 10th Bauer had the *Nailsea Manor* square in his sights, and at 0245 he fired a spread from his bow tubes.

John Slader later wrote:

> It was not a particularly loud explosion but by the time I had vacated my cabin *Nailsea Manor* was listing to starboard and as I passed the fore part of No.4 hatch I noticed the deck cargo was hanging over the port side. Beneath, a mass of flames could be seen in the shelter deck where the mail was stowed. In No.4 hold below, between where lorries and trucks had been secured, lay 1,000 tons of ammunition.

Captain John Hewitt wrote in his report:

> I rang the telegraph for the engines to stop and at the same time fired two rockets. The telegraphs were broken so I sent the First Mate down to the engine room and the engineer on watch stated that the main injection was

broken and he was unable to do anything. As I did not know whether the ship would capsize with the weight of the deck cargo, or the ammunition might explode, I gave six blasts and ordered the lifeboats away.

Urged on by the dangers threatening, the *Nailsea Manor*'s crew of forty-two abandoned ship promptly, with no one being injured in the process. The sinking ship still had way on her, and as the boats cast off and drifted astern it could be seen that Bauer's torpedo had blasted a large jagged hole in the hull on the waterline. Inside, in the hold, fire was raging out of control. Fortunately, HMS *Violet* was close at hand and Bauer was forced to beat a hasty retreat without delivering the *coup de grâce*, which would have caused a massive explosion, probably destroying the lifeboats and their crews.

Hewitt and his men did not have to endure long in their boats, being picked up by *Violet* and later transferred to another ship in the convoy, Ellerman's *City of Hong Kong*, which landed them in Freetown. John Slader remarked on their subsequent treatment:

> We arrived in Freetown on 14 October; Convoy WS 12 had arrived the day before, there being few occasions when the Sierra Leone River and the town were so congested. From the *City of Hong Kong* we were taken ashore to what could only be described as a doss house. Some 300 Distressed British Seamen (DBS) – seamen sunk by the enemy and rescued from the deep – were quartered there. Running water was scarce, it was far from clean, and the donkey's breakfast [bedding] far from wholesome. We later discovered it was a requisitioned school.

*

Having assuaged some of his repressed frustration by sinking the *Nailsea Manor*, Ernst Bauer now took up station in the western approaches to Freetown. Into his waiting arms nine days later sailed the United States Line's steamer *Lehigh*.

The 4,983-ton *Lehigh*, commanded by Captain Vincent P. Arkins, was an ageing relic of the closing days of the First World War and had just completed an Atlantic crossing with cargo for the Biscay port of Bilbao. As America was not yet at war with Germany, the *Lehigh*, with large Stars and Stripes painted on each side of her bridge and showing undimmed navigation lights at night, had crossed unmolested. The only inconvenience she had suffered was the discovery of four Spanish stowaways after sailing from Bilbao. Captain Arkins was faced with the daunting prospect of persuading the authorities at his next port, Takoradi in present-day Ghana, to allow him to land the unwanted passengers. Failing that, he would be obliged to carry the men back to the USA.

The *Lehigh* was 80 miles to the west of Freetown when on that fine clear morning in October U-126 sighted her. Bauer claimed that when he looked through the periscope he thought she was a Greek ship and that he only became aware of her American markings after he fired his torpedo. Whatever his reason for the sinking of this then still neutral ship, the news would not be well received either in Washington or Berlin.

Bauer's torpedo hit the unsuspecting American freighter in her after hold, blasting a large hole in her hull through which the sea poured unhindered. Radio Officer Sam Hakam later wrote:

> The torpedo struck without warning. There was a loud explosion followed by a towering plume of smoke and debris. My first reaction was, 'This is just like you see it in the movies'. But this was not the movies. This was for real.

Some thirty-five minutes after she was hit, the *Lehigh* was well down by the stern, and it seemed she would not stay afloat much longer. Captain Arkins gave the order to abandon ship, and his 40-man crew, accompanied by the four Spanish stowaways, who must by now have been regretting their choice of ship, left in four lifeboats.

When the *Lehigh* was hit, her main and emergency aerials came down and no SOS could be sent; but nearly two hours later the ship was still afloat, so Arkins put his lifeboat back alongside and Radio Officer Hakam and two others re-boarded her. Hakam wrote:

> I volunteered to go back with a couple of men, get the antenna up and get an SOS out. The Captain stood by. We almost had the job done when the ship gave a lurch. The Captain hollered for us to get off. He was afraid the suction of the ship going down might pull his boat under.

> We got off and pulled away fast. At a safe distance we stopped to watch the old S.S. *Lehigh* go down. It did not take long. The stern went down as the head raised up until the ship was straight up, then down it went with a rumbling roar leaving some debris behind.

Despite no SOS being sent out, Captain Arkins and his crew were picked up two days later by ships of the Royal Navy.

Ernst Bauer's new-found luck held, and early on the morning of the 20th he came across a small convoy consisting of two oil tankers under escort. He fired a spread of two torpedoes at the tankers, one of which hit the *British Mariner*, bound from Freetown to Curaçao in ballast. The other torpedo was a runner. The *British Mariner* was hit in her engine room and completely disabled. Three of her crew were killed, and the rest abandoned her. She remained afloat, and was later re-boarded and towed into Freetown, where she was declared a total loss. She served out the war in Freetown as a refuelling hulk for convoys.

CHAPTER SEVEN

An Unwelcome Caller

Having sustained serious damage in her collision with HMS *Clyde* in Tarafal Bay, U-67 was deemed unfit for further operations and ordered to return to Lorient. Before going north, Lorient instructed Günther Müller-Stockheim to meet up with U-68 on 2 October to hand over his surplus torpedoes and fuel. It was a disappointing end to the patrol, but Müller-Stockheim had no option but to comply.

The designated rendezvous point lay on a deserted stretch of coast some 270 miles north of Dakar which was as featureless as it was empty of life. Not even an animal track marred the surface of the undulating sand dunes backing the bay; there were no leading marks, no lights. That both U-boats found and entered the bay in the dead of night was no mean feat of navigation.

Seven torpedoes and 55 cubic metres of diesel oil were transferred from U-67 to U-68 overnight, the U-boats putting to sea again before dawn on the 3rd. U-67 turned north for Lorient and the repair yard, while U-68 headed south. Merten was under orders to proceed to Ascension Island to assess the possibility of lying in wait off there to ambush Allied ships sailing independently and unescorted between Freetown and the Cape of Good Hope. Should that not be profitable, he was to venture further south to St Helena with the same object in mind.

U-68 was to be the first U-boat ever to venture south of the Equator, where it was hoped she would improve on her abysmal record to date. Since being commissioned eight months earlier, she had torpedoed just one ship, the *Silverbelle* in Convoy SL 87. Operating as a lone wolf in an area where Allied ships least expected to be attacked, Merten hoped to make amends. But the sea around Ascension proved to be completely devoid of enemy ships, and after a few days of fruitless searching in the vicinity of the lonely island, Merten continued south for St Helena.

The island of St Helena, another tiny speck in the vast Atlantic Ocean, lies in latitude 16° south, and more than a thousand miles from the nearest mainland in any direction. St Helena was completely uninhabited when first discovered by Portuguese explorers in 1502, but it was recorded at the time that despite its volcanic origin the island was densely wooded and had a plentiful supply of fresh water.

For many years following its discovery St Helena remained unexploited, but being squarely in the path of the South-East Trades, when ships began rounding the Cape with cargoes from the East, it was inevitable that the island should become a convenient staging post in the long voyage home. The Honourable East India Company established a provisioning depot in 1654, and when the tea clippers and windjammers began calling regularly, St Helena, now with a small but firmly established population, assumed considerable importance in the maritime world. In 1834 the island became a British Crown Colony. The capital, Jamestown, where most of its inhabitants live, was built in a narrow valley which runs down to the sea in the north-west corner of the island. The anchorage in James Bay is sheltered from the worst of the Atlantic swell.

When steam superseded sail, and ships were no longer dependent on the trade winds, St Helena faded back into its original obscurity, and remained thus until the outbreak of war in 1939, when it became an important bunkering station. A fleet oiler was anchored in James Bay, and British warships patrolling the South Atlantic became regular callers.

The Royal Fleet Auxiliary tanker *Darkdale* arrived off James Bay on 4 August 1941 to take over as resident bunker ship from the Norwegian tanker *Nyholm*. Launched on the Clyde in July 1940 as the *Empire Oil* for the Ministry of War Transport, to be managed by Shell Tankers, she was requisitioned by the Admiralty in November of that year and renamed *Darkdale*. The 8,145-ton motor vessel was manned by a crew of fifty, which included four naval gunners. The latter were on board to service and supervise the manning of the tanker's armament, which consisted of a 4.7-inch anti-submarine gun, a 12-pounder HA/LA gun and an assortment of machine guns and rockets. In command was Captain Thomas Card.

In her short career before ending up at St Helena the *Darkdale* had sailed with three North Atlantic convoys carrying oil for the Admiralty from Curaçao, and had also run the gauntlet of the

U-boats alone, so she was well acquainted with the perils of war. Being assigned to St Helena, as yet untouched by the conflict, must have been a welcome relief for Card and his crew. And so it was – for a while, at least.

Anchored in James Bay, less than half a mile off the beach that fronts Jamestown, the *Darkdale* carried out her first refuelling operation within three days of arriving, supplying the light cruiser HMS *Orion*. The cruiser was followed two weeks later by the seaplane carrier HMS *Albatross*. Both ships were part of a force deployed to search for the German commerce raider *Atlantis*, which was then roaming the South Atlantic preying on unsuspecting Allied ships.

During August and September the *Darkdale* received a steady stream of callers, including the aircraft carrier HMS *Eagle*, the heavy cruiser *Dorsetshire* and the battle-cruiser *Repulse*. The work was not exacting, and far removed from the hell of the North Atlantic, where Allied merchant ships were falling to the U-boats like ripe corn before the reaper's scythe. The *Darkdale*'s crew settled down to a pleasant routine, with awnings stretched and liberty boats at the gangway. The population of St Helena welcomed them with open arms, and they reciprocated.

Towards the end of September 1941 the *Darkdale*'s tanks were running low, and on the 25th the Norwegian tanker *Egerø* arrived from Abadan with fresh supplies. When the Norwegian sailed again, the *Darkdale* had on board 6,000 tons of fuel oil, 850 tons of aviation spirit, 500 tons of diesel and a number of drums of lubricating oil. This was a highly inflammable mix of cargo, and there were times when Captain Card, acutely aware that he was anchored in a bay wide open to the sea, questioned the wisdom of those who had chosen the station.

It may be that James Bay was dangerously exposed, but it was not without protection. Since war had threatened the South Atlantic, the defences of Jamestown, originally set up when Napoleon was a prisoner on St Helena, had been considerably strengthened. The *Darkdale* was covered by a battery of 6-inch guns on Mundens Point at the northern end of the bay, while smaller calibre guns were sited on Ladder Hill Point at the southern end. Between the guns was a battery of high-powered searchlights. Both guns and searchlights were manned at all times. Added to all this was the tanker's own, not inconsiderable, armament.

The efficiency of those defences would soon be tested, for a little before midnight on 20 October U-68 began her cautious approach to St Helena. Merten had no welcoming lighthouse to guide him in, and the water being over 1,000 fathoms deep to within 5 miles of the land, soundings were giving no indication of the boat's position. Fortunately, the 2,700ft high summit of Diana's Peak was visible against the horizon. Then, at 0145 on the 21st, Merten sighted a cluster of lights which he identified as houses on the hill overlooking Jamestown. He decided to wait until dawn before closing the land.

At around 0500, when it was light enough to confirm that his navigation had been correct, Merten moved further in, submerging to periscope depth when within a mile of James Bay. He assumed his approach had been unseen from the shore at this early hour, but had not reckoned with the vigilance of an islander living in a cottage on the cliff-top above the bay. The man recognized the approaching craft as a submarine, probably hostile, and ran hotfoot into Jamestown to report his sighting to the authorities. He might just as well have saved his breath, for such was the complacency prevalent on St Helena at the time that no action was taken. As Jamestown awoke to the new day, life carried on much as it had done over the untroubled years since the death of Bonaparte. The man who would have been most concerned at the reported sighting, Captain Thomas Card of the *Darkdale*, was not informed.

The sight of the *Darkdale* lying quietly at anchor was like manna from heaven for *Korvettenkapitän* Merten. Her deep draught indicated that she was fully loaded or at least had a considerable amount of oil on board. An extract from U-68's log reads: 'Full of fuel, only at the bow can one see something of the waterline colour. I intend to blow it up this night, since by doing so there is the possibility of diverting suspicion to armed merchantmen.' Merten, who had previously visited St Helena in 1927 when a midshipman in a cruiser 'showing the flag' for Germany, also took careful note of Jamestown's improved harbour defences. Those big guns could easily blow U-68 out of the water, should she be discovered. He would have to tread warily.

Having completed his reconnaissance, Merten withdrew to await the coming of darkness. RFA *Darkdale*, meanwhile, was beginning another routine day. The crew were at work scrubbing decks, the galley fires were being stoked up and there was the smell of frying bacon in the air. No ships were due alongside for refuelling, and Tuesday 21 October – Trafalgar Day, some remembered – promised to be quiet and untaxing, an opportunity for a run ashore for some. In fact, when Captain Card received an invitation for himself, his Chief Engineer and Purser to dine with the island's Garrison Commander, he had no hesitation in accepting.

Card and his senior officers left the ship that evening, along with two off-duty seamen who had decided to investigate what little nightlife Jamestown had to offer, and two crew members were already on shore in the hospital with minor complaints. This left forty-three men on board the *Darkdale*, with Chief Officer Norman Miller in charge. The tanker's accommodation was blacked out, but as the risk of an enemy attack was considered so minimal as to be non-existent, she was showing regulation anchor lights.

Merten began his run in to James Bay as soon as darkness was complete. Lining up on the *Darkdale's* anchor lights, he approached on the surface, but slowly and cautiously. The sea was calm, the sky overhead cloudless and awash with twinkling stars. With such clear conditions it was just possible that the U-boat might be seen by some keen-eyed lookout on shore. But Merten had little cause to worry. The island of St Helena was so lulled into a false sense of security by its complete isolation that even the men manning the guns overlooking the bay rarely glanced out to sea.

Soon after midnight, Merten was close enough to the *Darkdale* to see the outline of the tanker clearly. She was lying with her bows facing to the east, her port side open to the U-boat. No movement could be seen on board, but since she was a British ship it was certain that her bridge would be manned, and that meant a wide-awake officer with binoculars. Merten decided to hit fast and hard. At 0043, with the range at 550yds, he fired a full spread of four torpedoes from his bow tubes, then quickly sheered away to starboard and headed back out to sea at full speed.

Thirty-two seconds after firing, U-68's log recorded that all four torpedoes had found their target. The first hit the British tanker aft in her engine room, the second went home amidships below the bridge, the third hit forward near the bow and the fourth amidships again.

The effect on the *Darkdale* was catastrophic, the multiple explosions literally blowing her apart. It was later claimed that Merten's third torpedo had missed its target, but whether it hit or not seems irrelevant. The entry in U-68's log says it all:

> Explosion tore the silence of the night apart. All we could see were flames, flames, and yet more flames burning as high as a house and flaring up repeatedly in the dark night sky, from bow to stern there were flames 20 or 30 metres high – there was nothing to be seen of the ship herself. It was one raging inferno, burning as tall as a house and three times wider than the ship had been . . . Ship is illuminated as by day, the whole coast, harbour, barracks and batteries are lighted up in a red glow.

As explosion after explosion rumbled across the harbour and echoed back from the surrounding hills, the reaction of Jamestown was instant. Lights flashed on, doors were thrown open, and within minutes the town's single street was thronged with men, women and children, all hurrying down to the harbour. The talk was that war had at last come to St Helena and the island was being shelled by a German surface raider. In that case the exodus should have been in the other direction, out of the town and into the safety of the hills, but this was not a time for rational thought.

Among the hurrying crowd were Captain Thomas Card and his senior officers, who had just left the Garrison Officers' Mess after being royally entertained by the Army and were on their way back to their ship when U-68 struck with such devastating force. As the night sky glowed red over the harbour, Card had no illusions about the source of the fire. His command, which the solitude of St Helena had seduced him into thinking was safe, had been cruelly hit. He began to run.

Reaching the wharf, Card found that his worst nightmare had indeed come to pass. Where his ship had once swung idly at her anchor there was now a sea of leaping flames surrounding and throwing into sharp relief the crippled *Darkdale* in her death throes. More explosions, with balls of fire soaring high in the sky like gigantic distress rockets, spurred Captain Card on to commandeer a boat, and with several other boats he put out to sea to rescue his men.

The rescue effort was doomed from the start. The boats' crews put their backs into their oars – there were no motor launches – but by the time they reached the anchorage the oil on the water was burning so fiercely that there was no way they could get close to the tanker. Captain Card could only watch while his ship became a funeral pyre for his crew. He was still there when, at 0530, the sky already paling with the coming of dawn, the burning wreck of the *Darkdale* suffered one last explosion. Five minutes later she was gone, leaving only untidy heaps of burning debris to mark her going.

Card later learned that two of the *Darkdale*'s naval gunners, who had been on deck when U-68 struck, had been blown into the water clear of the flames and picked up by a rescue boat. The remaining forty-one men, many of whom had been asleep when the tanker was torpedoed, had all perished with their ship.

Several days after the *Darkdale* went down, a Court of Enquiry was held in Jamestown to determine the cause of her loss. For some incredible reason, despite the testimony of the two survivors that they had seen a submarine on the surface, and despite the reported sighting of U-68 by an islander on the 20th, the Court ruled that the tanker had been sunk by an accidental explosion on board. It was as though St Helena did not wish to be associated with the war.

The islanders, meanwhile, were profoundly shocked at the tragic loss of so many lives with the *Darkdale*. On the Saturday following the disaster a memorial service was held on the wharf overlooking the spot where the tanker went down. It was a full turnout, with the Lord Bishop of St Helena officiating and the Governor, the Garrison Commander and the survivors from the ship in attendance. One hundred and twenty wreaths were laid on the water over the wreck. Captain Thomas Card later sent letters of condolence to the relatives of his lost men, saying: 'The Officers and Crew of the *Darkdale* were a fine body of men, no praise of mine can be high enough for them and it is with bitter regret and everlasting sorrow I have left them "asleep" in the deep waters of St Helena.'

The findings of the Court of Enquiry may have been accepted, but after 22 October 1941 no fleet tanker anchored in James Bay for more than a few days at a time, refuelling during the daylight hours and putting out to sea at night to return next morning. A expensive lesson had been learned.

*

While the people of St Helena mourned the loss of the *Darkdale*, U-68 was moving further south. Karl-Friedrich Merten, his appetite whetted by his recent and unexpected success in James Bay, was complying with his orders to hunt as far south as the old whaling station of Walvis Bay, which lies 750 miles north of Cape Town.

At about 0300 on 28 October Merten was cruising on the surface 730 miles due west of Walvis Bay, when a dark shadow was seen on the horizon ahead. The shadow hardened into the outline of a cargo ship on a southerly course. Merten increased speed and gave chase.

The southbound ship was the 5,297-ton Newcastle-registered *Hazelside*, on passage from Cardiff, via Durban, to Alexandria with supplies for the British Eighth Army in North Africa. The *Hazelside* had been with the UK–Freetown convoy OS 7 and had straggled in bad weather along with the *Nailsea Manor* and *Ger-y-Bryn*, all three ships carrying on deck large tank landing craft in sections. Unlike the luckless *Nailsea Manor*, the *Hazelside* had escaped Ernst Bauer's torpedoes. Now, confident she had left the threat of U-boat attack far behind, she was ambling down to the Cape, where the lights still shone bright and no guns were fired in anger. Had the authorities in Jamestown not been so eager to dissociate St Helena from the war, then the *Hazelside* might have been warned of the presence of a German U-boat in the South Atlantic. As it was, she was not zig-zagging, and most of those off watch, including Captain Evans, were sound asleep.

Korvettenkapitän Merten observed the British ship for a while, puzzled by her unusual deck cargo, but was satisfied that this was a target well worthy of sinking. At 0343, when the range was right, he brought the unsuspecting *Hazelside* to a sudden halt with one well-aimed torpedo.

Two of the *Hazelside*'s crew were killed by the explosion, but despite the late hour and the unexpected attack, Captain Charles Evans and the remainder of his men got away in two boats before Merten administered the *coup de grâce* eighteen minutes later. They were picked up by the southbound *Malayan Prince* and landed at Cape Town, but their ship with her vital cargo went to the bottom and now lies 3,000 fathoms deep.

U-68 lingered in the latitude of Walvis Bay, moving nearer to the coast, and three days later, at dawn on 1 November, the 4,953-ton

Bradford City hove in sight. The Cardiff-based motor vessel, under the command of Captain Henry Paul, was homeward bound from Mauritius with 9,500 tons of sugar in bulk, having called at Cape Town for bunkers.

When the *Bradford City* was hull up on the horizon, Merten took U-68 down to periscope depth and waited for the opportunity to strike. At 0645 he fired a spread of three torpedoes, one of which caught the loaded ship squarely amidships. She staggered and listed heavily to port.

Merten watched from periscope depth while the *Bradford City*'s crew lowered two lifeboats and rowed clear of the sinking ship. Anxious to be on his way, he took U-68 closer to his victim, but as he approached within 50yds, the U-boat began to porpoise out of control, diving beneath the *Bradford City* as she was going down. The two vessels collided, but it was a glancing blow, and U-68 survived with only a dented bow, surfacing 10yds on the other side of the ship. Merten later remarked, 'Thank God the enemy manned their lifeboats instead of their guns.'

All forty-five of the *Bradford City*'s crew were uninjured, but they fully expected to be machine-gunned when U-68 approached their boats. Much to their relief, Merten only wanted to know the name of their ship and her cargo. He then offered them fresh water and gave them a course to steer for the nearest land. This small act of mercy completed, U-68 motored away at full speed.

The *Bradford City*'s boats set course to the east, knowing full well that the only landfall they could expect was the barren and uninhabited Skeleton Coast. They had no other choice. The two boats separated during the night and did not meet again, but both reached land ten days later. Having survived the dangerous surf that pounds the shores in that region, the crew made camp on the beach, where several days later, by pure chance, they were spotted by a patrolling aircraft of the South African Air Force. They were eventually rescued by a search party sent overland from Walvis Bay.

*

U-68 had by this time been continuously at sea for fifty-one days, and her fuel tanks were at low ebb. She had no friendly neutral port nearby where she could refuel, but anticipating her needs, Lorient had made other arrangements. The armed merchant cruiser *Atlantis*, having been away from Germany for over a year operating with some success in the Indian and Pacific oceans, had rounded the Cape and was on her way north. She was ordered by Lorient to rendezvous with U-68 in a position 500 miles south of St Helena and there transfer sufficient fuel for Merten to reach home.

The 7,862-ton *Atlantis*, ex-*Goldenfels* of Hansa Line, had been requisitioned by the German Navy in 1939 and fitted out as a commerce raider. She was armed with six 150mm guns, albeit of 1906 vintage, a 75mm bow chaser, two twin 37mm and four 20mm anti-aircraft guns, as well as four torpedo tubes. Her maximum speed was only 17½ knots, but she had a range of 60,000 miles and carried two Heinkel He 114B float planes, invaluable assets for a raider acting alone. Under the command of *Kapitän-zur-See* Bernhard Rogge, and manned by officers and men of the German Navy, she had already sunk or captured twenty-two Allied merchant ships totalling 145,960 tons gross.

The meeting between U-68 and the *Atlantis* was delayed while Merten made a sweep into Walvis Bay, which proved to be empty of shipping, and it was not until 16 November that the two raiders kept their lonely assignation in mid-ocean. With her diesel tanks refilled, U-68 then continued to the north, the *Atlantis* following in her wake under orders to make another rendezvous with U-126 some 100 miles south of Ascension Island on the 22nd.

After inadvertently sinking the neutral American ship *Lehigh* on 19 October and damaging the tanker *British Mariner* on the following day, Ernst Bauer had combed the waters off Sierra Leone with no further success. His frustration was exacerbated when one of U-126's diesel engines began smoking badly, making it impossible for her to run at any speed on the surface without advertising her presence. Her engineers were unable to effect a repair. The boat was now two months out from Biscay and obviously in need of a thorough overhaul. When the order came to rendezvous with the *Atlantis*, Bauer contacted Lorient and requested that he be allowed to continue north after refuelling. His request was granted.

It was much to the credit of the navigators of both the *Atlantis* and U-126 that they came together in the empty waters south of Ascension and on the date specified, 22 November. Conditions for the refuelling operation were ideal, with fine clear weather and a low swell. U-126 came alongside the *Atlantis*, a pipeline was passed across and the transfer of oil went ahead. So smoothly was the operation proceeding, and so isolated was the spot, that when Rogge offered Bauer the luxury of a hot bath aboard the *Atlantis* he agreed without a qualm, leaving his First Watch Officer *Oberleutnant* Kurt Neubert in temporary command of U-126. Seven of the U-boat's crew also accepted an invitation to board the raider.

However congenial the atmosphere of the mid-ocean meeting, there was no relaxation of security. Lookouts were posted in the U-boat's conning tower, and at *Atlantis'* mastheads, but their visibility was limited to the horizon. It was unfortunate that two days earlier the raider's spotter plane had been damaged by a heavy landing on the sea and was out of action. Consequently, no long-range surveillance was possible, and this was to have disastrous results.

The wreck of the *Darkdale* lay undisturbed at the bottom of James Bay, her loss wrongly attributed to a shipboard accident. Then, on 2 November, the sloop HMS *Milford* arrived carrying divers to investigate a possible oil leak from the tanker. Their examination of the wreck showed that the *Darkdale* had been torpedoed, This was confirmed a few days later by Ultra decrypts of signals sent by U-68 to Lorient. British naval ships already in the South Atlantic searching for German surface raiders and their supply ships were alerted. This added danger to Allied shipping was doubled when Bletchley Park intercepted and decoded Admiral Dönitz's signals concerning the refuelling of U-126 by the *Atlantis*. The heavy cruiser *Devonshire* was ordered to sail from Simonstown to investigate.

The 13,000-ton *Devonshire*, commanded by Captain Robert Oliver, was fourteen years old but still able to maintain 32 knots, and packed a considerable punch with eight 8-inch guns and eight quick-firing 4-inch. Rounding the Cape, she headed north at full speed, and at dawn on 22 November, when Oliver calculated he was close to the rendezvous point specified by the Admiralty, he launched his Walrus spotter plane.

The Supermarine Walrus was a single-engined amphibious biplane. It had none of the fine lines of its German counterpart, but it had a top speed of 135mph, a range of 600 miles and was a superbly manoeuvrable aircraft. At 0710 on the 22nd *Devonshire's* Walrus sighted a suspicious merchant ship which was either stopped, or steaming very slowly. This was the raider *Atlantis* with

U-126 alongside, the latter then not being visible to the Walrus. Using the cloud cover, the pilot of the Walrus stayed out of sight, reporting his discovery by W/T to *Devonshire*.

Neither the *Atlantis* nor U-126 had any inkling that they had been discovered, and the refuelling continued until, at 0816, the three-funnelled *Devonshire* loomed over the horizon with her guns cleared for action.

The approaching cruiser was seen by a lookout at the raider's masthead who immediately warned the bridge. The reaction was instantaneous. U-126 was cut loose and she disappeared below the waves, leaving her commander luxuriating in his bath aboard the *Atlantis*. Rogge, realizing that he was heavily outgunned, presented his stern to the *Devonshire* and ran away at full speed. As he fled, Rogge ordered his wireless operator to send out the RRR signal, indicating they were under attack by an enemy surface raider and identifying his ship as the Dutch-flag merchantman *Polyphemus*.

The deception might have succeeded, except that Rogge was not aware that just a month earlier the raider attack signal had been changed from RRR to RRRR. It was only one letter, but Captain Oliver spotted the mistake and kept his distance, circling the stranger well out of range of any guns she might be carrying. At the same time he contacted London with a description of the suspect ship.

At 0934 Oliver received confirmation from London that the so-called *Polyphemus* was an imposter and that the description he had given closely matched that of the commerce raider *Atlantis*. *Devonshire*'s 8-inch turrets opened fire from a range of 17,500yds.

The end came quickly for the *Atlantis*. *Devonshire*'s gunners first bracketed her with three salvoes, then their fourth scored a direct hit on her No.2 hold, setting it on fire. It so happened that this hold contained the German ship's main magazine, and when, at about 1015, the flames reached the ammunition, a huge explosion ripped the *Atlantis* apart. She sank two minutes later.

Seven of the raider's crew of 350 were killed when her magazine went up, the rest ending up in the water in lifeboats or rafts. Under any other circumstances, *Devonshire* would have picked up the survivors, but Captain Oliver had been warned by the Walrus of the presence of U-126, and he lost no time in clearing the area.

The departing *Devonshire* left behind her a chaotic scene. Some 350 survivors from the crew of the *Atlantis,* a shamefaced *Kapitänleutnant* Ernst Bauer and seven members of U-126's crew, had speedily abandoned the sinking raider, many of them jumping into the sea minutes before the she blew up. Others had been lucky enough to launch lifeboats and inflatable rafts. The sea around them was littered with the charred remains of their ship.

This was the frightening reality that confronted *Oberleutnant* Kurt Neubert when he brought U-126 back to the surface. When Bauer was rescued from the sea to resume his command, Neubert was asked to explain his failure to torpedo the attacking British cruiser while he had the opportunity. Neubert said it had been his intention to do so, but that when he came back to periscope to assess the situation, one of *Devonshire's* salvoes of 8-inch shells had exploded all around U-126. Believing he was being depth-charged, Neubert had dived again.

On taking over his command again, Bauer's immediate priority was to rescue the men in the water before the sharks reached them. A total of 230 men were plucked from the sea, of whom as many as possible were accommodated below deck, while the majority were crammed shoulder to shoulder on the submarine's casings. Bauer then took the four lifeboats and five life-rafts in tow, and after consulting with *Kapitän* Rogge, set course for the coast of Brazil, more than 1,000 miles to the west. The prevailing west-running current would help, but with the procession of boats and rafts trailing behind, U-126 would not make any great speed. It promised to be a long and exacting voyage: two weeks at least, under a merciless sun during the day and with bitterly cold nights. How many of those on the U-boat's deck and in the open boats and rafts would survive was a matter of conjecture.

As soon as he was under way Bauer sent a signal to Lorient informing Dönitz of the situation and requesting assistance. The supply ship *Python,* which was in the area, was ordered to rendezvous with U-126 to take on board all survivors.

The motor vessel *Python* was a 3,664-ton banana carrier of the Hamburg-Kamerun Line, requisitioned by the German Navy primarily to refuel and re-supply U-boats in the South Atlantic. She met up with U-126 and her tow on 24 November and relieved her of all 350 survivors. As ordered, the rescue ship then set course for

Biscay. U-126, by then sixty-one days out from her base and sorely in need of a respite, followed in her wake.

On her way north the *Python* was ordered to meet with and refuel two U-boats. They were Merten's U-68 and U-A, the latter under the command of Hans Eckermann. Both were in desperate need of fuel. For *Kapitänleutnant* Lueders of the *Python* this was a routine request, one which would normally have been speedily dealt with, preferably at night. However, the Enigma signals sent to the U-boats concerning the rendezvous had been decrypted by Bletchley Park, and the heavy cruiser *Dorsetshire*, sister ship to the *Devonshire*, was ordered to intervene.

On the morning of the 30th *Dorsetshire*'s Walrus reported sighting an unidentified merchant ship which appeared to be stopped and was acting suspiciously. The British cruiser raced in to investigate and caught *Python* and the two U-boats in the act of refuelling, drifting and blissfully unaware of the danger threatening.

Alarm bells rang when the *Dorsetshire* came storming over the horizon, and the U-boats hastily cast off and dived. U-A got clean away, but U-68 in her haste to submerge had left a hatch open and was almost lost. Only the skill and experience of Karl-Friedrich Merten saved her. Meanwhile, the *Python* was making smoke and trying to show a clean pair of heels to the avenging *Dorsetshire*. But with the cruiser's 8-inch salvoes dropping nearer and nearer escape was impossible. Lueders stopped his ship and scuttled her.

Dorsetshire, aware of the submerged U-boats, kept her distance, which turned out to be a wise move. Merten was still occupied by his fight to keep U-68 at periscope depth, but Eckermann was back with U-A and fired a spread of five torpedoes at the British cruiser. Luckily, *Dorsetshire*'s lookouts were alert and the tracks of Eckermann's torpedoes were seen. The cruiser sheered away under full helm and steamed off at full speed, leaving behind her *Python*'s crew and the survivors she had been carrying to fend for themselves.

Admiral Dönitz now had 414 men in the water and a massive rescue operation to organize. He did not fail those men. U-68 and U-A were joined on 4 December by U-124, and U-129 arrived on the 5th, the four boats sharing the survivors equally between them, roughly fifty below and fifty on deck for each of them. Four Italian submarines were also rounded up and met the German boats off the Cape Verde Islands. With the survivors divided between them

China Steam Navigation's *Shuntien*. She foundered in a welter of foam. (*Swire & Sons*)

James Bay, St Helena, with Jamestown in background. (*Andrew Neum*)

The lone hunter, operating beyond the convoy routes. (*WWII in Pictures*)

Günther Hessler and his wife Ursula, Admiral Dönitz's only daughter. (*Sharkhunters*)

RFA *Darkdale*. A commemorative stamp. (*Shipstamp UK*)

RFA Darkdaie sunk by U-68 in James' Bay 22.10.1941

20p

ST HELENA

HMS *Unbeaten* in Gibraltar, a long way from her home base. (*Mrs B. Woodward*)

HMS *Clyde* in convoy. A rendezvous was arranged. (*Royal Navy*)

Lt. Cdr. Arthur Callaway DSO, RANR. A commanding figure in all respects. (*Australian War Memorial*)

HMS *Lady Shirley*. A highly efficient fighting ship. (*From a newspaper cutting*)

MV *Silverbelle*. A typical product of a North-East shipyard. (*Walter E. Frost*)

German U-boats off the US coast. Admiral King refused to listen. (*Hubpages.com*)

Operation *Drumbeat*. The Americans were totally unprepared. (*US wartime poster*)

St Paul's Rocks. No lonelier meeting place on earth. (*Armand F. Pereira*)

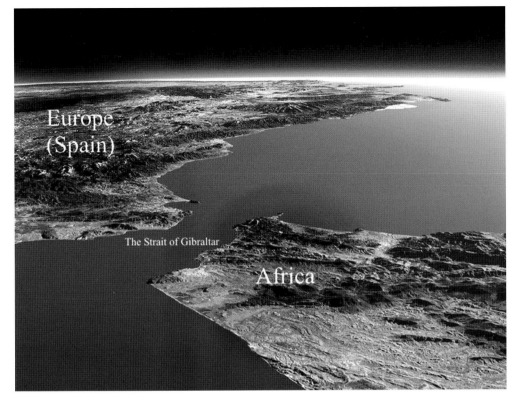

The Straits of Gibraltar. A frenzy of threshing propellers. (*Bing.com/Images*)

Tarafal Bay. An ideal spot for a clandestine rendezvous. (*True Beachfront*)

Lady Shirley lands her prisoners in Gibraltar. There was now really no need for such a show of force. (*Navegar-es-Preciso*)

Type IX U-boat under attack, closed up for a crash-dive. (*US Naval History & Heritage Command*)

the eight submarines were able to submerge comfortably. The long voyage back to Biscay began.

The Admiralty was by now aware that a substantial number of Axis U-boats were operating in the South Atlantic, and the hunt was on in earnest. Consequently, the eight overcrowded U-boats were forced to spend much of the daylight hours submerged. Progress was slow.

Only Johann Mohr in U-124 was prepared to take offensive action. He had on board 104 survivors in addition to a crew of fifty-two, and conditions below deck when submerged were becoming intolerable. Mohr determined that he must stay on the surface and run at full speed in order to shorten the voyage, and to this end he decided to create a diversion by attacking Ascension Island, thereby persuading British warships to concentrate their search in the south.

Mohr approached Ascension's Georgetown harbour in daylight on 9 December, hoping to emulate U-68's success in sinking the *Darkdale* off St Helena. There were no ships at anchor off Georgetown, so Mohr, still on the surface, moved in closer, his intention being to shell the Cable Station. Unfortunately for him, Ascension's defences had been recently strengthened by two 5.5-inch naval guns, manned by a detachment of Royal Artillery gunners. U-124 was sighted as she approached the harbour and came under accurate fire from the 5.5s. Mohr was forced to crash-dive and retreat out to sea. However, his deception bore fruit. All British warships in the area converged on Ascension, thereby allowing Dönitz's rescue flotilla free passage to the north. The eight submarines arrived back in Biscay at the end of December, and all survivors were landed at St Nazaire. So ended one of the most bizarre and successful rescue operations of the war.

CHAPTER EIGHT

East of Gibraltar

Further north, in the Straits of Gibraltar, the waters were a frenzy of threshing propellers. Bletchley Park had intercepted W/T traffic between Lorient and U-boats at sea indicating that the U-boats were about to break into the Mediterranean in force, and everything, including the two 40-year-old armed yachts *Rosabelle* and *Sayonara*, had been pressed into service.

Four anti-submarine trawlers were on constant patrol, steaming in line abreast 1½ miles apart, sweeping the Straits from end to end and keeping a constant visual and Asdic watch. Amongst them was HMT *Lady Shirley*, back in service after two months in Gibraltar under repair. Lieutenant Commander Arthur Callaway was still in command, and the trawler's crew was largely unchanged, except that the gaps left by the gunfight with U-111 off the Canaries had been filled. There had been only one change in her officers, Sub Lieutenant Allan Waller being replaced by Lieutenant Patrick Hardinge-Katon. Waller, hospitalized for further treatment of wounds received when the trawler *Tourmaline* was bombed and sunk in January 1941, had been seconded to the staff of Admiral Edwards-Collins and was in charge of Gibraltar's U-boat plot.

All this extra activity off Gibraltar was well meant, but it was too little, too late. A number of U-boats had already slipped through the Straits and had been in the Mediterranean for some months.

Towards the end of August 1941, the German Naval High Command, at the behest of Hitler, and despite the vociferous protests of Admiral Dönitz and his C-in-C Grand Admiral Raeder, had ordered the transfer of U-boats from the North Atlantic to the Mediterranean. They were to be based at Salamis in southern Greece to operate against British convoys supplying the Eighth Army in North Africa.

When Italy entered the war on the side of Germany in June 1940, Mussolini saw a not-to-be-missed opportunity to recreate the old Roman Empire in North Africa which had once stretched from

Morocco to the Red Sea. He ordered General Graziani, who commanded a force of 200,000 motorized troops in Italian-occupied Libya, to move eastwards and cross the frontier into Egypt. The British garrison in Egypt, heavily outnumbered, was forced into a headlong retreat. Within three days, Graziani was 70 miles deep into Egypt and at the gates of Sidi Barani. Here, possibly astounded by the ease of his advance, the General called a halt to consolidate.

This unexpected lull in the fighting gave the British troops, led by the experienced General Wavell, an opportunity to recover from the humiliation of their forced retreat and to regroup. Reinforced, they then launched a fierce counter-attack, pushing the Italians back into Libya. Graziani's men had no stomach for a fight on equal terms, and their retreat soon became a rout. Sidi Barani fell to Wavell, followed by Bardia, Tobruk, Derna and Benghazi. By early February 1941 the British were 300 miles into Libya and Mussolini was begging Hitler for help.

General Erwin Rommel's Afrika Korps landed in North Africa in late February, and the battle-hardened German troops took charge of the rapidly deteriorating situation in the Western Desert. Within days, Wavell's barnstorming advance had come to a full stop. Britain responded, as she has so often done down through the ages, by calling in the Royal Navy.

Arms, ammunition and provisions for Rommel's army were carried across the Mediterranean from Italy by convoys of small ships, and it was at this jugular that the Royal Navy struck. Cruisers and destroyers based at Malta swooped on Rommel's convoys, and before long nearly three-quarters of the supplies intended for the Afrika Korps were ending up on the sea bed. It soon became clear that unless Germany could regain control over her shipping lanes in the Mediterranean the war in the Western Desert would be lost. For Hitler, whose Panzers had swept through northern Europe with such ease, the humiliation would be too much. He refused to listen to the advice of his admirals, and so made one of the biggest mistakes of his infamous reign.

On 26 August the Führer issued his order for the U-boats to enter the Mediterranean, and three weeks later Heinrich Driver took U-371 out of Brest and headed south. He was followed at intervals by Hans Heidtmann in U-559, Udo Heilmann in U-97, Hans-Diedrich von Tiesenhausen in U-331, Helmuth Ringelmann in U-75 and Wolfgang Kaufmann in U-79. Their aim was to slip through the heavily defended Straits of Gibraltar and to so harass British shipping that the Royal Navy would be forced to divert its ships from attack to defence.

Admiral Dönitz, who had served in U-boats in the Mediterranean during the First World War, knew the dangers and difficulties to be encountered in this land-locked sea. Shallow water and frequently smooth seas would make it virtually impossible to hide from the constantly searching British aircraft and surface ships. As a result, the U-boats would have to spend much of their time below the surface in water with a temperature often in excess of 21° C. The heat in the confined space of a submarine's hull would become unbearable, resulting in slow reactions and questionable decisions.

It soon became clear that the Admiral's reservations were well-founded. Reports began to reach Lorient of the difficulties being experienced by the first U-boats to enter the Mediterranean. Commanders complained that the British supply convoys they had been sent in to destroy consisted largely of small, shallow-draught vessels which were extremely difficult to torpedo and were so heavily escorted that surfacing to use guns was out of the question. After a month in action, the six U-boats had succeeded in sinking just two barges, a small Greek coaster and a 758-ton oil tanker. Three of the boats, having expended all their torpedoes with little gained, were already on their way home. But Hitler, as uncompromising as ever, refused to accept defeat and ordered Dönitz to send in more boats.

U-81, a Type VIIC completed at Bremen towards the end of April 1941, was the first of the second batch of U-boats to be sent south. Commanded by 26-year-old Friedrich Guggenberger, she sailed from Brest on 29 October and almost immediately ran into trouble in the Bay of Biscay. Surprised on the surface by two aircraft of RAF Coastal Command, she was severely damaged by machine gun fire and depth charges. Guggenberger managed to extricate her from danger, and returned to Brest for repairs. She sailed again on 4 November, arriving in the western approaches to the Straits of Gibraltar on the afternoon of the 12th.

Armed with only the briefest advice on how to slip through the Straits undetected and a copy of the Sailing Directions for the area, Guggenberger decided to travel at night, on the surface, and hug the northern coast to take advantage of a 2-knot ingoing tide. He submerged to await nightfall.

Surfacing again just after 1800, U-81 rose into a black, moonless night and prepared to transit this narrow stretch of water that had been dominated by the Royal Navy for nearly 240 years. It was a daunting prospect. Working up to full speed, Guggenberger closed the Spanish coast, and with the help of the east-flowing tide U-81 was soon making a good 18 knots through the water. For those in the conning tower of the U-boat it was an exhilarating experience, but nerve-wracking at the same time. The lights were burning brightly on the Spanish shore, casting a glow on the water, and groups of fishing boats were lighting up the Straits further out. The possibility of the U-boat's silhouette being spotted by lurking British patrol boats was very real.

The danger increased when, passing close to the town of Tarifa, U-81 was momentarily caught in the rotating beam of its lighthouse. Fortunately, she slid through into the darkness unseen by enemy eyes. Then, less than two hours after she had begun to run the Straits, she was past Gibraltar's Europa Point and relatively safe. Guggenberger now took her back down to periscope depth to pass the rest of the night at a more sedate pace.

When Guggenberger surfaced at dawn on the 13th to fix his position he received a signal from Lorient instructing him to make a rendezvous with U-205, which had entered the Mediterranean on the heels of U-81. The two boats were to locate and attack a squadron of British warships sighted by an Italian reconnaissance aircraft off Cape de Gata on the afternoon of the 12th. The position given for the enemy ships was vague, but as they were said to be steering west, Guggenberger was able to work out a rough interception course. All attempts to contact U-205 were unsuccessful.

Guggenberger's calculations bore fruit, and at around 1400 on the 13th the distinctive mastheads of group of warships were visible through his periscope. Moving closer, he realized that this was no routine British patrol. What he had sighted was in fact the aircraft carrier HMS *Ark Royal* returning to Gibraltar after delivering replacement fighter aircraft to Malta. She was accompanied by the 31,000-ton battleship *Malaya* and a destroyer escort. Few U-boats had ever been offered such a tempting array of targets.

Approaching as near to the enemy ships as possible without risking discovery, Guggenberger set his sights on the high-sided carrier and emptied his bow tubes at her. Three of his torpedoes missed their target, but the fourth went home, bringing *Ark Royal* to a shuddering halt. She immediately took on a heavy list to starboard.

Much to Guggenberger's surprise, retaliation was very slow, and he was able to take U-81 deep and creep away. Then, when he thought he had escaped detection, the dreaded ping of Asdics was heard and the depth charges came raining down. In the hours that followed, U-81 was subjected to more than 100 depth charges dropped by the escorting destroyers, but she eventually escaped with nothing more than a few broken gauge glasses and a thoroughly frightened crew. *Ark Royal* was taken in tow, but sank before reaching the safety of Gibraltar. With the exception of one man killed by the exploding torpedo, the carrier's entire crew were saved, but her aircraft, unable to take off because of the heavy list, were lost with her.

The loss of HMS *Ark Royal* was a serious blow to Britain's navy, as at the time three other carriers were under repair, leaving none free for service in the Mediterranean. Without air cover, British supply convoys would be under threat. The situation became even worse when, eleven days later, Hans-Dietrich von Tiesenhausen's U-331 sank the battleship *Barham*.

HMS *Barham*, at 33,000 tons and with eight 15-inch guns, was a formidable warship. She was also jinxed – or so it was said. Launched in 1915, she began her career by colliding with her sister-ship *Warspite* and suffering serious damage that put her out of service for three weeks. At the Battle of Jutland in June 1916 she came under heavy fire and spent another month in the repair yard. Between the wars, she went the rounds showing the flag without incident, but in December 1939, with Britain at war again, she ran down the destroyer HMS *Duchess* in fog, sinking her with the loss of 124 men. A few weeks later, *Barham* was torpedoed by U-30 in the Atlantic and was out of action until April 1940. She then moved into the Mediterranean, where in May 1941 she came under attack by Italian bombers off Crete, although on this occasion the ill-fated battleship sustained only minor damage.

Six months passed without incident, then on 25 November, while in company with the battleships *Queen Elizabeth* and *Valiant* and a destroyer escort, HMS *Barham* was on her way to intercept an Italian convoy when what little luck she still possessed ran out. U-331 broke through the escort screen and approached within

750yds of *Barham* before firing a spread of three torpedoes. At such close range the huge warship was a target not to be missed. All three of von Tiesenhausen's torpedoes went home, blasting an enormous hole in the battleship's armour-plated hull. She lurched heavily to port as the sea poured in, and moments later she was on her way to the bottom.

Many years later, one of the survivors, Richard Laland, Able Seaman in the *Barham*, wrote:

> The Germans were at the gates of Alexandria at that time and we were accompanying destroyers trying to stop their supplies. We had no idea there were U-boats in the area.
>
> We were standing by a ladder two decks below on the messdeck when there was a huge explosion. It was by an air vent from the engine room that was hit and all this smoke came pouring up.
>
> We looked at each other and said, 'Right, let's get up top!' By the time we got on deck the ship was listing at a 45 degree angle. We climbed over the guard rail and started running down the side of the ship. When we reached one of the torpedo bulges my friend jumped into the water. I dived in head first, but as I did the ship rolled again and I smashed my head on the hull and was knocked unconscious.
>
> I was disorientated but reached out and felt the ship. I was trying to push myself away when I got blown away by this massive explosion as the magazine went up. I didn't know which way was up or down and that was it, I'm going to die – I had given up and remember thinking, I hope it's quick.
>
> I shot to the surface. It was the strangest thing. I saw one of my shipmates in the water and asked him, 'Where's the ship?'
>
> He replied, 'It's gone.'

Richard Laland was picked up by an Australian destroyer, along with another 840 survivors out of a total complement of 1184 officers and men. So ended the career of one of the Royal Navy's most blighted warships.

*

In the midst of all this mayhem at sea, in the Western Desert the Eighth Army had launched Operation Crusader, primarily aimed at relieving the vital port of Tobruk, which had been surrounded and cut off by Rommel. Mistakenly, the German High Command believed Crusader to be the opening move in a British and French seaborne invasion of Morocco. Dönitz was told, 'This places Italy and our whole position in the Mediterranean in a situation of acute danger. The importance of retaining our position in the Mediterranean necessitates a complete reorientation of the focal areas of U-boat activities until the situation has been restored.' With no room for argument, Dönitz was ordered to send another ten U-boats into the Mediterranean and to station fifteen more in the western approaches to the Straits of Gibraltar.

This was clear madness. The whole *raison d'être* for the U-boats lay in the North Atlantic, where the great Allied convoys sailed between America and Britain and, at the best of times, only thirty-four boats were available for operations. Admiral Dönitz was convinced – and for good reason – that the war would be won or lost in the North Atlantic sea lanes, and he protested vigorously against the transfer of any more of his U-boats to the Mediterranean, both to Admiral Raeder and to the Führer himself, but neither would listen. The Naval War Staff created a new post of *Führer der U-boote* Mediterranean, who was attached to the staff of Admiral Wiechold in Rome and supposedly subordinate to Lorient, but Dönitz feared he was losing control of his beloved U-boat arm.

The consequences of Hitler's misguided policy were already in evidence. With the exception of a small group of U-boats operating off Newfoundland, Allied convoys in the North Atlantic were now largely unmolested. Sinkings had fallen significantly, down from 200,000 tons in September to 60,000 tons in November. At the same time, in the Mediterranean, the U-boats were suffering. U-95 had been sunk by the Dutch submarine O-21, U-208 was sunk by the corvette HMS *Bluebell*, U-206 was caught on the surface and sunk by aircraft, and U-432, U96 and U-558 were all damaged by air attack. On 16 November U-433 was sent to the bottom by the corvette *Marigold* when south of Malaga. And now others were queuing up to enter the Straits of Gibraltar.

U-374 sailed from Brest at the end of November, her orders being to break into the Mediterranean and reach the Italian port of La Spezia, where she was to be based. A Type VIIC built at Kiel and commissioned in June 1941, she was under the command of *Oberleutnant-zur-See* Unno von Fischel, the son of Admiral Hermann von Fischel, who himself had commanded a U-boat in the 1914–18 war.

Although U-374 had spent forty-four days in the North Atlantic on her first war patrol, she had achieved little, sinking only one small ship, the Bristol steamer *Rose Schiaffino* of 3,349 tons. Crossing the Atlantic unescorted with a full cargo of iron ore for Cardiff, she had gone down like the proverbial stone when von Fischel torpedoed her, and none of her crew of forty-one survived. Apart from this comparatively easy victory, U-374 was unblooded.

U-374 was still 500 miles out in the Atlantic when von Fischel first received news that British air and sea patrols had been stepped up in the Straits of Gibraltar and the approaches. At that time a very large convoy, some fifty-five ships, was assembling in Gibraltar, all loaded and headed north. Security was at a maximum. Already on the night of 6 December another boat, U-375, had come under heavy sea and air attack when attempting to enter the Straits. She had narrowly escaped destruction by retreating back into the Atlantic, and two more days would pass before she was able make another attempt.

Forewarned, Unno von Fischel arrived in the western approaches to the Straits on the night of 10/11 November and moved in with extreme caution, dropping down to periscope depth when he came in sight of the land. Having thoroughly reconnoitred the area, he surfaced at midnight and closed the coast of Morocco. By this time the moon had gone down and the night was dark, with further cover being provided by rain squalls sweeping in from the Atlantic. There were few lights visible on the African shore, and there seemed little chance of U-374 being seen by unfriendly eyes. To make doubly sure, von Fischel reduced speed, so that the beat of the boat's diesels was barely audible. U-374 was no more than a dark shadow gliding ghost-like on the mirror-calm water as she entered the Mediterranean.

At 0345 on the 11th, the four British anti-submarine trawlers on patrol off Gibraltar had reached the eastern limit of their search area and had reversed course to begin another westerly leg. The constant steaming up and down to no apparent avail was soul-destroying work, for although the Asdics pinged and binoculars searched the horizon, only the odd Spanish or Moroccan fisher-man was moving. The four trawlers were in line-abreast, with HMT *Lady Shirley* nearest to the African side. On her starboard beam was the *St Nectan*, with Lieutenant Osborne RANR keeping watch on the bridge. Osborne had just taken over the watch and had already swept round with his binoculars, taking particular notice of the *Lady Shirley*, commanded by fellow Australian Henry Callaway. There was a cold front moving in from the Atlantic, bringing with it a series of fierce squalls, and from time to time sheets of stinging rain swept across the small flotilla, sluicing down the decks of the patrolling trawlers and temporarily reducing visibility to zero.

Satisfied that everyone was on station, Osborne turned away to consult the chart. Then, without warning, the heavens opened and another torrential downpour descended. Osborne, with his nose pressed to the spinning clear-view screen in the wheelhouse window, could see nothing of the horizon ahead, and the other trawlers on either beam had disappeared from sight in the rain.

For a long twenty-five minutes Osborne stared into the wall of cascading water, praying that there were no fishing vessels in their path and that none of the other trawlers had wandered off course. Then, as quickly as it had come, the rain cleared, and there, all around, was sea and sky washed clean by the deluge. The two trawlers on his starboard side were still there, wallowing in the chop set up by the squall, but when Osborne looked to port, where the *Lady Shirley* had been, there was an empty space. Osborne searched with his binoculars ahead and astern. Nothing but wave-tops.

An hour passed without sight nor sound of the missing trawler. Then, at 0510, the armed patrol yacht *Sayonara*, which was on station in the area, broke radio silence to report: 'Cable Enterprise blown up, have eleven survivors on board.' This was followed a little later by another signal from *Sayonara* reporting that her fellow patrol yacht *Rosabelle* had been blown up and sunk. *Sayonara*'s messages caused some confusion. There was no record of a ship called *Cable Enterprise* being in the Mediterranean or its immediate vicinity. Furthermore, there had been no flashes seen, no explosions heard, no cries for help over the radio, no soaring distress rockets. The *Sayonara* did in fact pick up survivors, twelve in all, and they were from the *Rosabelle*, which had sunk with the loss of thirty lives.

Signalman Neville Wilson, who was serving in the *Lady Shirley* when she sank U-111 and had since transferred to the trawler *Arctic Ranger*, intercepted both of *Sayonara's* signals. He later stated:

> I had heard some dull explosions and then came these two signals about *Cable Enterprise* and *Rosabelle*. Not until 9 am were we informed that *Lady Shirley* had vanished. It was a very confused situation. *Arctic Ranger* had been helping another trawler to shadow a French convoy; at 10.30 am we completed this support duty and went off to join in the hunt for the missing *Lady Shirley*. We carried out an intensive search east of Gibraltar but there was no trace of her.
>
> We could hardly conclude that she had been torpedoed, since there was not even the smallest trace of wreckage, or of the many loose items scattered about her decks which I knew from experience would have floated off had she been tin-fished. There was nothing at all to explain her mysterious disappearance.

Sub Lieutenant Allan Waller, who had been on duty in the control tower in Gibraltar during the night, later wrote:

> At about 0500 the Naval Control of Shipping yacht *Sayonara* signalled she had picked up survivors of a ship which had blown up. Next came a signal from a ship (I do not know which one) that the NCS yacht *Rosabelle* had blown up and sunk. The situation was confused and unclear but at daylight all the ships in the area searched the Straits for survivors and wreckage. In the case of the *Lady Shirley* there was nothing. Nothing
>
> Late in the forenoon I was called back to the tower to see if I could identify items of wreckage which had been brought in by the searching ships. With me was Lieutenant Commander 'Nobby' Clarke RNR, who had been commanding officer of the *Rosabelle* . . . She was a yacht built in 1901, she had been used as an examination vessel. Forty years old, she was in a bad condition. Clarke had complained she was unseaworthy, with the result that he had been temporarily relieved of command. It is interesting to note that officially *Rosabelle* was 'sunk by explosion,

probably torpedoed by a U-boat, Straits of Gibraltar'. Clarke could have been right about the state of his ship.

I was unable to identify any of the pitiable bits and pieces. Nobby Clarke recognized some scrollwork as coming from the *Rosabelle*.

It has always been a mystery to me why the two small 'spanner' rafts kept on top of *Shirley*'s asdic bridge had not been found. These small rafts were only secured by light brackets to prevent them rolling off, so they would have floated off. There must have been buoyant items on the upper deck which should have surfaced. The area where she disappeared was known and small, and it had been thoroughly searched. I discussed this with Lt. Osborne who had been the last person to see her. He was sure that he heard no explosion but this could have been muffled by the heavy rain squall. Neither had an underwater explosion been detected by the asdic set and operating conditions had been quite good. In effect, no one on board the nearest ship had heard or seen anything. *Lady Shirley* is officially described as 'sunk by U-boat, Gibraltar Straits, 11 December 1941'.

I have never believed this. I think she was sunk by sabotage. On 18 January 1942, I was getting ready to go on watch at 1800 in the Tower. The house Middleton is just outside the South Dockyard Gate, as I left the house there was a terrific explosion and a huge smoke ring rose and drifted quite rapidly over the south end of the Upper Rock. North Pavilion Road is a sharp incline and the road consists of mule steps. Middleton was still sufficiently high enough to enable me to look over the wall by the house into the dockyard, already a large fire had broken out in the corner of the dockyard by the small dry dock. I ran into the dockyard. In the corner had been a 'trot' of three trawlers; *Imperialist* alongside the quay heading, then *Erin* and outside the small *Honjo*, a minesweeper. The *Erin* had blown up and sunk immediately. The *Honjo* was on fire from stem to stern and adrift with, already, a dockyard tug that was endeavouring to get a line aboard. Somehow the *Honjo*'s crew managed to get a line ashore to us and we held her bow against the quay wall while Surgeon Commander and his team (they must have moved quickly as the dockyard surgery was some distance away behind the Tower) went aboard to attend to some badly injured men. In a short time the injured men and the rest of the *Honjo*'s crew were ashore and the tug was towing the blazing ship into the middle of the harbour clear of all ships.

It was believed that a time bomb had been placed in one of *Erin*'s depth charges. This could have been done quite easily. Security could not cover everything. Thousands of Spaniards came to work in Gib, mostly in the dockyard. One, acting as agent for the Germans, could have placed the charge. It was a Sunday evening, no Spanish workmen about, what better time?

It would have been easy to plant a bomb in one of the *Lady Shirley*'s depth charges. *Erin* had sunk instantly, as *Shirley* must have done. The Germans had a reason for sinking *Shirley*, the action had been well publicised, a full report appearing in the Gibraltar Chronicle on 10 October. It had been broadcast. All the national papers had reported it, many with illustrations, comparing the size of the U-boat and *Lady Shirley*.

Six men died as a result of the *Erin* and *Honjo* incident, and it was later established that the explosion was the work of Spanish saboteurs trained, financed and equipped by Berlin. It was, in fact, the latest of a series of largely unsuccessful attacks on the Gibraltar garrison which had begun earlier in the year. A bomb had been exploded in the North Tunnel in February, followed by an attempt to blow up the airstrip, but neither explosion caused significant damage. Then, in June Intelligence foiled a plan to attach a mine to a merchant ship in the harbour. Apart from these relatively minor incidents, the Spanish saboteurs, of whom 183 were known to be active in Gibraltar, failed to make their mark until the *Erin* was blown up.

It may be that the *Lady Shirley* did fall victim to the saboteurs, but what evidence there is points towards Unno von Fischel and U-374. Allan Waller wrote later:

Another thing. If, as suggested, the Germans had smarted under little *Shirley*'s defeat of a U-boat and sought revenge upon her, why hadn't they jumped to announce the glad news of her sinking? In my position on the U-boat plot, information came to hand from all kinds of quarters and it was part of my job to read all the U-boat reports; but the Germans made no claims about *Shirley* – none whatsoever.

The answer to Waller's query is simple. Von Fischel did in fact inform Lorient on the 11th that he had sunk two escorts in the Straits of Gibraltar, and this was recorded in Admiral Dönitz's War Diary. U-374's commander had no opportunity of identifying the ships he had sunk as it was a very dark night, and according to his log the U-boat was heavily engaged by several British ships during the encounter. She returned their fire, then dived and remained submerged for some hours.

It seems certain that the armed yacht *Rosabelle* was sunk by U-374, but the identity of the other vessel remains unclear until this day. The *Sayonara* named her as the *Cable Enterprise*, but Admiralty records make no mention of a ship of that name being sunk, or indeed being in the area at the time. As there were no survivors left to tell the tale, the fate of HMT *Lady Shirley* must forever remain unclear, although the consensus of opinion is that she must have been the other recipient of von Fischel's torpedoes.

In the last three months of 1941 nineteen U-boats were lost in the Mediterranean and one more in the Bay of Biscay on passage to the Straits of Gibraltar. In the same period sinkings of Allied ships in the North Atlantic had fallen to an all-time low. Meanwhile, on 7 December, Japanese carrier-based aircraft had mounted the surprise attack on the US Pacific Fleet at Pearl Harbor, and at the same time Japanese troops had landed on Malaya's east coast. At long last America had been drawn into the war, and the fortunes of Hitler's U-boats were about to change.

CHAPTER NINE

The Middle Sea

When he was satisfied that Gibraltar was well out of sight astern, Unno von Fischel brought U-374 back to the surface and rang for full speed. In response, the U-boat's engineer officer, *Leutnant* Leonhardt, appeared in the conning tower to report that as a result of the severe depth-charging during the night one diesel was out of action and could not be repaired at sea. This was uncomfortable news, for after the devastation U-374 had caused in the Straits of Gibraltar, British warships would by now be out in force searching for her. The remainder of the passage was made in nervous anticipation of retribution by sea or by air, and at a reduced speed of about 9 knots. The U-boat's new home port of La Spezia, near Genoa, was not reached until 14 December.

Repaired, refuelled and re-provisioned, with her crew rested, U-374 sailed from La Spezia on the 18th and headed south for North African waters. Von Fischel's orders were to join with a group of six other U-boats already engaged in harassing British convoys running supplies from Alexandria to the beleaguered garrison of Tobruk.

Tobruk, 70 miles behind the front line in German-occupied territory, was a very painful thorn in General Rommel's side. The heavily fortified port, manned by a large force of British and Commonwealth troops plus an armoured brigade, was in effect barring his way to Egypt. As well as being surrounded by the tanks and guns of the Afrika Korps, Tobruk was under constant bombardment by German and Italian planes, and to continue to hold out the city needed an uninterrupted supply of arms, ammunition and men. This could only come by sea, and in small, fast merchantmen escorted by destroyers. The 18-hour run from Alexandria by the 'Tobruk Ferry', as the Allied supply convoys had become known, was made in the dead of night, the ships timing their arrival off Tobruk with the coming of dawn. Invariably, their arrival would coincide with the appearance of enemy bombers overhead, so there was no time for niceties. The ships stayed alongside just long enough to literally dump their cargoes on the quay and to take on board wounded troops, and sometimes prisoners of war, before hurrying back out to sea. Many failed to clear the breakwaters, and Tobruk harbour was littered with the wrecks of bombed ships.

Convoy TA 5, consisting of a handful of fast merchantmen escorted by the Hunt-class destroyers *Hasty*, *Heythrop* and *Hotspur* and the corvette *Salvia*, arrived in Tobruk on the morning of 23 December. After the usual frenetic turnaround, in this case mercifully free of air raids, the convoy left port again in late afternoon for the return run to Alexandria.

With Convoy TA 5 was China Steam Navigation's *Shuntien*, a small passenger/cargo vessel built in Hong Kong and registered in London. The *Shuntien*, under the command of Captain William Shinn and with British officers and a mixture of Chinese and Maltese crew, had spent all her working life on the China Coast until requisitioned by the Admiralty in August 1941. She was ideally suited to serve the Eighth Army, being just over 3,000 tons gross, 300ft long, of shallow draught, with a service speed of 16 knots and capable of reaching 20 knots should the need arise. She also had generous passenger accommodation, albeit of a basic nature, and was equipped to carry large numbers of deck passengers, something she had done as a matter of routine on the China Coast.

On this occasion, after offloading her supplies in Tobruk, the *Shuntien* had taken on board for the return trip 1,100 German and Italian prisoners of war and their guard of forty men of the Durham Light Infantry. In all, including her crew of seventy and eighteen naval gunners, the *Shuntien* thus had a total complement of over 1,200 men. To say that the little ship was overcrowded would be an understatement, but it was not a situation that troubled Captain Shinn and his officers. In their years on the China Coast they had often carried a deck full of passengers and their luggage.

Contrary to the popular belief promoted by holiday brochures, the Mediterranean is not always all blue skies and flat calm seas. In the winter months, vigorous depressions sweep in from the Atlantic bringing gale-force winds and rough seas. The relatively shallow water accentuates the sea and the swell, making it heavy going for smaller ships. When Convoy TA 5 left the shelter of

Tobruk harbour on the afternoon of the 23rd it ran straight into a howling north-westerly gale which, with the wind and sea on the port quarter, promised an uncomfortable night for the ships.

The night, when it came, was dark and full of menace, a heavily overcast sky hiding what moon there was. Running before the rising swell, the *Shuntien* took on a shock-like movement, shaking herself like a wet terrier every time her stern lifted and her propeller raced. The tightly packed mass of prisoners crowding her open decks suffered worst. Already stunned and frightened at the loss of their liberty, they quickly succumbed to the horrors of seasickness. Even for the *Shuntien*'s crew, hardened as they were to the rigours of the 'Tobruk Ferry' in winter and sure in the knowledge that morning would see them safely behind the breakwaters of Alexandria, it was a bad night. The ship was in a constant state of alert for U-boat attack, although with such foul weather and a strong destroyer escort around them, no one was giving serious thought to the enemy. But he was out there in the darkness, riding out the storm and waiting for them.

U-559, a Hamburg-built boat commissioned in the previous February by *Kapitänleutnant* Hans Heidtmann, had been among the first U-boats to enter the Mediterranean from the Atlantic. Slipping unseen through the Straits of Gibraltar on 26 September, when the weather was still fine and warm, she had had an untroubled run to her new base at Salamis in Greece. From there she was assigned to support the Afrika Korps by attacking Allied shipping on the coasts of Egypt and Libya. To date, however, she had succeeded in sinking only one ship, namely HMAS *Parramatta*. It had taken just one torpedo to dispose of the Australian sloop; her magazine had blown up and she sank in minutes. Four weeks later, Heidtmann, keeping vigil in his storm-lashed conning tower, was hoping for another such easy victim, but in view of the weather he feared he would be disappointed. Then out of the night came Convoy TA 5.

On the bridge of the *Shuntien*, Captain William Shinn regarded the weather with similar disgust, but it was now 24 December and he was confident that he could at least look forward to a peaceful Christmas in Alexandria. This would give him the opportunity to celebrate the remarkable and recently received news that his wife had just given birth to triplets.

As he peered anxiously into the darkness, Shinn heard the distinctive thud of exploding depth charges, and his dreams of home evaporated. The war was back again. HMS *Salvia*, keeping station close on the *Shuntien*'s port beam, had an Asdic contact and was attacking the unseen enemy. But the corvette's reaction was too late. Hans Heidtmann had already fired his torpedoes and was running away.

Heidtmann had aimed well. One of his torpedoes ploughed into *Shuntien*'s port side abreast her after hold. The explosion blew away the entire stern section of the little ship. Five minutes later, her bows lifted high and she foundered in a welter of foam. There had been no time to lower boats or jettison rafts, no time to send out a distress call. The one-time China Coaster had gone, leaving behind her a few scraps of wreckage, a spreading patch of oil and hundreds of men struggling in the rough seas. As luck would have it, HMS *Salvia* was close by and she immediately moved in to pick up survivors.

Salvia, under the command of Lieutenant Commander John Miller, was one of the first Flower-class corvettes to enter service. Launched in the summer of 1940, she was built along the lines of an Antarctic whaler, with a raised forecastle and a well deck forward of the bridge. The corvettes earned themselves the reputation of being able to 'roll on wet grass', but they were eminently seaworthy little ships. The *Salvia* was no exception. In spite of the rough seas, and with her well deck awash for much of the time, she performed a small miracle in plucking from the water an estimated 460 survivors from the sunken *Shuntien*, including Captain Shinn and sixty-three of his crew. The destroyer HMS *Heythrop* picked up another nineteen. The numbers on board the *Shuntien* are in dispute, but it is believed that at least 900 men lost their lives, most of them German and Italian prisoners of war. Hans Heidtmann may have scored a notable victory in sinking the ship, but it was largely at the expense of his own countrymen and their allies.

The *Salvia* had been on full submarine alert while carrying out the rescue, with extra lookouts posted and her Asdic probing the depths, but U-559 had not lingered to view her triumph. However, Lieutenant Commander Miller's caution was fully justified, as another danger now threatened the convoy. U-79, commanded by *Kapitänleutnant* Wolfgang Kaufmann, had sailed from Salamis only two days earlier and had arrived off the Libyan coast just as TA 5 was passing. Kaufmann, whose only success since entering the Mediterranean in early October had been the sinking of the small gunboat HMS *Gnat*, lost no time in bearing down on the convoy. Unfortunately for Kaufmann, the escorting destroyers *Hasty* and *Hotspur* lay directly in his path, and the U-boat was caught in their Asdic beams as it approached. A barrage of well-aimed depth charges followed, and U-79 was unceremoniously blown to the surface. Faced with two vengeful destroyers, Kaufmann opted to scuttle his boat, and thus he and all his crew survived, hauled from the water by HMS *Hotspur*.

HMS *Salvia*, meanwhile, was under way again and following in the wake of the convoy. With nearly 500 survivors on board, many of them potentially hostile if given the opportunity, Lieutenant Commander Miller decided to make a lone high-speed dash for Alexandria. But the little corvette, a survivor of so many brushes with the enemy, was never seen again. Searching for her, a sister-corvette, HMS *Peony*, found a patch of oil some 100 miles west of Alexandria, but no wreckage or survivors.

Enemy reports show that *Salvia* had the misfortune to steam into the sights of Joachim Preuss in U-568 who had been lying in wait for such an opportunity. Preuss, who had brought U-568 in through the Straits of Gibraltar only two weeks earlier, was credited with being partly responsible for bringing America into the war against Germany. While on patrol in the North Atlantic in October 1941, U-568 was involved with other U-boats in a pack attack on Convoy SC 48, whose inexperienced Canadian escorts were losing the fight. Although the United States was still then officially neutral, the Canadians' call for help brought three US Navy destroyers based in Iceland racing to the rescue. Preuss, knowingly or not, torpedoed one of them, USS *Kearny*, and although she did not sink, eleven of her crew were killed. *Kearny* hit back at U-568, subjecting her to a severe depth-charging that continued throughout the night. The battered U-boat escaped, and USS *Kearny* reached Iceland under her own steam. Two months later, after Pearl Harbor, Hitler declared war on the United States of America, citing the 'unprovoked attack' on U-568 as a provocation.

When HMS *Salvia* was sighted by U-568 in the small hours of Christmas Eve 1941, Joachim Preuss fired a spread of four torpedoes at close range. One of his torpedoes went home and was sufficient to break the corvette in two. Her ruptured fuel tanks spilled heavy bunker oil on to the sea, which then caught fire. In the midst of this conflagration, both halves of the stricken ship sank. Those who did not go down with her died a horrible death by burning. The exact figure is not known, but it is certain that at least 550 men lost their lives.

*

U-374 had arrived off the coast of Libya on 22 December, by which time Operation Crusader was in full flood and British troops, having relieved Tobruk, were pushing relentlessly westwards. Endlessly patrolling up and down off Mersa Matruh waiting for passing convoys, Unno von Fischel and his men spent a miserable and fruitless Christmas. Not that many of their fellow country-men and women fared much better, for all was not well back in Germany.

In early summer Hitler had mounted Operation Barbarossa, sending nearly four million troops across the border into Russia, along with their tanks, guns and vehicles, all supported by over 2,700 aircraft. Once and for all the evil of Bolshevism was to be wiped out, while Germany's borders would spread ever outwards towards the eastern horizon.

It was a dream that had been dreamed 129 years before by one Napoleon Bonaparte, and like his it was doomed to abject failure. Hitler, like Napoleon, had sent an army into Russia ill-equipped for the Soviet winter, and in December 1941, with the temperature on the Eastern Front at –42° C, the German generals were losing twice as many men to the bitter cold as to the Russian guns. It even came to the point where collections were being made on the Home Front of warm clothes, woollens, furs, anything that could be sent to make life easier for the troops in the East. And as if that was not enough, for the first time strict food rationing had been imposed in Germany. This did nothing to improve the morale of an already questioning civilian population. Christmas 1941 in Germany would be marred by austerity.

Meanwhile, in Britain, events had taken a turn for the better. The devastating air raids of the summer were a thing of the past, and factories were moving back into full production. There was still a steady haemorrhage of merchant ships to the U-boats, at the rate of nearly 200 a month, but shipyards all over the country, on the Clyde, the Tyne and the Mersey, were beginning to catch up. Even sleepy West Country seaside towns, once renowned for building ships to meet the Spanish Armada, had been pressed into service to build small vessels, merchant and naval. And then, on 7 December, came Pearl Harbor.

On board U-374 they listened with envy to the intense wireless traffic generated by the attack on Convoy TA 5, but that was as near as they got to the war. No convoy, not even a single enemy ship, darkened their horizon. The year 1941 drew to a close with von Fischel moving towards the conclusion that his present assignment was a complete waste of time. Then, late in the morning of 8 January 1942, the waiting finally came to an end.

At the time, U-374 was out of sight of the coast, on dead reckoning about 30 miles to the west of Mersa Matruh, and had just reversed course to run the easterly leg of her patrol. The short Mediterranean winter was showing signs of coming to an end, it being a fine, warm day with a light offshore breeze and a barely rippled brilliant blue sea. Twenty-one-year-old Ordinary Seaman Johannes Ploch was on lookout at the after end of the conning tower, scanning the sea astern. Shortly before noon, he became aware of several smudges of smoke on the horizon to the west. He immediately informed the officer of the watch, who called von Fischel to the bridge. By then the masts and funnels of a small convoy were visible astern.

The convoy, an offshoot of the 'Tobruk Ferry' consisting of half a dozen merchantmen heavily escorted by destroyers, was returning to Mersa Matruh after delivering supplies to Benghazi for the Eighth Army, which was then regrouping after the relief of Tobruk. The ships were within four hours of reaching their destination, and having come this far unscathed, were steaming along with confidence.

As the convoy drew near, von Fischel took U-374 down to periscope depth and manoeuvred into position for an attack. The ships being eastbound, he correctly assumed that they were empty; closer examination revealed that they were escorted by three destroyers. What von Fischel could not know was that these destroyers, HMS *Legion*, HMS *Maori* and the Norwegian-manned HNMS *Isaac Sweers*, were part of the elite 4th Destroyer Flotilla, fresh from the Battle of Cape Bon and the rout of an Italian cruiser force running supplies to the Afrika Korps in Tripoli. The group was led by *Legion*, under the command of 39-year-old Commander Richard Jessel RN. HMS *Legion*, commissioned in December 1940, already had a formidable reputation, having led the assault on the Lofoten Islands in the Norwegian campaign. She had also been with the *Ark Royal* when she was torpedoed, going alongside the carrier to take off survivors.

While U-374 was at periscope depth and waiting for the convoy to approach, aircraft, presumably British, were seen overhead. In these clear waters there was a danger that U-374 might be seen from the air, but von Fischel resisted the urge to dive deep. No bombs came raining down but, unknown to von Fischel, the U-boat had been detected by Asdic, and HMS *Legion*, accompanied by the *Isaac Sweers*, was racing ahead of the convoy to attack.

When von Fischel did become aware of the new threat he put U-374 into a steep dive and went as deep as possible. She must then have been very near the bottom, and therefore difficult to detect, or so von Fischel hoped. However, he had underestimated the skill of *Legion*'s Asdic operators. They easily found the U-boat, and over the next two hours the two destroyers dropped a total of forty-three depth charges, most of which exploded close to U-374. The damage caused by the blast was considerable: the submarine's bow tubes were jammed, leaving her unable to fire torpedoes, her wireless was put out of action, depth gauges were smashed and the stuffing boxes on both her propeller shafts developed serious leaks. Water was entering her hull, and it was imperative to surface before the batteries were affected and began giving off deadly chlorine gas. To Unno von Fischel's great relief, at that point Commander Jessel decided the need to escort the convoy safely into port was paramount, and he broke off the attack.

When darkness came, as soon as he judged it safe to do so, von Fischel brought U-374 to the surface to assess the damage inflicted by the depth-charging. It was so serious that von Fischel decided it would be too dangerous to submerge again. U-374 therefore set course for Messina, on the surface and at a speed of between 10 and 11 knots. Her survival was now in the hands of the gods.

On the morning of 12 January, the British submarine HMS *Unbeaten* was at periscope depth and patrolling off the southern approaches to the Straits of Messina. Three days earlier she had been in a patrol line off the Gulf of Taranto with HMS *Thresher* and the Polish submarine *Sokół*, but had been ordered south to cover Messina. Since arriving at the southern approaches to the Straits she had been keeping a lonely vigil, seeing nothing more than wheeling sea birds and the occasional Sicilian fisherman rolling her gunwales under in the choppy seas. *Unbeaten*'s captain, Lieutenant Commander Edward 'Teddy' Woodward, had been given no specific target, but was keeping a close watch on the Italian shore 4 miles distant, as well as to seaward.

Unbeaten was a long way from her home base in Holy Loch, on Scotland's west coast. She was a small submarine, just 630 tons displacement, having a top speed on the surface of only 11½ knots and armed with four bow tubes, a 3-inch deck gun and three .303 machine guns. She carried a complement of thirty-three.

Since arriving in the Mediterranean in April 1941, *Unbeaten* had been engaged in harassing Italian convoys carrying supplies to Rommel's Afrika Korps, but with little success. Based on Malta, her first action had been against the small Italian merchantman *Silvio Scaroni*, which she encountered on 19 May. Woodward fired his bow tubes at the vessel and spectacularly missed with all four torpedoes. The *Silvio Scaroni* disappeared over the horizon unscathed. For the next four weeks *Unbeaten* searched in vain. Then, on 16 June, while patrolling south of Messina, Woodward was presented with the opportunity of sinking the large Italian troop transport *Oceania*, but again his spread of four missed the target. Another month elapsed before *Unbeaten* encountered two enemy schooners and attacked on the surface. Having fired forty-three rounds of 3-inch at the sailing ships, Lieutenant Commander Woodward experienced the humiliation of seeing them escape, apparently unharmed. In August *Unbeaten* was in the vicinity of the island of Pantelleria, and Woodward had the 11,348-ton Italian troopship *Esperia* in his sights. He fired three torpedoes, but again they all missed their target.

By this time Teddy Woodward had concluded either that there was something seriously wrong with his periscope, or that he was jinxed. Then, at the end of August, came his first success, when he torpedoed and sank a 373-ton Italian sailing vessel. It was small recompense for an otherwise barren voyage, but Woodward hoped that it signalled a turning point in *Unbeaten*'s fortunes. It was no such thing, however, and from then on the horizon remained stubbornly empty.

Unbeaten was back at sea again on 4 January 1942, sailing from Malta in company with HMS *Thrasher* and the Polish *Sokół*. The three submarines had orders to form a patrol line across the Gulf of Taranto. They arrived off the Gulf on the 6th, but found nothing except white horses and the occasional fisherman. Woodward was more than relieved when, shortly after midnight on the 9th, he received a signal from Malta ordering him to move to the west and take up a patrol in the southern entrance to the Straits of Messina. No specific reason for the order was given. *Unbeaten* arrived off Messina in the early morning of the 10th and dutifully began to patrol the approaches, but before long it became obvious that this was going to be yet another pointless exercise.

For the next forty-eight hours *Unbeaten* tracked back and forth across the approaches to Messina, submerged during the day and on the surface at night, but no ship of any importance came her way. Then, at 0200 on the 12th, a dark and stormy night, a brilliant red flare was seen to the north, between *Unbeaten* and the land. Woodward recognized the flare as the type used by U-boats, and immediately submerged to periscope depth and stayed there for the remainder of the night, hydrophones listening for any sign of movement.

The passage northwards from the Libyan coast had been a nightmare for Unno von Fischel. With U-374 unable to dive, and her faulty diesels barely able to deliver much more than 10 knots, he had spent a nail-biting forty-eight hours scanning the horizons for danger. Trimmed right down, with only her conning tower showing above water, U-374 made a small enough target, but her enemies were many. British warships, most of them radar-equipped, combed these waters incessantly for such a target, while overhead enemy aircraft criss-crossed the sky during the daylight hours. Now, with dawn breaking and the Italian and Sicilian coasts in sight, one on each bow, and the safety of the Straits of Messina ahead, von Fischel at last felt able to relax. He blew ballast and brought the U-boat's casings above water. This was the last mistake he would ever make.

At about 1015, Lieutenant Aston Piper, who had the watch in *Unbeaten*'s control room, received a report of HE bearing 065° at 1,800yds. Piper searched on the bearing with the periscope, and two minutes later saw what was no more than a dark smudge on the horizon. Unsure of what he was seeing, he called the Captain to the control room. Woodward took over the periscope and after studying the target for some minutes identified it as the conning tower of a submarine; as he knew of no other British submarines in the area, he concluded it must be either German or Italian.

Increasing to *Unbeaten*'s full underwater speed of 11 knots, Woodward altered course to put the stranger ahead. With the range down to 1,300yds, it could be seen that the target was a fully surfaced German U-boat, easily identified by its distinctive green and grey camouflage stripes. Woodward ordered the depth settings of his torpedoes to be reduced to 10ft, took careful aim, and at 1023 fired a full salvo of four from his bow tubes.

Johannes Ploch had just finished his watch on lookout and was in the conning tower when two of Woodward's torpedoes hit home in U-374's pressure hull. The explosive effect of two 21-inch torpedoes, each packed with 805lbs of TNT and travelling at 40 knots, was awe-inspiring. The German submarine was literally ripped apart, and she sank in a swirl of angry water.

Ploch was blown clean over the side from the conning tower and came to struggling in a sea of spreading oil and splintered wooden slats, the latter the remains of the casing decking. That was all that was left to mark the passing of U-374, Unno Fischel and forty-two of his crew.

Four miles from land and in rough water, Ordinary Seaman Ploch would have joined his dead comrades had it not been for Lieutenant Commander Woodward. Sweeping the horizon with his periscope, he had caught a brief glimpse of a hand waving and realized there was a man in the water alongside the submarine, probably in danger of being drawn into her threshing propellers. He immediately went astern on both engines and, surfacing at the same time, drew clear of the survivor. Still in shock, and coated in diesel oil, Johannes Ploch was dragged from the sea and taken below. The rescue had been completed in just four minutes.

After reporting the sinking of U-374 to Malta, Woodward continued with his patrol, but a week was to elapse before a likely target came his way. This was the 6,468-ton Italian tanker *Rondine* which, along with the steamer *Rapido*, was being escorted on passage from Syracuse to Taranto by the motor torpedo boat *Giuseppe Cesare Abba*. Woodward fired four torpedoes at the tanker, but was forced to dive in a hurry when the *Abba* intervened. It was never confirmed whether Woodward's torpedoes found their mark, but it seems likely that the *Rondine* escaped undamaged.

Unbeaten ended her fifteenth Mediterranean war patrol in style. While entering harbour at Malta on the surface she was attacked by six enemy fighter aircraft and was slightly damaged. Her next success did not come until 1 March, when she encountered and attacked the Vichy French convoy S 14 off the coast of Tunisia. With one well-placed torpedo *Unbeaten* sank the 5,417-ton French steamer *PLM-20*, before being forced away by the escorts.

Woodward's second major success came the next day. In almost a carbon copy of the U-374 incident, and within a few miles of the same spot in the approaches to the Straits of Messina, he surprised the Italian submarine *Guglielmotti* on the surface. Woodward wrote in his report:

> At 0634 sighted U Boat bearing 125 degrees distance 2200 yards, turned onto a 130 degree track and increased speed. At 0640 fired a dispersed salvo of four torpedoes, after one minute forty seconds after firing one explosion was heard, HE stopped and U Boat was heard breaking up. Surfaced to attempt to pick up survivors of which there were about twelve, but a fighter aircraft forced *Unbeaten* to dive and clear the area. All survivors appeared to be wearing 'collar' life jackets. Aircraft and E Boats were observed in vicinity of survivors, a distant depth charge attack of twenty-four charges was carried out by three E Boats at 0850, on 19 March arrived Malta.

An Italian report later stated that the *Guglielmotti* had been on passage from Taranto to Messina. The torpedo boat *Francesco Stocco* arrived on the scene, dropped seventeen depth charges and picked up one body. The source reported that there were no survivors from the *Guglielmotti*.

Unbeaten's two-year tour of the Mediterranean waters came to an end on 1 April 1942, when she was seriously damaged during an air raid on Malta. It was then decided to send her home for repairs, and to give Lieutenant Commander Woodward and his men some well-deserved leave.

On completion of her refit, *Unbeaten* sailed from the Clyde on 23 October, under the command of Lieutenant Donald Watson DSC, RN. After landing a secret agent on the coast near the Spanish port of Vigo, she was ordered to begin an anti-shipping patrol in the Bay of Biscay. On 6 November Watson received orders to intercept an enemy blockade runner said to be crossing the Bay on her way home from the Far East. The search for the enemy ship was unsuccessful, and *Unbeaten* was then directed to rendezvous with another submarine off Bishop Rock and assist with escorting an inbound convoy.

On the morning of 11 November a Wellington of No.172 Squadron RAF Coastal Command reported it had sunk a U-boat in the Bay of Biscay. *Unbeaten* was known to be in the vicinity of the sinking, and it was feared she might have been the mistaken victim of the attack. That afternoon she was asked to report her position, but she failed to reply. She did not show up at the arranged rendezvous off Bishop Rock, and was never heard of again. It was assumed she had been sunk by the Wellington.

CHAPTER TEN

U-514 and Drumbeat

In the autumn of 1941 Hitler's U-boats were already operating off Newfoundland, and when, on 7 December, the Japanese attacked Pearl Harbor, he grasped the opportunity to pay back America for the help she had been giving Britain on the North Atlantic convoy routes. At that time only the Type IX U-boat was capable of sustained action off the American east coast, and there were just five of these boats available. These were sent across the Atlantic in early January 1942, initially to attack shipping off Newfoundland. Operation Paukenschlag (Drumbeat), known to the U-boat men as the 'American Hunting Season', had begun.

Reinhard Hardegen in U-123 fired the opening shot of Drumbeat, sinking the 9,076-ton Liverpool steamer *Cyclops* off Cape Sable, Nova Scotia, on 12 January 1942. The veteran *Cyclops*, thirty-six years old and a vessel of another age, was said to be a lucky ship, having survived the rigours of the oceans for so long, as well as two attacks by U-boat in the war of 1914–18. Under the command of Captain Leslie Kersley, she was homeward bound from the Far East with a general cargo and also carried seventy-eight Chinese ratings on their way to Halifax to supplement the crews of other British ships. The *Cyclops* had a total complement of 182 on board, which for a ship of her size meant her limited accommodation was seriously overcrowded.

U-123 put an end to the *Cyclops'* many years of voyaging with one torpedo fired in the darkest hours of the morning of 12 January. The British ship was abandoned at once, but finding she was still afloat when daylight came, Captain Kersley put his boats back alongside and re-boarded. This proved to be an unwise move, for half an hour after the last man was back aboard, Reinhard Hardegen delivered the *coup de grâce* with a second torpedo. The *Cyclops* sank in five minutes, taking with her forty-one crew members and forty-six of her Chinese passengers.

Although the US Navy had been warned by British Intelligence that the U-boats were crossing the Atlantic, the Americans were totally unprepared for what followed. This was, in the main, due to the attitude taken by Admiral Ernest King, C-in-C of the US Navy, who was fiercely protective of America's independence. King refused to listen to what he described as 'a bunch of Limeys' telling him how to run his navy. As a result, American merchant shipping on the Atlantic coast paid a terrible price.

Reinhard Hardegen reported to Admiral Dönitz:

> They simply weren't prepared at all. I assumed that I would find a coast that was blacked out – after all, there was a war on. I found a coast that was brightly lit. At Coney Island there was a huge ferris wheel and roundabouts – I could see it all. Ships were sailing with navigation lights. All the lightships, Sandy Hook and Ambrose lights were shining brightly. To me this was incomprehensible.

Further south, off Cape Hatteras, the farce was repeated. Hardegen's First Watch Officer Horst von Schroeter later recalled:

> We had up to twenty steamers in sight at one time. We could tell, because they were all sailing with lights burning. After a sinking the steamers would extinguish their navigation lights for a short while, but they felt so uncomfortable without them that they would light them up again after half an hour or so . . . for us it was like target practice – there was no defence, the steamers weren't even zigzagging.

Hardegen also commented on the careless use of radio by the Americans:

> A most important contribution to the success of this and the previous operation was made by the enemy's unrestricted use of the 600 metre band. Emergency calls were intercepted every day, often giving the position, course and speed of the ship. By plotting these, a good idea of the traffic routes could be obtained, so that targets could be easily found.

Pressing home their advantage, the U-boats moved south to the busy shipping lanes off Florida, where they found a similar situation prevailing. If anything, the killing here was even easier. Lying on the sea bed during the day, they surfaced after dark to be presented with a procession of Allied shipping, navigation lights burning brightly and silhouetted against the glare of lights ashore. The local authorities were so convinced that the war would never come to them that they had not even bothered to dim the street lighting on the foreshore. Many of them argued that such a move would have a disastrous effect on the tourist season, which was then in full swing. U-boats were hard pressed to fire their torpedoes fast enough, and when these were exhausted, deck guns were used with impunity. There was no opposition, and at one stage so many U-boats were working on the surface in close proximity that they also burned navigation lights at night to avoid colliding with one another.

Too late, the US Navy made an effort to organize convoys, but their best ships were in the Pacific fighting the Japanese. Only a handful of Coastguard cutters and small patrol boats, backed up by a few obsolete aircraft, were available for escort duty. Furthermore, the men manning these ships and aircraft had only the most basic training in anti-submarine operations. It was a hopelessly one-sided contest; the battle-hardened U-boat men simply ran rings around the opposition. Sated with their success in the north, they moved south into the Caribbean and Gulf of Mexico, sinking, slaying and pillaging like the buccaneers of an earlier age.

On 12 April Admiral Dönitz made the following entry in his War Diary:

> The following situation in the America area emerges from U-boat W/T messages and reports from C.O.s who have returned:
>
> Anti-S/M activity immediately under the coast has increased. Destroyers, Coast Guard ships and escort vessels are patrolling the steamer routes, sometimes ships are escorted by escort vessels in particularly endangered areas (Hatteras). In spite of these measures, the successes of the U-boats have so far remained at the same level. Before the U-boat attack on America was begun it was suspected that American anti-S/M activity would be weak and inexperienced; this conjecture has been fully confirmed. Anti-S/M vessels have no Asdic, some are equipped with hydrophones. The crews are careless, inexperienced and

little persevering in a hunt. In several cases escort vessels, Coast Guard ships and destroyers, having established the presence of a U-boat, made off instead of attacking her. This can only be the only explanation of the fact that so far no losses occurred from D/C hunts in shallow water (20 metres).

Air activity has also increased considerably. Boats are forced by it to remain submerged by day near the coast. On full-moon nights it is dangerous owing to the numbers of aircraft involved and the boats are forced to transfer their attacking areas further out to sea.

On the whole, however, the boats' successes are so great that their operation near the coast is further justified and will continue.

With regard to disposition on the coast, so far the boats have been given freedom of action in all areas which their fuel stocks will allow them to reach. With the appearance of the first U-tanker (U-459) the range and operational endurance of the boats will be extended when they have been supplied and the number of boats in the operational areas will increase. This will inevitably mean new allocation of attacking areas. If the stretches of coast which the Americans have to defend are extended, they will need to increase the number of anti-S/M vessels considerably. These anti-S/M vessels cannot be raised as fast as all that, there will continue to be particularly favourable points for attack and from time to time anti-S/M vessels will of necessity have to be withdrawn from coastal stretches which are specially defended. At least anti-S/M activity will not be increased in the latter areas.

The U-tanker U-459, under the command of *Kapitänleutnant* Georg von Wilamovitz-Moellendorff, carried out her first refuelling at sea on 22 April, when she met up with the Type IXB U-108 500 miles north-east of Bermuda. She was the first of what Dönitz envisaged as a fleet of twenty-four supply boats to be stationed in the Atlantic.

U-tankers, displacing 1,668 tonnes on the surface and with a range of 9,300 miles at 12 knots, carried, as well as diesel oil, extra torpedoes, ammunition and spare parts, and had on board a machine shop capable of undertaking minor repairs. They were also able to supply drinking water, fresh food and freshly baked bread. Included in their complement of fifty-three was a doctor, as well as spare personnel to replace sick or injured crew. They were, in fact, floating supply bases, each able to keep twelve Type VIIs operational for an extra month, or five of the larger Type IX boats at sea for an extra two months.

The big disadvantage of the supply U-boats, or *Milchkühe* (milk cows) as they became known, was that they were slow to dive, leaving them very vulnerable to attack from the air. To compensate for this weakness, they mounted two 37mm and one 20mm AA guns, but as their casualty rate showed, this was not enough.

U-514, a Type IXC under the command of Hans-Jürgen Auffermann, had played her part in Operation Drumbeat when on her first war patrol. She opened her score modestly by sinking the 167-ton British sailing vessel *Helen Farsey* off Bermuda on 6 September, but five days later Hans-Jürgen Auffermann followed the example set by Günther Müller-Stöckheim and penetrated the harbour of Bridgetown, Barbados at night. From a distance of about 3,500yds Auffermann fired a total of six torpedoes at two ships lying at anchor. They were the Vancouver-registered *Cornwallis* and the Norwegian motor vessel *Betancuria*. Fortunately for the two merchantmen, a torpedo net stretched across the harbour below the surface against any such eventuality, took the brunt of the attack. Only one torpedo penetrated the net, hitting the *Cornwallis* in her No.2 hold. The Canadian ship sank in shallow water, but was later raised and towed to Trinidad for repairs.

Auffermann's luck improved on the 15th of the month, when he sank the 3,297-ton British steamer *Kioto*. On the 16th, however, U-514 was caught on the surface by a patrolling American aircraft and severely damaged. She escaped by diving, but suffered further damage from depth charges when a destroyer arrived on the scene.

By skilful manoeuvring, Auffermann took U-514 out of harm's way to the east, spending the next four days carrying out emergency repairs, after which he moved south. Cruising off the Amazon delta on the 28th, he encountered a two-ship convoy escorted by the US destroyer *Roe*. He attacked, sinking the 2,730-ton *Ozório* and the 5,742-ton *Lages*, both Brazilian-flag vessels, while the inexperienced American destroyer chased its tail. The sinkings did not go down well in Brazil, which only a month earlier had been coaxed into joining the war on the side of the Allies.

U-514's final success was in South American waters on 11 October, when she torpedoed and sank the American merchantman *Steel Scientist* off the coast of Dutch Guiana. The *Steel Scientist*, on a voyage from Suez via the Cape to Paramaribo with 200 tons of general cargo and 1,800 tons of salt ballast, did not die easily. Aufferman stopped her with a torpedo in her engine room, but it took a further two torpedoes to sink her, a heavy price to pay for a twenty-one-year-old ship with a cargo of little consequence. However, this latest conquest brought U-514's score to 17,354 tons in just over three weeks. With his torpedoes exhausted, Auffermann now considered he was justified in setting course for Lorient. He was sent on his way by a patrolling American aircraft, which straddled U-514 with a stick of depth bombs, but once again she escaped. Four weeks later, just before daybreak on 8 November, as U-514 crossed the Bay of Biscay and began her run in to Lorient, Operation Torch, the invasion of French North Africa, was launched.

*

For some months past a frantic Joseph Stalin had been pressing Britain and America to open up a Second Front, an invasion of continental Europe to take the pressure off Russian forces struggling to halt the advance of Hitler's Panzers into the Soviet Union. A direct assault across the Channel, which is what Stalin was asking for, was then beyond the capability of the Allies, and Churchill came up with an alternative plan to strike at the 'soft underbelly' of Europe. He proposed an invasion of French North Africa aimed at clearing the Germans out of Morocco and Algeria, to be followed by landings on Sicily and thence an advance into Italy. It was a workable plan, and despite the opposition of some American generals who proposed an instant gung-ho assault on the beaches of north-western France, Churchill's wisdom prevailed.

Operation Torch began at dawn on 8 November 1942, with 74,000 British and American troops storming ashore at Casablanca, Oran and Algiers. At the same time, General Montgomery, who had finally stopped Rommel's forces at El Alamein, was advancing west, carrying all before him. The days of the Germans in North Africa were numbered. At the same time, on the other front, in the

Far East, the Japanese had been halted and were being slowly winkled out of their island conquests. It seemed that the tide of war was finally turning in favour of the Allies – except in the North Atlantic, where Hitler's U-boats were back in force again and exacting a fearful toll.

Historically, most of Britain's oil had come from the Middle East via the Suez Canal, a route which was now closed. Alternative supplies were being brought in from the Caribbean, but with Torch in progress much of this oil was being diverted to North Africa. By the end of November 1942 Britain's reserves were running dangerously low.

On 25 December 1942 U-514 was 420 miles due west of Madeira, bound for the warm waters of the Caribbean. Overhead, the sky was a flat, brooding overcast, the wind no more than a gentle zephyr, and the only waves in sight were those generated by the U-boat as she slid through the flat calm sea. The Christmas tree was aloft, the half-dozen bottles of Bordeaux saved for the occasion had been retrieved from their hiding place, and in the tiny galley the goose was in the oven. For obvious reasons, Christmas aboard the U-boat would be a subdued affair, but for the first time since leaving the dangerous waters of Biscay, U-514's commander, Hans-Jürgen Auffermann, felt at peace with the world, however transient that state of mind might be.

It had not been an easy passage so far. Leaving the shelter of Lorient harbour sixteen days earlier, U-514 had sailed into one of the worst winters ever known in the North Atlantic. Inching her way across the Bay of Biscay in the teeth of a force 10 southerly with 60ft waves, pitching and rolling crazily, her conning tower constantly awash, she had endured and survived the wrath of the great ocean – but only just. The one saving grace had been that the extreme weather had kept at home the enemy's air reconnaissance with their horizon-hopping radar and blinding searchlights that turned night into day. It was well said that any U-boat caught on the surface by them was not long for this world.

U-514 was Auffermann's first command. She was a long-range boat, a Type IXC of 1,120 tonnes displacement, with a top speed of 18 knots on the surface and 7¾ knots submerged. Built with operations in the Indian Ocean and Pacific in mind, she had a maximum endurance of 13,450 miles without refuelling, and was armed with a 105mm deck gun, two 20mm AA guns and six torpedo tubes. Like all U-boats of her class, she had an Achilles heel which could prove crucial, being slow to crash-dive when the need arose. In spite of this one failing, her potential to hit the enemy hard was undeniable. Twenty-nine-year-old Auffermann had commissioned her in Kiel only four months earlier, and she had already proved her worth in Operation Drumbeat.

U-514 was not alone when, on that grey December day she left Lorient and set course for the open sea. Sailing in close company was U-125, commanded by *Kapitänleutnant* Ulrich Folkers, another Type IXC also bound for the happy hunting grounds of American waters. But before they would be free to sail west the two boats had been assigned to play nursemaid to a blockade runner.

With all her ports under siege by the Royal Navy, Germany was running short of many vital raw materials obtainable only in the Far East. This had led to the formation of a small fleet of blockade runners, fast merchant ships sailing alone and carrying precision tools and other high technology goods out to Japan, then returning with oil, rubber and high-grade ores. By the end of 1942 two of these ships were leaving German ports every month. Some got through, others were sunk or captured, but the risks were justified by the need.

The blockade runners were escorted across the Bay of Biscay by surface ships and aircraft, after which U-boats took over, shadowing the merchantmen until they reached longitude 30° west, east of the Cape of Good Hope, and were relatively safe from attack by British forces. On this occasion U-514 and U-125 had been charged with escorting the tanker *Germania*, which was making a dash for the Cape to bring back a cargo of fuel oil from the East. Two other boats, U-563 and U-706, were also called in to help protect the tanker.

The *Germania* did not sail from Bordeaux until 12 December; meanwhile, the four U-boats assigned to her were obliged to kill time at a pre-arranged position some 180 miles to the west of Cape Finisterre. When the *Germania* eventually arrived at the rendezvous at dawn on the 14th, Aufferman and Folkers took up positions 30 miles ahead and to port and starboard of the tanker. The other two boats were stationed in a similar manner astern. Running on the surface, the U-boats were well placed to spot and intercept any threat to the blockade runner.

With the continuing bad weather assisting, all went well for the first twenty-four hours; then luck turned against them when, in the early afternoon of the 15th, they sailed straight into the midst of a northbound British convoy. Despite the heavy seas and poor visibility, the *Germania* was sighted by one of the convoy escorts, the Hunt-class destroyer HMS *Tanatside*, which immediately hauled out to investigate. The escorting U-boats were too far away to intervene, and realizing the game was up, the master of the *Germania* scuttled his ship.

Admiral Dönitz wrote in his War Diary:

> With reference to the escort of 'Germania': Of the boats detailed for the protection of the 'Germania' one was near the ship. The sinking though, as anticipated, could not be prevented. How the other three ships were placed in relation to the ship is not known. In any case they were useless. A real support for a blockade runner could only be formed by an all round screen at a distance of 50–60 sea miles from the ship. With a range of visibility of 10 sea miles – a favourable supposition – 15 boats would be needed during the day, a number by no means available. But even this protection is theoretical, as, owing to the necessity of submerging in the event of aircraft, difference in fixes, deterioration of visibility, the possibility of not being able to report the sighted enemy before submerging, and other incidents, the position could be changed entirely.

In view of Admiral Dönitz's interpretation of the situation, it is to be wondered why he allowed the U-boats to be used in this way. But the Führer had spoken.

After conducting a fruitless search for survivors from the *Germania*, U-514 and U-125 were ordered to continue their voyage. Three days later, on the 18th, they received a signal from Lorient instructing them to join a pack being assembled to intercept a southbound convoy sighted earlier in the day by U-441. Several hours later, being unable to gather together sufficient boats to mount a credible attack on the convoy, Lorient cancelled the operation. Aufferman and Folkers then resumed their passage to the west. However, by this time U-125 was experiencing serious problems with her diesels and was unable to keep up. She was left behind to rendezvous with U-461, which carried the spare parts she needed to repair her engines. U-514 carried on alone.

*

Oil tankers from the Caribbean were routed first to Guantanamo Bay, the US Navy base in Cuba, where convoys were assembled for the passage up the East Coast to New York or Halifax, Nova Scotia. From there they sailed in convoy across the North Atlantic. The distance steamed was in excess of 6,000 miles, as opposed to the 3,400 miles the direct route would have taken. Including the time spent waiting for convoys, this could prolong a voyage by up to four weeks, and it also put the vulnerable tankers at the mercy of the U-boats packs which lay in wait on the North Atlantic seaways. Things came to a head as Operation Drumbeat was stepped up and 100,000 tons of shipping were being lost on the American eastern seaboard every month, the majority of the ships being tankers loaded with oil for the Atlantic crossing.

Emboldened by the success of his Type IX boats in American waters, Dönitz decided to send in a task force of six Type VIICs to assist in reaping the rich harvest on offer. The smaller U-boats had a limited range, but they were more manoeuvrable and quicker to dive than the Type IXs, and supported by a U-tanker they promised to achieve equal success.

Among the six new entrants was U-442, built and commissioned at Danzig and under the command of *Korvettenkapitän* Hans-Joachim Hesse. Born in Ostfriesland, on Germany's bleak northern coast, 36-year-old Hesse joined the German Navy soon after leaving school and had served as gunnery officer in surface ships until transferring to the U-boats in 1940.

U-442's first operational patrol had not been an outstanding success, and she had almost come to an untimely end when involved with the *Veilchen* (Violet) Group in an attack on Convoy SC 107 off Cape Race at the end of October 1942. She was on her way to the happy hunting ground of America's east coast when she was called in to join *Veilchen* in a mass assault on an eastbound convoy.

SC 107 was a cosmopolitan collection of thirty-nine merchantmen, nineteen British, six American, five Greek, four Norwegian, one Swedish and one Icelandic, escorted by a destroyer and four corvettes of the Royal Canadian Navy. This was a convoy of the utmost strategic importance, carrying a quarter of a million tons of military supplies and fuel for the proposed Anglo/American landings in North Africa. The convoy had been compromised by the interception and decryption by German Intelligence of a carelessly sent radio message, and the 13-strong *Veilchen* Group was in hot pursuit. In the mêlée that ensued, *Veilchen* sank fifteen ships totalling 82,817 tons, and damaged four more. Three U-boats were lost, and U-442 all but made that four.

The 6,690-ton steamer *Hatimura* of the British India Steamship Company had been torpedoed by U-132 and was straggling astern of the convoy when Hesse in U-442 came across her. Confident of an easy kill, he moved in and torpedoed the helpless ship at close range. To his horror, the *Hatimura* blew up with a thunderous roar, showering the immediate vicinity with burning wreckage. Included in the steamer's cargo had been 250 tons of gunpowder, 200 tons of TNT, and 300 tons of incendiary bombs. Even worse, U-132 had just surfaced alongside the *Hatimura* and was about to deliver her *coup de grâce* when the British ship suddenly erupted as a result of U-442's torpedo. A huge piece of wreckage dropped on U-132, ripping open her pressure hull, and she sank, taking all her crew with her. Miraculously, it would seem, of the *Hatimura*'s total complement of ninety, only four lost their lives.

This disastrous occurrence signalled the end of U-442's maiden war patrol, for she was recalled a few days later. She returned to sea on 20 December under orders to join the other Type VIICs selected to operate off the coast of Brazil. Hesse was still smarting from the disgrace of his first patrol, for although he was blameless he could not avoid being implicated in the loss of U-132. His mood did not improve when, leaving the River Loire, he ran straight into the teeth of the raging storm.

Christmas Day 1942 was just another nightmare in a spate of recurring nightmares for Hans-Joachim Hesse. Lashed in the conning tower of U-422 as she crashed from crest to trough of the mountainous seas, her casings continuously awash with foaming green water, he was nearing the point of exhaustion. Since sailing from St Nazaire five days earlier he had had little except for endless mugs of strong coffee and had been denied the luxury of sleep apart from the odd catnap snatched on his feet. He was conscious that the day was special, and vaguely aware that there should be celebrations, but the unrelenting sea demanded his complete attention.

CHAPTER ELEVEN

The Spanish Main

While *Kapitänleutnant* Auffermann and his crew raised their glasses to toast 'wives and sweethearts' in the comparative comfort of the temperate thirties, and U-442 fought her lonely battle with the raging elements on the outer fringes of the Bay of Biscay, 3,000 miles away in the Caribbean Sea the sun was just rising over the island of Curaçao.

Lying 60 miles off the coast of Venezuela, Curaçao was first colonized by the Spanish in 1499, and for the next 400 years was famous only for its prolific orange groves. The fruit of these trees is inedible but it produces a delicious orange liqueur. Named for the island, the fiery sweet curaçao was much favoured by the pirates of the Main. Today it still pleases the palates of discerning drinkers worldwide, but takes second place to the liquid gold that succeeded it.

In 1815 Curaçao fell into Dutch hands and 100 years later, when the Royal Dutch Shell Company established a refinery to process Venezuelan oil on a large scale, the island began to prosper. When war broke out in 1939, Curaçao was producing 150,000 barrels of petroleum products a day, and along with Aruba, its neighbouring island, assumed immense strategic importance for the Allies. In December 1941 the US Army took over the defence of both islands.

With America in the war, in January 1942 Germany decided the time was ripe to disrupt Allied oil supplies in the Caribbean. The task was handed to Admiral Dönitz, who sent in the newly formed *Neuland* (New Land) Group of five German and two Italian submarines, with the primary object of attacking the refineries on Curaçao and Aruba. The original plan was to shell the shore installations with the U-boats' deck guns, but the commanders involved with *Neuland* decided more would be achieved by torpedoing tankers anchored in the open harbours. Certainly, in view of the large calibre guns known to be defending the refineries, this would be less risky.

Werner Hartenstein in U-156 opened the campaign. Arriving off Aruba on 13 February, he spent forty-eight hours studying the coast, at periscope depth during the day and on the surface at night. He concluded that no one on shore appeared to be taking any precautions against attack, and in the early hours of the 16th he surfaced off the Lago refinery near St Nicolaas. Two tankers were in the anchorage, the 4,317-ton *Padernales* and the *Oranjestad* of 2,396 tons, both flying the British flag. Moving in closer, Hartenstein torpedoed the *Padernales*, killing eight of her crew and setting her on fire. The explosion and ensuing conflagration galvanized the *Oranjestad* into action, and she made a frantic attempt to weigh anchor and escape. It was too late; before the tanker could move Hartenstein stopped her with another torpedo, killing fifteen of her crew. The sky above St Nicolaas was lit up like day as both tankers and the sea around them burned fiercely.

Emboldened by his easy success, Hartenstein penetrated deeper into the harbour and torpedoed the 6,452-ton American tanker *Arkansas*, which was berthed alongside the jetty. Fortunately for her crew, the *Arkansas* was empty and gas-free at the time. There were no casualties on board, and the ship remained afloat.

With no retaliation forthcoming, Hartenstein then ordered his gunners to shell the refinery with the 105mm deck gun. And at this point his luck changed. In the confusion of the night, U-156's gun's crew forgot to remove the tompion from the muzzle of the gun before opening fire. The first round exploded in the barrel, killing one of the gun's crew, Heinrich Büssinger, and seriously wounding Gunnery Officer Dietrich von dem Borne. The 37mm AA gun was then brought into action, but its small shells had little effect ashore. After firing sixteen rounds, Hartenstein gave up, using a farewell torpedo to further damage the *Arkansas* before leaving the harbour. Once at sea, Hartenstein assessed the state of his deck gun and found that after sawing off the shattered end of its barrel the gun could still be of limited use.

A witness to the attack on shore, Captain Robert Rudkin of the US Army garrison, reported:

> Flaming oil spread over a wide area under a steady wind. We dashed outside. I could hear cries out in the waters which I learned were infested with barracuda. There came a steady stream of tracer bullets from the dark of the ocean – aimed at the refinery.

While Werner Hartenstein was busy causing mayhem on Aruba, U-67, with Günther Müller-Stockheim in command, had entered

Curaçao's Willemstad harbour. He fired four torpedoes at two anchored tankers, but all four failed to explode. Müller-Stockheim did, however, succeed in setting fire to the small Dutch tanker *Rafaela*. Meanwhile, Jürgen von Rosenteil in U-502 was in action off the Venezuelan mainland, torpedoing three small feeder tankers, two British and one under the flag of Venezuela.

The *Neuland* Italian boats, now increased to five, were allocated a patrol area on the Atlantic side of the West Indies, where they achieved what was for them unprecedented success. Over a period of four weeks, from 20 February to 23 March, they sank fifteen ships of various nationalities, totalling 92,846 tons gross. At the same time, Max-Hermann Bauer in U-126 was ravaging shipping using the Windward Passage between Cuba and Haiti, where, uncontested, he disposed of another 41,000 tons of Allied shipping, most of it under the American flag.

The US Navy's Caribbean Sea Frontier Force, which consisted of three small Coastguard cutters and a few training craft, with fourteen obsolete Army observation planes in support, was powerless to intervene in the face of Group *Neuland*'s lightning attack. It was not until 28 February, when Ernst-August Rehwinkel in U-578 sank the destroyer USS *Jacob Jones* off the coast of New Jersey with the loss of 138 crew, that the threat was taken seriously. Only then were a few First World War-vintage destroyers found to supplement the meagre defence force, but the U-boats continued to strike with little fear of retribution.

On the night of 18 February, the 6,940-ton tanker *British Consul* lay at anchor in Port of Spain, Trinidad. She was fully loaded and ready to sail, but as U-boats had been sighted off the port her Master, Captain G.A. Dickson, had decided to postpone leaving until daylight on the 19th. The British tanker was displaying only dimmed anchor lights, but anchored near her was the American steamer *Mokihana*, which was brightly lit overall. It was as if, even at this stage, the Americans were completely ignoring the war they were now involved in. For the *Mokihana* a rude awakening was about to arrive.

Shortly after midnight, Albrecht Achillies' U-161 slid into the harbour unseen, turned under full helm and emptied her stern tubes at the anchored ships. One torpedo went home just forward of the *Mokihana*'s bridge and broke her back. She sank in shallow water, a total loss. Achillies' second torpedo hit the *British Consul* in the vicinity of her engine room. She was burning fiercely as she settled on the bottom. Despite the late hour, with most of the crews of both ships asleep, there were no casualties. For Achillies it had been a ludicrously easy sortie and, perhaps as a gesture of contempt for the state of the island's defences, he left the harbour with his navigation lights burning.

Not every attack was as successful. Three months later, in the early morning light of 19 April, Ernst Kals brought U-130 to the surface off the Bullen Baai tank farm on Curaçao and opened fire at the petroleum storage tanks with his 88mm deck gun. This time no hits were scored, no fires were started, and when a gun ashore returned his fire, Kals beat a hasty retreat.

As spring turned to summer, the *Neuland* boats were sinking 10,000 tons of shipping a day in the Caribbean and on the Eastern Seaboard, and at long last the Americans were forced to accept that the war on their doorstep was a reality. Convoys were organized for tankers plying between the islands and the Venezuelan oilfields, but the help of a corvette escort group offered by the Royal Navy was refused. By the beginning of May the total tonnage sunk by Group *Neuland* was nearing half a million tons, most of the ships lost being loaded tankers.

Concerned at the mounting losses, much of it British shipping, the Admiralty again offered help, but again in vain. Admiral King had not changed his mind. He was firmly of the opinion that the British were trying to 'teach him how to suck eggs', and he refused to accept any advice or help. The truth was that after three years of war the Royal Navy had got the measure of the U-boats in the Atlantic and were quite justified in offering to show the Americans how it was done. The situation on the Eastern Seaboard was now so serious that immediate action was needed.

Many years later, US war correspondent Arch Whitehouse commented:

> The Germans had a field day in the Caribbean, where they concentrated on tankers moving in and out of Aruba and other South American ports. The weather was salubrious, the water warm, and the Germans could call on the help of agents in Central America, Panama, and other tropical spots. They became more audacious with each success and after torpedoing a ship would come to the surface

and display their bronzed bodies as they took snapshots or movies of their victims bobbing about on rafts or in overcrowded lifeboats.

Winston Churchill wrote in his memoirs:

> It is surprising indeed that during two years of the advance of total war towards the American continent more provision had not been made against this deadly onslaught. With all the information they had about protective measures we had adopted, both before and during the struggle, it is remarkable that no plans had been made for coastal convoys and for multiplying small craft. Neither had the coastal air defence been developed. Thus it happened that in these crucial months an effective American defence system was only achieved with painful, halting steps.

*

Meanwhile, the situation on the North Atlantic front was also worsening. The exceptionally harsh winter had exacted a heavy toll of the tanker traffic, many of these deep-loaded ships suffering serious weather damage. Nearly a quarter of the British tanker fleet was in dock under repair, and its numbers were being severely depleted by the activities of Hitler's U-boats. Operation Torch was being starved of the oil and petroleum required to maintain its momentum. Although aware that the risks involved were considerable, Churchill now proposed that instead of sailing in coastal convoys to New York or Halifax before crossing the Atlantic, tankers from the Caribbean should sail direct to Gibraltar. The proposal was agreed, but shelved through lack of suitable escorts. Consequently, by mid-December 1942 British oil reserves had been reduced to just 300,000 tons, and with the average consumption running at 130,000 tons a month, the position was serious enough to warrant risks being taken. Once more, it was time to put Winston Churchill's considered judgement to the test.

All this conspired to rob the crew of the British tanker *Empire Lytton* of their Christmas in port. Much to their disgust, their ship was hurried out of Willemstad, Curaçao early on the morning of 25 December. However, even more so in war than in peace, commercial shipping functions seven days a weeks, 365 days a year, public holidays being subordinate to the trade. There were mutinous mutterings in the messrooms, but no more.

The 9,087-ton *Empire Lytton,* a wartime replacement owned by the Ministry of War Transport and managed by Harris & Dixon of London, was on her second voyage. Commanded by Captain John Andrews, she had a crew of forty supplemented by seven naval gunners. Built at a time when every plate and every rivet counted, she was a basic ship, box-like in the hull with a complete absence of fine lines but able to carry maximum cargo with maximum economy. On this occasion she had on board 12,500 tons of high-octane aviation spirit, every shipowner's dream of a high freight cargo, but every shipmaster's nightmare. One carelessly exposed flame, or an inadvertently struck spark, and she was likely to blow sky-high.

Following the *Empire Lytton* out of Willemstad harbour were five other loaded tankers, the Norwegian-flag *Albert Ellsworth,* the US-flag *Florida* and three tankers of the British Tanker Company, *British Dominion, British Glory* and *British Vigilance.* All were fully loaded with Venezuelan oil or petroleum products, and together formed Convoy OT 3S. Escorting them were a group of small patrol boats of the US Navy. The convoy was bound for Trinidad, 450 miles to the east.

At that point, Captain Andrews had no orders regarding the destination of his cargo other than that at Trinidad the *Empire Lytton* was to join another coastal convoy which would take them north to New York, before setting out to cross the Atlantic for an as yet unspecified port in Britain. It promised to be a long, tedious voyage.

The passage to Trinidad passed without incident, and the six tankers arrived off the island at daylight on the 27th. There the *Florida* and the *British Glory* left, bound on to Pernambuco. The four remaining tankers were then taken to an anchorage off Port of Spain.

During the course of that day other loaded tankers began to arrive, and by nightfall there were nine anchored in close proximity. Convoy TM 1 was now assembled, and comprised the British ships *Empire Lytton, British Dominion, British Vigilance, Oltenia II* and *Cliona,* the Norwegians *Albert L. Ellsworth, Minister Wedel* and *Vanja* and the Norwegian-manned, Panama-registered *Norvik.*

Before the darkness closed in completely, a column of four grey-painted warships entered the bay and dropped anchor within hailing distance of the tankers. They were the guardians of the proposed convoy, ships of the Royal Navy's Escort Group B5, the H-class destroyer *Havelock* and the Flower-class corvettes *Godetia*, *Pimpernel* and *Saxifrage*. Commanding the escort, in HMS *Havelock*, was 40-year-old Commander Richard Boyle DSC, RN, a distinguished and experienced leader. *Godetia*, which was Belgian-manned, was under the command of Lieutenant Alan Pierce OBE, RNR, *Pimpernel* was commanded by Lieutenant Frederick Thornton RNR and Lieutenant Norman Knight RNR commanded *Saxifrage.*

Havelock and her corvettes, their hulls battered and streaked with red rust, had been shepherding convoys in the North Atlantic with Escort Group B5 since late 1940, and had just completed a nine-month-long tour of escort duty working with the US Navy on the Eastern Seaboard. Consequently, they could hardly be judged as being at peak efficiency. They were, in fact, tired ships, desperately in need of major maintenance, and their crews in need of rest. With the Royal Navy stretched to its utmost limits with convoy work, there was little prospect of either.

With breakfast over the next morning, 28 December, the masters of the waiting tankers were ferried ashore to attend a convoy conference in Port of Spain called by the local Naval Control of Shipping Officer. Captain Andrews of the *Empire Lytton* and Captain Andreassen of the *Vanja* were unable to join the others, as both ships had developed serious engine problems. This did not bode well for the coming voyage.

The conference was an informal affair, with only seven ships' captains, their radio officers, the commanders of the four escorts and a lone US Army Air Force officer present. The NCSO opened the proceedings, then handed over to Commander Boyle, who outlined the convoy discipline and signals procedure. He also announced that, in the unavoidable absence of Captain Miller of the *British Dominion*, who had been previously appointed to act as Convoy Commodore, Captain Alfred Laddle commanding the *Oltenia II* would take over that role. This would involve coordinating all movements of the merchant ships and liaising closely with the Escort Commander. Although he had no previous experience as convoy commodore, Captain Laddle accepted the added burden with good grace.

The intended route was not discussed, and the tanker captains assumed it would be the usual long slog via Guantanamo Bay and New York or Halifax, followed by the North Atlantic crossing. They were told that shortly before sailing they would receive sealed envelopes on board containing courses to be steered, and these envelopes were not to be opened until clear of the land. This was a sensible precaution, but when Boyle broke the news that the convoy was to leave port that afternoon there was some consternation.

Meanwhile, back at the anchorage, Captain Laddle's chief officer, Kenneth Bruce, was having doubts about the security of the convoy. When the *Oltenia II* had completed taking on her liquid cargo at Port Firtin, on the southern coast of Trinidad, she had gone alongside the quay in Port of Spain to load what was described as 'special cargo'. This turned out to be 1,000 Sten guns, 500,000 rounds of ammunition and 750 drums of lubricating oil. This was not an unusual extra in wartime, but what disturbed Bruce was that the cargo had been left lying on the quay unguarded, the guns and ammunition plainly marked ALGIERS, and the drums GIBRALTAR. German agents in Port of Spain – and they were said to be legion – would have had no difficulty in deducing the destination of the convoy or, for that matter, its probable route.

Six of TM 1's tankers sailed late that afternoon, leaving behind yet another of their number wrestling with engine problems. The 8,375-ton *Cliona*, owned by the Shell Tanker Company and commanded by Captain James Rendall, was a comparatively new ship but she had been a long time on voyage. Crossing the Atlantic in ballast, she had been ordered to leave her convoy and proceed independently to Guantanamo Bay and then to Curaçao to load fuel oil for the Admiralty. By the time she reached Trinidad, she was over a month into her voyage, running short of provisions, and her engines were sorely in need of a thorough overhaul. Fortunately, *Cliona*'s engine problems proved to be short-lived, and she joined up with the convoy before dusk.

When it became evident that the *Empire Lytton* and *Vanja*, both with engine defects, would not be ready to sail with the convoy, Commander Boyle detailed the corvette *Godetia* to stay behind with them. As it happened, this suited *Godetia*'s commander, Lieutenant Alan Pierce, for his ship also had her problems. She had limped into Port of Spain with one of her two boilers shut down and the other just barely able to keep up steam. She, too, needed time for repairs.

It was nearly midnight on the 28th before *Godetia* finally led the two delayed tankers out through the breakwaters of Port of Spain. Had Lieutenant Pierce then known that a German U-boat was out there lurking in the darkness, he might have delayed the sailing until morning.

U-124, commanded by *Korvettenkapitän* Johann Mohr, was on her tenth war patrol with an impressive record behind her, having disposed of forty-two Allied ships totalling 196,295 tons, including two warships. So far, however, her foray to the American Eastern Seaboard was proving to be fruitless. Then, just as dawn broke on 28 December, when the U-boat was 50 miles to the east of Trinidad, Mohr was delighted to see a heavily-laden merchantman heading in towards the island. She was slow-moving and sailing alone. The sea was flat calm, visibility excellent, the sky clear of any snooping aircraft and the target moving at the speed of a horse-drawn brewer's dray; this was every U-boat commander's ideal opening to a day. Approaching as close as he dared, Mohr blew open the hull of the enemy ship with a single torpedo.

The 4,692-ton British tramp *Treworlas*, twenty-one years old and flagging after a lifetime in the punishing charter trade, was nearing the end of a 10,000-mile passage from the Red Sea, and she had on board a cargo of 3,000 tons of manganese ore. She sank in just sixty seconds, her deadweight cargo taking her down like a slab of concrete tossed into a pool. Only nine men out of her total complement of forty-seven survived.

More than pleased that he had at last justified some of the diesel burned in reaching these far waters, Mohr decided to remain in the area to see what else would come his way. And so it was that at 0300 on the morning of the 29th the three late-comers to Convoy TM 1, the tankers *Empire Lytton* and *Vanja* with their escorting corvette, crossed his path.

Much to Lieutenant Pierce's chagrin, *Godetia* still had only one boiler functioning, and the three-ship convoy was obliged to go at the corvette's best speed, which was an erratic 11 knots. This should have been a repeat of the *Treworlas* episode for Johann Mohr, only on a grander scale. Unfortunately, his recent good luck had turned. He emptied all his tubes at close range, but every torpedo missed the target.

Although the sea was calm and the tracks of Mohr's torpedoes must have been clearly visible, even in the dark, it appears that no one aboard the tankers or their escort was aware that they had been under attack. It was only when, at first light, a Catalina of the US Navy patrolling overhead spotted U-124 on the surface 7 miles ahead of the stragglers that the alarm was raised. *Godetia* put on a brave face and raced towards the spot at her best speed, but U-124 had dived by the time the corvette arrived. Pierce made a perfunctory show of dropping a few depth charges, but they exploded in vain.

Incidentally, it was ironic, although not evident to either commander, that this was the second meeting between U-124 and a corvette named *Godetia*, albeit not Lieutenant Pierce's *Godetia* but her short-lived predecessor K-72. Late in the evening of 25 August 1940, U-124, then under the command of Georg-Wilhelm Schulz, had attacked Convoy HX 65A as it was passing through the Minches. Schulz sank two 5,000-ton British steamers, but was forced to execute a hasty crash-dive by HMS *Godetia*, one of the escorting corvettes. In his haste to escape, Schulz underestimated the depth of water in the Minches, and U-124 grounded on rocks at 300ft. The U-boat remained passive on the bottom while *Godetia* carried out a random depth charging. The charges fell wide, causing no damage, but the grounding had blocked U-124's bow tubes, and her attack capability was severely reduced. Much to Schulz's humiliation, when notified of the damage, Lorient assigned U-124 to weather reporting duties for the remainder of her patrol. The first *Godetia*, after a promising start, had a short and not particularly promising career. It ended prematurely when she was sunk in collision with the British merchantman *Marsa* in the North Channel on 6 September 1940.

Having been forced to break off his pursuit of the three-ship convoy off Trinidad, Johann Mohr reported his contact to Lorient, and was told to remain in the area. No one seemed to make the connection between these ships and TM 1, which was then only just over the horizon.

Godetia and her two late starters caught up with the main convoy at dawn on 29 December and merged in with the other ships. TM 1 was then steaming in five columns abreast, and on a course of 070° at 9 knots.

Leading the first, or port, column was the 8,309-ton Norwegian *Albert L. Ellsworth*, commanded by Captain Thorvald Solheim.

A 5-year-old tanker originally owned by Onstad Shipping of Oslo, she now sailed under Admiralty jurisdiction and was carrying 11,473 tons of light crude oil consigned to the Royal Navy at Gibraltar. Astern of her came another Norwegian, the lately joined *Vanja*. Also registered in Oslo and under Admiralty control, she carried a similar load of light crude.

Column 2 was led by the 6,394-ton *Oltenia II*, a 15-year-old ex-Romanian tanker seized by the Royal Navy in 1941. She was being managed for the Ministry of War Transport by the British Tanker Company. Commanded by Captain Arthur Laddle, the newly-appointed convoy commodore, she had a British crew of sixty and was loaded with 9,806 tons of heavy crude oil, 732 drums of lubricating oil and the arms and ammunition openly displayed on the quayside in Port of Spain. Following her was the *British Dominion*, a 6,983-tonner of the same company, under the command of Captain Joseph Miller, who carried with him a crew of fifty-two. The *Dominion* was one of the high-risk members of the convoy, having in her tanks a highly volatile 9,000 tons of high-octane aviation spirit.

The British Tanker Company also headed Column 3, with its 8,093-ton *British Vigilance*. She was a new ship, launched as the *Empire Vigilance* in May 1942 by the MOWT. With a cargo of 11,000 tons of benzine, she was a ship to be handled with care. In command was plain-speaking Welshman Captain Evan Owen Evans, and with him a crew of fifty-three. In her wake came another wartime replacement, Harris & Dixon's *Empire Lytton*, with Captain John Andrews in command. Carrying 12,500 tons of high-octane fuel, she was another floating bomb primed to go off at the slightest provocation.

At the head of Column 4 was the 9,555-ton *Norvik*, an early example of a flag of convenience ship. Norwegian-owned and manned, she sailed under the flag of the Republic of Panama. Commanded by Captain Knut O. Bringedal, her cargo tanks contained another 13,021 tons of Admiralty crude for the Navy in Gibraltar. Astern of her was the 8,375-ton *Cliona* of the Royal Dutch Shell Group, British-manned and British-flagged, with Captain James Randell in command. She was loaded with light crude oil.

The starboard column, Column 5, consisted of just one ship, the 6,833-ton Sunderland-built *Minister Wedel*, owned by Karl Bruusgaard of Oslo and on Admiralty service. Her commander was the youthful 27-year-old Captain Wilhelm Wilhelmsen, who headed a crew of forty-two. The *Minister Wedel* had loaded 8,920 tons of fuel oil in Trinidad before sailing.

All TM 1's tankers were armed with a 4-inch anti-submarine gun; some also carried a 12-pounder dual-purpose gun. To comply with the Geneva Convention, both guns were mounted in the stern, and were to be used for defensive purposes only – in other words, when running away from the enemy. For defence against air attack, two 20mm Oerlikons and four .303 machine-guns were strategically mounted on the boat deck and bridge. It was an impressive amount of armament for merchant ships, but these guns were of no use against a U-boat at periscope depth, and that is where the main threat would come from.

The only really credible defence offered by Convoy TM 1 lay with Commander Boyle and his escorts. These he disposed to form a thin screen around the tankers, with *Havelock* on the starboard bow, *Godetia* on the port bow and the other two corvettes, *Saxifrage* and *Pimpernel*, bringing up the rear on the port and starboard quarters respectively. This, to say the least, was poor protection for a convoy of nine slow-moving tankers carrying between them 25 million gallons of highly inflammable cargo on a 3,500-mile passage through U-boat-infested waters. Certainly, the sight of these four brave warships was of little comfort to the tankers' captains, who were to be the first to attempt a direct passage across the open Atlantic to Gibraltar.

Admiral Dönitz, ensconced in his chateau overlooking the River Loire at Kerneval near Lorient, had been alerted to the sailing of TM 1 by his agents in Port of Spain. From the information he was given he was still uncertain of the route the tankers would follow, but he strongly suspected that this would be a direct crossing to Gibraltar. He began to call in his U-boats.

As TM 1 set out to cross the Atlantic, the *Delphin* (Dolphin) Group of six Type VIIC boats was making a rendezvous to the west of Madeira. The group consisted of U-381 (Graf Wilhelm-Heinrich Pückler und Limburg), U436 (Günther Seibicke), U-442 (Hans-Joachim Hesse), U-571 (Helmut Möhlmann), U-575 (Günther Heydemann) and U-620 (Heinz Stein), with the Type XIV U-463, commanded by Leo Wolfbauer, acting as supply tanker and store ship.

Dönitz's plan of action was for the *Delphin* boats to make a sweep across the Atlantic to the Brazilian coast in the hope that TM 1 would be caught in their net. U-125 and U-514, already somewhere to the west, were to join up with the group when it reached them.

While Dönitz gathered his U-boats together, the code breakers at Bletchley Park, having thoroughly mastered the U-boat Enigma code, were busy reading his radio traffic. Their conclusion was uncannily accurate. They reported to the Admiralty: 'A group of six U-boats is proceeding to a patrol line the exact position of which is uncertain. It is possible that this line is west of Madeira and is designed to intercept American Casablanca convoys.'

An Admiralty report estimated that at that time no fewer than 169 U-boats were operating in the North Atlantic. And yet, with all these alarms bells ringing loudly, TM 1, a convoy vital to the continuation of Operation Torch, was sent to sea under the protection of just one destroyer and three corvettes. It can only be presumed that in routing the tankers direct to Gibraltar the planners in Whitehall thought it would slip by the enemy unseen. They could not have been more wrong.

CHAPTER TWELVE

A Chance Encounter

The next three days passed without incident, and Convoy TM 1, steering a north-easterly course, moved deeper into the Atlantic. The first of the prevailing trade winds were making themselves felt, but after the oppressive heat of Trinidad they were a welcome relief. With the sea still relatively calm, now would have been the time to press on at increased speed, but Commander Boyle resisted the temptation. His corvettes had limited fuel capacity, so he set the convoy speed at 8 knots to extend their range. For most of the tankers this was a little more than half speed, and views were expressed that such slow progress was a risk too far.

When a warm tropical dawn ushered in the first day of 1943, TM 1 was only 650 miles north-east of Trinidad. The head winds were freshening, and in the prevailing adverse current the convoy's speed was further reduced. For the tanker crews, many of them living on top of a high octane cargo, this seemed to be tempting providence.

The air cover provided by Catalinas of the US Navy had ceased after twenty-four hours, but the ocean was still unsullied by any sign of the enemy. And there was good news from *Godetia*: she had at last completed her repairs and was functioning on both boilers. This news was soon to be offset by a report from the Belgian corvette that the main transformer of her radar had burnt out and she could not effect repairs. This meant the escort ships had lost a quarter of their capacity to see in the dark and was a serious handicap. However, as the first such convoy to sail to Gibraltar by the direct route it was thought that TM 1 still held the element of surprise – but things were about to change.

It was a huge coincidence that in this great empty ocean Trinidad-bound U-514 happened to be on a collision course with the convoy. Hunter and hunted were closing on each other at a combined speed of 16 knots. And some 350 miles astern of U-514, U-125 was also converging on them. The two U-boats were operating independently, and neither Hans-Jürgen Auffermann nor Ulrich Folkers was aware of the approach of TM 1.

U-514 was also conserving her fuel, motoring on the surface at an economical speed through calm seas. The sky overhead was blue and untroubled, the horizon empty all around. The war seemed a million miles away. Taking advantage of this temporary lull, Aufferman was content to allow most of his crew on deck during daylight hours. The touch of the warm sun on their pale skin was a much needed tonic, sufficient to chase away the dark shadows of those storm-filled days behind them.

Sunday, 3 January dawned over Convoy TM 1 with the weather showing signs of deterioration. The sky had clouded over and the wind was from the north-east at force 4, just enough to whip up a chop on what had been a calm sea. Rain squalls were on the horizon, the visibility was fair to moderate. There was no lack of vigilance in the ships, but nobody gave serious thought to anything untoward happening in these relatively untroubled waters. Trouble might come later, but now normal routine prevailed.

Aboard the convoy's vice-commodore ship *British Vigilance*, sailing in the lead of the centre column, preparations were under way for Captain's Inspection. Decks were being scrubbed, cabins and forecastles cleaned, galleys and pantries made spotless.

Then, as the morning wore on, there was an abrupt change of mood. Flag signals raced up the halyards of the Commodore's ship, *Oltenia II*, and her signal lamp began to flash urgently. Word had been received from the Admiralty that a U-boat had been detected in the area, with the distinct possibility that an attack on the convoy was imminent. All thought of normal routine was dropped, lookouts were doubled up and guns were manned. TM 1 was back on a war footing.

Commander Boyle brought his escorts into a state of immediate readiness, but there was little else he could do except continue to look and listen. Not wishing to reduce the convoy's speed any further, he delayed ordering a zig-zag pattern, reasoning that it was better to press on.

Unaware of the approaching convoy, no one was more surprised than *Kapitänleutnant* Auffermann when, at about twenty minutes past four that afternoon, one of his lookouts reported smoke on the horizon ahead. All sunbathing was summarily suspended, and there was a rush of half-naked men for the hatches before they were slammed shut. U-514 went down with a roar of escaping air and, levelling off at periscope depth, Auffermann moved in to assess the target.

The minutes ticked by, and the column of smoke became a spreading cloud. Then masts and funnels became visible, followed by the box-like hulls of a several merchantmen. It soon became apparent to Auffermann that he had stumbled on an eastbound convoy. He surfaced again and used his binoculars to confirm that the ships were loaded tankers and that the convoy's escort was unusually small. He instructed his wireless operator to send a *Kurzsignal* (short-signal) sighting report to Lorient.

The coded burst of Morse, sent at 250 words per minute, was so brief that none of the wireless operators of the convoy's ships, whiling away the watch by scanning the airwaves, were aware of the transmission .

On receiving U-514's signal, Admiral Dönitz took personal charge of the operation. His War Diary for the day reads:

> 3 January 1943: At 1624 U-514 reported enemy convoy in DQ 9288, course 090. U-125 was ordered to proceed at maximum speed. Group Delphin at high cruising speed, course 170, and to attack this convoy. Convoy of some 10 ships in DQ9297 at 1730, course 070, speed 9 knots. Destroyers ahead and on each side . . .
>
> The convoy sighted in DQ 93 by U-514 is probably one formed of tankers proceeding from Trinidad to Gibraltar. Although Group Delphin is almost 900 miles from the convoy and there was little chance of maintaining contact until the Group arrived, the order was given to stalk the convoy at maximum continuous speed, because of the pressing need to attack tanker traffic to Gibraltar . . . The centre boat of Group Delphin was about 360 miles away, all boats were in a westerly position i.e. ahead of the convoy. It was calculated that the first boat would reach the convoy in about 20 hours.

After further thought, Dönitz ordered Auffermann to make a lone attack on the convoy in order to delay the tankers until the arrival of the *Delphin* boats, which had meanwhile gone off on what turned out to be a wild goose chase.

Only minutes after U-514's sighting report was received in Lorient, Nicolai Clausen in U-182 radioed that he had sighted a westbound convoy of between eleven and fifteen ships 420 miles due west of Madeira. The *Delphin* boats, now ten strong, were then in 30° W, and already moving in a south-westerly direction to meet Auffermann's convoy 900 miles away. The newly sighted convoy, GUS 3, was only 360 miles to the east of *Delphin* and might easily be reached in less than twenty-four hours. Not surprisingly, Dönitz decided to go for what seemed to be the easy option and ordered the pack to reverse course and operate against the westbound ships.

The option turned out to be anything but easy. What Clausen had discovered was a convoy of twenty-one fast American merchantmen returning in ballast from the North African beach-heads. The Americans had by this time learned the bitter lessons of Operation Drumbeat and were taking no risks with their ships, even if they were in ballast. Unknown to Lorient, Convoy GUS 3 was escorted by the 32,000-ton battleship *New York*, the light cruiser *Philadelphia* and nine destroyers. Dönitz, accustomed to operating against poorly escorted British convoys, made the mistake of ordering an all-out attack on GUS-3.

When U-182 approached Convoy GUS 3 under the cover of darkness she was immediately picked up by the destroyer *Earle*'s radar. *Earle* was joined by USS *Parker*, and the two destroyers pounced on the unsuspecting U-boat like terriers after a rat. Caught in the American searchlights, U-182 was subjected to a barrage of shells and forced to crash-dive. Clausen and his men then spent a very uncomfortable seven hours underwater being bounced around by pattern after pattern of depth charges. U-182 eventually escaped, but by the time it was safe for her to surface, Convoy GUS 3 was 100 miles ahead.

On the following night, four more *Delphin* boats made contact with the convoy and, unaware of the size of the escort force, moved in eagerly to attack on the surface. The American destroyers were ready for them, searchlights and guns manned. What followed was a rout, in which the U-boats were promptly driven off and forced to flee underwater.

*

After receiving reports of 'very heavy depth charge attacks', Dönitz conceded defeat and ordered the *Delphin* boats to withdraw and continue on their original course towards U-514's eastbound convoy. Even though Aufferman had reported losing touch with TM 1, this seemed to be a more attractive option.

By now Bletchley Park had pinpointed the position of the *Delphin* pack, and it was rightly surmised at the Admiralty that an ambush was being set up for the Gibraltar-bound tankers. TM 1 was ordered to make a bold alteration of course to the south after dark, with the object of bypassing the waiting U-boats by 100 miles or more. This made good sense, but it also presented Commander Boyle with a dilemma.

It was obvious that Boyle's escorts would soon be called upon to manoeuvre at high speed, in which case it was necessary for them, and in particular the corvettes, to refuel before the action began. The weather at the time was described as 'light North-East Trades, force 4, moderate sea', which was just about quiet enough to allow oiling.

The Panama-flag tanker *Norvik* had been designated as fleet oiler for the convoy, but when an attempt was made that afternoon to refuel HMS *Havelock*, the tanker's gear proved inadequate for the job. The destroyer managed to take on board only six tons of fuel before a combination of rough seas and *Norvik's* faulty gear halted the operation. The topping up of the corvettes' tanks would have to wait until a later date, which Commander Boyle realized could prove to be more of a problem. The change of course ordered by the Admiralty was taking the convoy into an area where the North-East Trades were blowing at their strongest.

After TM 1 had been sighted, Auffermann took U-514 back to periscope depth. There was an air of eager anticipation in the U-boat as she lay in wait for the enemy ships to come to her. She had been continuously at sea for twenty-five days, and by this time Hans-Jürgen Auffermann and his crew were thoroughly bored with watching Atlantic dolphins at play. It was time for action.

As the convoy of tankers drew slowly nearer, the sun dipped below the horizon and darkness began to descend. At about 1800, when the light had completely gone, Auffermann gave the order to surface.

It was a very dark night, with no moon, and to Auffermann's amazement he saw that the tankers had switched on their navigation lights, dimmed but clearly visible in the darkness. The convoy was not zig-zagging and appeared to be completely oblivious of any danger threatening. This was too good to be true.

Auffermann watched as the ships came round in unison on to a new more easterly course, then chose his first target carefully, finally settling on the leading ship of the centre column. She was large and deep-loaded. Possibly a whale factory ship, he thought.

Chief Officer John Butterwick had the watch on the bridge of the *British Vigilance* and had just been joined by Captain Evans. The two men were discussing the diversionary alteration of course when there was a shout from the apprentice of the watch. He reported seeing a dark shape and a bow wave on the port bow at about 400yds. Seconds later there was a loud explosion, and the tanker staggered as she was hit. A tall column of water and petrol shot skywards from the bows. The cargo ignited, and the whole fore part of the ship was suddenly engulfed by flames and dense black smoke. Captain Evans later reported:

> The cargo immediately caught fire forward, but the flames seemed to be confined to the port side with dense smoke. The Chief Officer ordered steam to be turned on to the tanks through the smothering valves. I rang the engines to be put full astern to take the way off but received no reply. I ordered the crew to stand by the boats aft and rang the alarm for boat stations.

Steaming in line directly astern of the *British Vigilance* was Harris & Dixon's *Empire Lytton*. On her bridge Chief Officer Alfred De Baughn was on watch. The night being fine and dark, the ocean wide and empty, De Baughn was pacing the starboard wing of the bridge, his thoughts far away as he savoured the silence of the night. Then, at 1845, the darkness ahead erupted in a sea of flame, quickly followed by the muted thump of the exploding torpedo.

Jerked out of his reverie, De Baughn instinctively ordered the helm hard to starboard, and when Captain Andrews arrived on the bridge seconds later the ship was already swinging clear of the blazing tanker ahead. Andrews now took over the con, bringing the *Empire Lytton* back on course as the stricken *British Vigilance*, on fire from stem to stern, drifted past on the port side.

As the burning wreck dropped astern, in the light of the flames Andrews caught sight of the low outline of a submarine on the surface broad on the *Empire Lytton*'s port bow. Without giving a thought to his own highly volatile cargo, he hauled his ship over to port, and headed straight for the U-boat, intending to ram.

It was a brave, perhaps foolish gesture, and it was just as well that Hans-Jürgen Auffermann had no intention of lingering to meet it. U-514's twin diesels increased their tempo, black smoke rolled back from her exhausts and she shot across the *Empire Lytton*'s bows, clearing the tanker's tall stem by no more than 20yds.

It was a near miss, but U-514 was not to escape completely unscathed. The *Empire Lytton*'s first-trip apprentice Basil King was in the starboard wing of the bridge when the U-boat crossed the bow. With his adrenaline running high, the 16-year-old rose to the occasion like a grown man, strapping himself into the harness of the starboard Oerlikon and opening fire on the U-boat as she cleared the bows.

By now, Aufferman was running away from the avenging tanker as fast as his diesels would take him. This, unfortunately, was not fast enough, for one of U-514's motors was not developing full power. This gave young Basil the opportunity to spray the U-boat with 20mm Oerlikon shells. Captain Andrews later estimated that of the 300 rounds fired at least 200 hit their target. At the same time, the *Norvik*, leading ship of Column 4, had opened fire with her 4-inch, bracketing the escaping U-boat with her first two shots.

Others now joined in. Captain Joseph Miller of the *British Dominion*, rear ship of Column 2, wrote in his report:

> The periscope of the submarine was sighted on the starboard side of the BRITISH VIGILANCE immediately after she had been torpedoed. We immediately opened fire with our Oerlikon gun to indicate the position of the submarine, which was too fine on the bow for the 4″ gun to bear. The OLTENIA II opened fire at the time with her 4″ gun but I do not know if she scored any hits.

Aufferman very wisely decided the time had come to submerge and take his chances under water. But even by diving deep U-514 could not hide from TM 1's escorts. On the word from Commander Boyle, *Havelock* and the three corvettes executed 'Operation Raspberry', dropping back astern of the convoy and then moving forward again, methodically saturating the area where the U-boat was believed to be with depth charges. Miracles were being worked for U-514 that night, for once again she escaped serious damage, although Auffermann and his crew were badly shaken up.

Aboard the *British Vigilance* Captain Evans was attempting to establish some semblance of order out of the chaos reigning. His first thought was to get the way off the ship so that the lifeboats would not be dragged under when they were launched. He rang full astern on the bridge telegraph, but there was no response from the engine room. The telegraph chains had been cut. Someone was still down there, however, for when Evans was leaving the bridge the engine shuddered to a halt and then went astern.

In the wireless room abaft the bridge the Chief Radio Officer was following the emergency procedure and doing his best to get away an SOS. It was a near-impossible task. The tiny cabin was filled with choking black smoke, the lights had failed and, groping about in the darkness, the R/O discovered that both the main and emergency transmitters had been smashed by the blast.

Captain Evans later described the catastrophic situation:

> There was a dense pall of smoke rising from forward which completely enveloped the bridge but as the flames broke through the smoke I found that there was no one left on the navigating bridge. I hurried down to my cabin to collect the ship's papers and my life jacket, but the electricity had failed and I was only able to find my protective hood and emergency outfit. Armed with these I made my way aft. By this time the ship's midships section was clear of personnel, so I went aft to the port boat, the crew were inclined to be a little panicky so I calmed them down and assisted with the boat. The boat was lowered in an orderly manner and a number of the crew abandoned ship in it. I then turned my attention to the starboard boat.

On the starboard side of the after deck, Chief Officer John Butterwick was supervising the lowering of the *British Vigilance*'s motor lifeboat with the help of Chief Engineer Roland Marshall. The two officers were struggling to maintain order amongst a panicking crew.

Perversely, although the *British Vigilance* had been hit on the starboard side, the whole of the port side of the ship was engulfed in flames, and the sea on that side was also ablaze. This had prompted a stampede to the opposite side, where a large number of ratings were scrambling into the starboard lifeboat before it was lowered. It was pure, unrestrained panic, and disaster threatened.

Eventually, Butterwick and Marshall restored a semblance of order, but when the motor boat hit the water it was dangerously overcrowded.

Captain Evans' report continues:

> By this time the vessel must have been on fire fore and aft as I heard the ammunition exploding overhead on the boat deck, I was under the impression that I was alone on the vessel. The benzine had been blown all over the deck and there were small patches of fire about the ship. On looking over the stern of the ship I saw two dark objects in the water close to each other which I took to be the two lifeboats. I found the 2nd Officer still on board and later came across an Able Seaman still clinging to the boat ladder over the starboard side near the water. The ammunition was exploding rapidly and the three of us took shelter in the lee of the house on the starboard side of the poop deck. Looking forward the flames seemed to be confined to jets from the valve spindles and gear which were blazing fiercely on the fore and aft bridge. The ship had now fallen off bringing the wind abeam on the port side, and there was a certain amount of flame drifting across the deck.

The three men were trapped in the after part of the tanker with the fire all around them. The ready-use ammunition for the *British Vigilance*'s guns was exploding, and the air was full of flying shrapnel. Flames were spurting out of the engine room ventilators, indicating that the ship was also well alight below decks. The way was now off the her, and she had swung beam-on to the wind, which was blowing the flames right across the deck. The whole vessel was rapidly becoming a blazing inferno, and Evans realized that unless they quickly found some means of abandoning ship they would be roasted alive.

The *British Vigilance*, as with all oil tankers of her day, was a ship of two parts. Her engine room and funnel were right aft, and around them were grouped the engineers' accommodation and crew's quarters. Amidships was the bridge housing, which contained the navigation bridge, deck officers' accommodation and officers' saloon. The two sections were joined by an open catwalk, often referred to as the 'flying bridge', to provide safe passage between the two ends in bad weather. In case the bridge was cut off from aft for any reason, two sets of lifeboats were carried, usually two full-sized boats over the engine room and two smaller boats alongside the bridge house.

Second Officer Alan Newby made a brave attempt to reach the bridge but was beaten back by the flames now licking around the catwalk. The ready-use ammunition for the 4-inch gun on the poop had now begun to explode, and the position of the survivors was becoming untenable. It was clear that if they were to live, the three men would have to brave an ordeal by fire. Covering their heads as best they could, with Captain Evans in the lead, they made a determined dash along the catwalk, reaching the bridge breathless and singed but otherwise unharmed.

They found the starboard lifeboat alongside the bridge to be intact, but it was a wooden boat, and in the intense heat it might burst into flames at any minute. Working quickly, their desperation fanned by the advancing flames, they cleared away the boat and lowered it. As soon as it hit the water, they shinned down the manropes and cast off from the burning ship.

Captain Evans later reported:

> We put the oars out and experienced great difficulty in getting the boat clear of the ship. The Able Seaman who had been rescued from the boat ladder was exhausted and of little use. The sea was ablaze in patches ahead of the vessel and on the port bow, nevertheless the only way we could get clear of the ships was to take the boat forward, as the vessel was gradually drifting astern. On nearing the bow I saw there was a huge hole where the torpedo had struck in the side of the vessel, and was afraid the boat would be drawn into the hole. I made the Able Seaman hold up an asbestos blanket to keep the flames off whilst the 2nd Officer and I made a tremendous effort to clear the ship. We finally managed to clear the ship and continued to pull away in case the ship should blow up. We then rested for a few minutes, when well clear, and heard a loud explosion from the ship and the flames on the foredeck increased into a solid mass rising to a great height.

The three survivors settled down to wait out the night, but their ordeal was brought to an end two hours later, when the corvette

Saxifrage found them. Captain Evans' first thoughts when he boarded the corvette were for the rest of his crew. Fifteen who had got away in the port lifeboat were already on board *Saxifrage*, picked up soon after leaving the ship, and from them Evans learned of the fate of the motor lifeboat. This boat, with Chief Officer Butterwick in charge, had been so overwhelmed by some panicking crew members that when it left the side of the *British Vigilance* the waves were lapping over its gunwales. The overloaded boat drifted away from the ship and then capsized, throwing its occupants into the water. Only two men found refuge on the upturned boat's keel. They were later joined by two others who had jumped overboard from the ship. One of these was the Chief Radio Officer who, having been forced to abandon the wireless room, had jumped over the side and swum clear of the burning oil. By now the sea was rising, and the four survivors were soon in danger of being washed off their precarious perch by the breaking waves. Fortunately for them, the empty port lifeboat, which was on fire, drifted up alongside them. They scrambled aboard the boat, which was otherwise intact, and after a desperate struggle put out the fire. There were no oars in the boat, so they used their hands to paddle around looking for any other survivors in the water. They found two men still alive, but apart from that there were only lifeless bodies. Captain Evans later wrote in his report:

> We had to board the corvette quickly as she was in a hurry, action stations were sounding as we climbed on board. Shortly afterwards 'Action Stations' was cancelled and the corvette returned again to search for the remainder of the survivors. We could see red lights in the water, but some of the crew did not have their lifejackets on. Whilst picking up other survivors 'Action Stations' again sounded and the corvette rejoined the convoy. But returned to the vicinity again after this attack had died down. Several more men were rescued from the water, making a total of 27, but again she was recalled to the convoy. After this she could not return and I regret to state that the remainder of the crew of the BRITISH VIGILANCE were lost.

When the final count was made, it was revealed that of the *British Vigilance*'s total complement of fifty-four, twenty-seven men had lost their lives. This grievous loss was largely due to an outbreak of panic caused by the fire on board. At the Board of Inquiry held into the loss of his ship Captain Evans said he was nauseated by the actions of some of his crew. He told the Court, 'I have never sailed with such a bad crew generally. Their behaviour when the ship was torpedoed was disgusting.' On reflection, however, it must be said that being trapped on board a burning ship containing 11,000 tons of highly inflammable benzine is not conducive to good discipline.

Evans watched the demise of his ship from the deck of *Saxifrage*. She was still visibly afloat at 1030 that night and 'blazing fore and aft'. By midnight she was a mass of flame on the horizon, and when dawn came on the 4th she was still there, but now only a column of black smoke marked her funeral pyre. In fact, the *British Vigilance*, a credit to her Scottish builders, was still afloat three weeks later when, quite by chance, she was sighted by U-105.

U-105, under the command of Jürgen Nissen, was not enjoying a good year. Sailing from Lorient in June 1942, she had been attacked by a patrolling Sunderland while crossing the Bay of Biscay and severely damaged. She took refuge in the neutral Spanish port of El Ferrol, and later in the month returned to Lorient for repairs. She did not sail again until 22 November, and it was not until three weeks later, on 14 December 1942, that she landed her first prize, which was hardly a great achievement. The 6,578-ton British tramp *Orfor* was on her way to various ports in the West Indies carrying 7,000 tons of gunny sacks for the sugar trade. Sailing alone, she was easy meat for Nissen's torpedoes and she went down when hit in the engine room. The *Orfor*'s Master and twenty-one of his crew were lost, but the remainder abandoned ship in two lifeboats. One of these boats sailed 600 miles to land on Desirade Island, Guadeloupe, while the other was picked up by the armed yacht HMS *Black Bear*.

U-105 spent another barren month cruising the Caribbean, before she chanced on the 67-ton sailing barque *C.S. Flight*, which was on its way from Curacao to Barbados carrying a human cargo of West Indian labourers. Forty-nine innocents lost their lives when Nissen forced them to take to the water by spraying the barque with 20mm cannon fire.

When he came across the smoke-blackened wreck of the *British Vigilance* on 24 January 1943, Jürgen Nissen, having heard all the prodigious tales of endless conquests in the Caribbean, was a disappointed man. The burnt-out *British Vigilance* was no great prize, but perhaps better than nothing. It cost Nissen another two torpedoes to sink her.

Without leaving the convoy to the mercy of other U-boats which might be in the area, Commander Boyle was unable to take effective action against U-514. Fortunately for him, and for the ships of TM 1, Aufferman was in no position to mount further attacks. Thanks to the sustained and accurate fusillade of 20mm shells aimed at the fleeing submarine by young Basil King, U-514 ended up with a leaking torpedo tube cap, a fractured oil cooler and damage to her main radio transmitter. This left Auffermann trailing behind the convoy and with only intermittent communication with Lorient. Eventually, he lost contact with TM 1 altogether, and would never regain it. Dönitz's other forward scout, Ulrich Folkers in U-125, failed to find TM 1 and due to U-514's faulty radio was unable to make contact with Aufferman.

The torpedoing of the *British Vigilance* should have been a warning to the Admiralty that TM 1 was urgently in need of extra protection, in the form of another destroyer at the very least, to augment Commander Boyle's pitifully small escort force. As nothing was forthcoming, it must be assumed that with Operation Torch in full flight, there were just no other escorts to spare. This was to have dire consequences for Convoy TM 1.

CHAPTER THIRTEEN

The Wolves Gather

Having put so much effort into the pursuit of TM 1, Admiral Dönitz was understandably furious with Hans-Jürgen Auffermann for failing to keep the tankers in sight. He regarded the convoy as of vital importance to the Allied campaign in North Africa, and nothing short of its complete destruction was acceptable. Thanks to Auffermann's original sighting report, Dönitz at least had a rough idea of the location of the convoy, but the ocean was wide, and unless he acted swiftly he feared he might lose it altogether.

From the course being steered by the tankers when last sighted, Dönitz deduced that they would pass through the 200-mile gap between Madeira and the Canary Islands. Accordingly, he ordered the *Delphin* boats to spread their net to cover this gateway to Gibraltar. The pack had by now swelled to ten boats, namely U-134 (Rudolf Schendel), U-181 (Wolfgang Lüth), U-381 (Wilhelm-Heinrich Graf von Pückler und Limburg), U-436 (Günther Seibicke), U-442 (Hans-Joachim Hesse), U-511 (Fritz Schneewind), U-522 (Herbert Schneider), U-571 (Helmut Möhlmann), U-575 (Günther Heydemann) and U-620 (Heinz Stein). Others were on their way to join them. This was to be a do-or-die operation.

In the midst of all this frenzied activity, which involved a constant stream of radio traffic between Lorient and the U-boats, Bletchley Park had not been idle. At this stage, thanks to the efforts of the Royal Navy, the British cryptographers were reading Dönitz's Enigma signals with comparative ease, often within hours of transmission. And it was as a result of this that the Admiralty diverted TM 1 to pass south of the Canaries, thereby hopefully avoiding the *Delphin* ambush by more than 100 miles. However, because of the need to conceal Bletchley Park's activities from the enemy, Commander Boyle could not be informed of the reason for the change of course. Not that this would have bothered Boyle at the time; he had a far more pressing problem to deal with. The merchant ships of his convoy were carrying thousands of tons of fuel oil of all grades, and yet, through a quirk of the weather, the ships guarding them were about to become useless for the want of a few tons of that oil.

Early on the morning of 4 January, *Havelock*'s radio operators tuned into what appeared to be a U-boat transmitting close by. HF/DF bearings indicated that it was somewhere astern of the convoy. *Godetia*, having more fuel to spare than the other escorts, was ordered to drop back and investigate. The corvette drew a blank and rejoined the convoy, having wasted a great deal of her precious fuel. Matters were brought to a head during the course of the morning, when *Saxifrage* signalled that she was down to her last four tons of diesel.

Boyle's mind was made up for him. He knew that if he maintained course to pass south of the Canaries, as the Admiralty had ordered, the weather would get worse by the hour, for the North-East Trade's were at their strongest in that latitude. In order to refuel his ships he had to go north in search of better weather. Without more ado, he reverted to the convoy's original course of 055°, which would take it between the Canaries and Madeira. He advised the Admiralty of his decision.

Much to Commander Boyle's relief, when the sun came up on the morning of the 5th the convoy was moving into calmer waters. During the day, the Anglo Saxon tanker *Cliona*, which also carried the necessary gear for oiling at sea, was able to supply *Havelock* and the corvettes with full tanks. Although Boyle was well aware of the shortcomings of his small escort force, he now at least had the fuel to put up a credible defence against a determined attack by U-boats. It was perhaps just as well that he was unaware of the size of the pack Dönitz was putting up against him, or the fact that by reverting to the original course he was sailing right into its open arms.

Unfortunately, it just so happened that while Boyle was busy refuelling his ships, Lorient chose to change its Enigma settings by adding a fourth wheel to the coding machine. Forty-eight hours would pass before Bletchley Park was able to break the new code and continue reading the torrent of signals flying between Dönitz and the U-boats. This retrieved their advantage over the German Admiral, and with both U-514 and U-125 out of the running, Dönitz had no one tracking TM 1, and could only speculate as to the convoy's intentions.

The *Delphin* pack now comprised twelve U-boats and had set up a 120-mile-long patrol line 600 miles to the west of the Canaries and sweeping westwards. The convoy of loaded tankers, blissfully unaware of the danger it faced, adhered to its original course of 055°.

At 1600 on the 8th, U-381, the third boat from the northern end of the patrol line, sighted the elongated cloud of smoke that heralded the arrival of TM 1. The convoy was then 700 miles west of the Canary Islands, steaming at 9 knots and on full alert following the loss of the *British Vigilance*.

Admiral Dönitz, who by now was beginning to doubt the wisdom of the ambush he had set up, was delighted when U-381's sighting report came in. He ordered her to stay close to the convoy and act as a beacon for the other U-boats to home in on.

U-381's career so far had been singularly unproductive. A Type VIIC built by the Howaldt yard in Kiel, she was commissioned under the command of *Oberleutnant* Wilhelm-Heinrich Graf von Pückler und Limburg in February 1942. Now on her third war patrol, with almost a year in service, she had yet to open her score. Her lack of success may have been just bad luck, or it may have been that 30-year-old von Pückler und Limburg, who came of a long line of former German princes, was a very cautious commander. Who is to judge? However, on this occasion, presented with what must have been the softest of targets, the Count was forbidden to attack, even if he was of a mind to do so.

The *Delphin* pack now included U-511 and U-522, who were outward bound from Lorient, and U-181 and U-134, both inbound from the Atlantic. In all, the pack now totalled thirteen U-boats. Commander Boyle's small escort force was about to be overwhelmed.

With the burning wreck of the *British Vigilance* fading away into the darkness astern, TM 1 had closed ranks, the *Empire Lytton* moving up to take the place of the torpedoed ship. Commander Boyle, calculating that the greatest danger lay to the north, rearranged his escort force to best advantage. *Havelock* took up station on the port bow, with *Godetia*, the most experienced corvette, guarding the port quarter. *Pimpernel* was on the starboard bow, with *Saxifrage* on the starboard quarter. The weather was set fair, and for the next five days TM 1 progressed smoothly towards its destination. At the same time, Dönitz's 120-mile-long wall of U-boats moved relentlessly westwards.

Things started to go wrong for TM 1 in the late afternoon of the 8th, when the convoy was some 600 miles off the Canaries. The weather was still fine and clear, with a light south-easterly breeze, slight sea and moderate swell; about as good as it ever gets in the North Atlantic. As darkness began to close in, *Godetia* and *Pimpernel* reported to *Havelock* that their radars had failed and they were unable to effect repairs. Both ships had been many months on the American coast without proper maintenance – as, indeed, had all of the B5 Escort Group – and the results were beginning to show. At the same time, *Havelock*'s HF/DF began to give trouble. At this crucial point Commander Boyle was rapidly losing his ability to seek out the enemy on the surface.

It was a dark, moonless night, and with the weather still showing a kind face, everything was to TM 1's advantage. The general feeling in the ships was that if they could get through the next twelve hours safely, the worst would be over. No one was yet aware that U-381, trimmed down with only her conning tower above water, was following in their wake and faithfully reporting the convoy's every move to Lorient and the other members of the *Delphin* pack.

U-436 was the first boat to make contact with TM 1 in answer to U-381's call. A Type VIIC built in Danzig in 1941, she was under the command of the experienced *Kapitänleutnant* Günther Seibicke, who had won the Iron Cross 2nd Class and Iron Cross 1st Class in the first year of the war while serving in minesweepers. Transferring to the U-boat arm in April 1941, Seibicke had quickly made a name for himself by sinking 37,000 tons of Allied shipping in the North Atlantic. Now he was about to make a bid for the coveted Knight's Cross.

Havelock was keeping station some 2½ miles off the port bow of the convoy when, at 1930, her radar picked up a tiny echo 1¾ miles astern and just ahead of the first ship of the outer port column. Commander Boyle immediately turned under full helm, and steamed back to investigate. As *Havelock* settled on her new course, the masthead lookout reported a U-boat on the surface right ahead. Boyle rang for full speed, and warned those below decks that he was about to ram.

Seeing the enemy destroyer racing towards him with her bow-wave foaming, Günther Seibicke fired a spread of three torpedoes at the nearest tankers, then cleared the conning tower and executed a crash-dive. *Havelock* was just too late to open fire with her 4-inch, but as the sea closed over U-436 the destroyer's Asdic locked firmly on to her.

Seconds later, *Havelock* ran over the patch of disturbed water left by the diving U-boat, and Boyle dropped a pattern of five depth charges set to shallow depth. As the charges exploded with a muffled roar, throwing plumes of spray high into the sky, the loud thump of a torpedo going home was heard. One of Seibicke's random spread had scored a hit.

The Norwegian-flag tanker *Albert L. Ellsworth* had drawn the short straw when she was nominated as lead ship of TM 1's outer port column. For Captain Thorvald Solheim, being put in such an exposed position was akin to being the proverbial sacrificial lamb. Not that Solheim and his ship were strangers to the Atlantic battle. They had been in the thick of the action even before Norway was drawn into the war.

In February 1940 the *Albert L. Ellsworth*, homeward bound with a cargo of oil from the Caribbean, picked up thirty-four survivors from a fellow Norwegian, the 4,114-ton motor vessel *Snestad*. The *Snestad*, outward bound in ballast for Philadelphia, had been torpedoed on the previous day by U-53 when 100 miles west of the Outer Hebrides. Twenty-four hours later, the *Albert L. Ellsworth* was passing south of the Faroe Islands when she also had the misfortune to cross the path of Max-Herman Bauer and U-50. Bauer fired two torpedoes, both of which exploded prematurely but very close to the Norwegian tanker. Like the unfortunate *Snestad*, she was a neutral-flag ship, and as such supposedly immune from attack; the unexpected thunder of the exploding torpedoes caused panic amongst the seventy-six men on board. Lifeboats were launched and the ship abandoned, two men being lost in the scramble to get away.

Bauer came back later in the night to find the *Albert L. Ellsworth* still afloat. He used two more torpedoes on the derelict ship, but again they proved to be duds, one failing to explode, the other veering off course and missing the target altogether. Bauer thought he had scored a hit, and left the scene believing the tanker was sinking.

At first light next day the *Albert L. Ellsworth* was still there, drifting aimlessly and rolling in the long swell. Rather shamefacedly, the survivors of the two Norwegian ships took their lifeboats back alongside the abandoned tanker and re-boarded her. She reached Bergen two days later, and was back in service again at the end of the month.

When Norway fell in the spring of 1940, the *Albert L. Ellsworth* was on passage from Marseilles to Gibraltar, and like most Norwegian merchantmen she opted to come under British control. She was attached to the Royal Fleet Auxiliary and regularly carried cargoes across the Atlantic for the Admiralty. Now, at 2037 on 8 January 1943, the tanker's voyaging finally came to an end.

Günther Seibicke's torpedo struck the *Albert L. Ellsworth* on her port side in the vicinity of No.6 cargo tank. She caught fire and within minutes was blazing furiously, lighting up the night sky, a flaming beacon guiding the rest of the *Delphin* boats on to their target.

After four years of hazardous Atlantic crossings Solheim and his men had grown accustomed to the terrible risks they faced day by day, and this time there was no panic as the tanker was abandoned. Solheim and those with him on the bridge got away in one of the amidships boats, while the majority of the crew lowered the after boats and cleared the burning ship. Only one man, Second Engineer Georg Julien, was left behind. He had been on watch below when the torpedo struck, and his first instinct was to take the engine room ladder at a run and get on deck before the ship exploded or went down under him. It was only when he reached the upper deck that he remembered the engine was still running and the ship was surging ahead at full speed. He realized that to attempt to lower the boats when the tanker was making so much way through the water would be nothing short of suicidal. With total disregard for his own safety, the engineer went back down into the bowels of the doomed ship and stopped the engine.

When Julien returned to the deck he found that all the lifeboats had already left the ship; he now had the choice of dying in the flames or taking his chance in the sea. He chose the latter, hurling himself overboard and swimming clear of the burning oil on the water. Fortunately for him, he was seen, and one of the lifeboats came to his rescue.

Just a few seconds after the *Albert L. Ellsworth* was hit, another of Seibicke's torpedoes slammed home in the hull of the next ship in line, the British-flag *Oltenia II*, commanded by the convoy commodore Captain Alfred Laddle.

The demands of war had brought the *Oltenia II* a long way from her usual trading area. In the halcyon days of peace she had spent much of her time carrying oil from Abadan to Indian ports and, as was the case with most British ships habitually trading in the Indian Ocean, she carried British officers and Lascar (Indian) ratings. This arrangement suited the shipping companies, as Lascar crews were cheaper to employ and less prone to indiscipline than European seamen, and at the same time the Indian Government welcomed the jobs provided. There was, however, a down side in that many of the Lascar seamen saw the war as being a European business and wanted no part of it. This was the case with the *Oltenia II*'s Indian crew. Following the horrific sight of the *British Vigilance* going up in flames, they had refused to venture below decks, spending their time huddled together on the open deck. And that is where they were when two of Günther Seibicke's torpedoes exploded in the *Oltenia II*'s engine room. The only two men on watch below, Second Engineer Hugh Purdie and Fifth Engineer Thomas Hickey, were killed instantly.

Chief Officer Kenneth Bruce had the watch on the *Oltenia*'s bridge when U-436 struck. Momentarily stunned by the deafening explosion, he rushed to the after end of the bridge to see that the whole of the stern section of the tanker was ablaze, with 'flames on the port side aft as high as the funnel'.

Captain Laddle arrived on the bridge seconds later to find his ship dead in the water and settling rapidly by the stern. She had been hit in her most vulnerable compartment, and her back was broken. Laddle gave the order to abandon ship.

Chief Officer Bruce made his way to the port midships lifeboat, of which he was to take charge. There he found the tanker's Third Officer and Fourth Engineer attempting to clear away and lower the boat, while a group of about twenty Indian crew looked on. Bruce took charge, but was unable to persuade the ratings to help. With considerable difficulty, the three officers succeeded in getting the boat into the water, by which time the *Oltenia II*'s after deck was awash. The waiting Lascars then boarded the boat with a rush.

On the starboard side of the bridge Captain Laddle was supervising the launching of the other midships boat. When the boat was in the water and the crew embarked, Laddle told them to wait alongside while he went to his cabin to collect the ship's papers.

While he was away, the *Oltenia II* took her last plunge. Captain Alfred Laddle was never seen again, presumably having been trapped in the accommodation when the ship went down.

With the crash of Günther Seibicke's torpedoes still echoing across the water, the convoy's escorts were galvanized into action. As prearranged, the destroyer and the three corvettes converged on the submerged U-boat, intent on smothering her with depth charges.

But on this occasion, confusion came over the convoy's response. *Pimpernel*, racing back at full speed, narrowly avoided colliding with the *Cliona*, rear ship of Column 4. The corvette was forced to make a bold alteration to starboard, thus running across the bows of the other tankers in the rear. It was very dark, and the Norwegian-flag *Vanja*, rear ship of the outer port column, mistook the corvette for a U-boat and opened fire on her with every gun she could bring to bear. Fortunately for *Pimpernel*, the *Vanja*'s gunners were not on good form.

Havelock had more luck. As she dashed aft her radar picked up a small echo close astern of the rear tankers. Boyle fired starshell, which lit up the night sky and revealed a U-boat on the surface at 1,000yds. True to form, U-436 had resurfaced and was shaping up for another attack. She dived as *Havelock* approached, but was picked up by the destroyer's ASDIC and subjected to a pattern of fourteen depth charges. As the U-boat twisted and turned, trying to escape, *Havelock* followed up with another pattern. When the thunder of the charges subsided, contact had been lost, but a heavy underwater explosion was heard. Boyle believed he had either sunk or damaged the U-boat, but his optimism was misplaced. U-436 had in fact escaped unharmed and slipped away.

While *Havelock* was pursuing U-436, *Pimpernel*'s Asdic operators obtained a contact on the starboard quarter of the convoy. The corvette altered to investigate, her radar showing a small echo consistent with a U-boat's conning tower bearing 120 degrees at 2,200yds. As he moved in, Lieutenant Thornton fired starshell, which showed up a U-boat on the surface. With the range at 1,500yds, *Pimpernel* opened fire with her 4-inch, but after only one round was fired, the unidentified U-boat, which was about 1,500yds off, slipped beneath the waves. The corvette's Asdic locked on to the escaping U-boat and Thornton went after her, dropping a ten-charge pattern. Contact was lost in the turbulence caused by the explosions, and a box search was carried out until the U-boat was found again about half an hour later. Thornton continued the pursuit with two further depth charge attacks, and shortly after the second attack a loud underwater explosion was heard. The Asdic contact faded gradually about eight minutes later. Disappointingly, no oil or debris came to the surface, and it was assumed, correctly as it transpired, that the U-boat had got away.

The violent reaction of TM 1's escorts may have done little damage to the attacking U-boats, but it did induce them to withdraw, allowing *Havelock* to search for survivors from the torpedoed tankers.

While the guns roared and the depth charges exploded around him, Chief Officer Bruce was fighting his own battle to escape the pull of the sinking *Oltenia II*. It was a desperate fight, for although the lifeboat contained twenty-three men, only Bruce and the other two Europeans were prepared to bend their backs to the oars. The twenty Indian crew refused to lend a hand, sitting passively in the boat awaiting whatever fate had in store. This was decided for them when, as the three officers fought vainly to get clear of her, the *Oltenia II* went down with a rush, creating a powerful vortex which capsized the lifeboat, throwing all its occupants into the water.

Kenneth Bruce later wrote in his report that he was sucked down with the sinking ship to a great depth. When the tanker finally released its grip on him he shot to the surface, coming up directly under the capsized boat. He dived again, swam clear, and surfaced to find the other survivors seated astride the keel of the boat.

A lesser man might have given up there and then, but Bruce, by virtue of his rank, was no stranger to a challenge. Thick oil was coming to the surface from the sunken *Oltenia II*, forming a black, suffocating film on the water, and Bruce realized that unless the boat was righted all their lives would be in danger. It would not be easy, but if all the men on board cooperated by hauling on the gripes and throwing their weight on one side, it could be done.

Bruce called for the effort to be made, but only the Third Officer and Fourth Engineer responded. The Indians preferred to chant a prayer and hope for divine intervention. The lifeboat remained up-ended, floating on its buoyancy tanks, while the sea around it was gradually becoming covered in thick, black oil.

Angry and frustrated, Bruce looked around for another option. It was then that he became aware of one of the ship's wooden life-rafts drifting nearby. There were four men on the raft, two of the *Oltenia II*'s radio officers and two quartermasters. They were all that remained from Captain Laddle's boat, which had also capsized when the tanker went down.

The raft and the lifeboat came together, and on Bruce's instigation eight men from the boat were transferred to the raft, leaving fifteen clinging to the keel of the lifeboat. And that was how the lifeboats of the *Albert L. Ellsworth* found them at dawn. Later, HMS *Havelock* sighted the now crowded boats, and all survivors were taken on board. She already had some *Oltenia II* survivors on board, many of whom had been in the water and were covered in black oil. Some had swallowed the oil and were in danger of choking on their own vomit. Although *Havelock* had a doctor on board with a fully equipped sickbay, there was little that could be done for these unfortunate men other than cleaning the oil off with soap and water. This was a long and laborious process, patiently carried out by the destroyer's crew, but sometimes in vain. Some of the worst cases died. In all, of the total complement of sixty on board the *Oltenia II* seventeen men, six British officers and eleven Indian ratings, lost their lives in the sinking. Chief Officer Kenneth Bruce, the senior survivor picked up by *Havelock*, expressed his gratitude for the treatment he and the others had received on board the destroyer, saying, 'We were given every attention and shown all possible kindness by the officers and crew.'

After the furore caused by the torpedoing of the *Oltenia II* had died down, the rest of the night passed quietly for the battered Convoy TM 1 as it gathered together its scattered remnants. Out of the nine tankers that sailed from Port of Spain, only six now remained, and for every mile they progressed eastwards the danger was increasing.

*

While TM 1 licked its wounds, to the south-west, off the coast of Dutch Guyana, U-124 was back in the war. Still smarting at the thwarting of his attack on the *Empire Lytton* and *Vanja* as they hurried to catch up with the rest of the convoy, Johann Mohr had taken U-124 into fresh pastures. At first, the waters to the south of Trinidad proved barren, then late on 8 January, when he was about 50 miles north of Paramaribo, Mohr struck gold.

Convoy TB 1, bound from Trinidad to Bahia, consisted of twelve ships, eight American, two British, one Dutch and one Panamanian, and was escorted by four coastal patrol (PC) of the US Navy. The latter were formidable little warships of 450 tons displacement with a speed of 20 knots, miniature destroyers in fact. They were well armed, each with one 3-inch dual purpose gun, one 40mm and three 20mm cannons, two rocket launchers, four depth charge throwers and two depth charge racks. With this strong escort force TB 1 should have been safe from most enemy predators, but the merchantmen were an ageing lot, and with the convoy's speed set at 6 knots they were very vulnerable.

Johann Mohr had little difficulty in penetrating the escort screen, and at thirty minutes to midnight on 8 January he attacked with a spread of three torpedoes.

The 7,713-ton New York-registered tanker *Broad Arrow*, commanded by Captain Percy Mounter and bound for Rio de Janeiro with 8,207 tons of diesel and fuel oil, was first in the line of fire. One of Mohr's torpedoes hit her squarely in her after magazine, and the resulting explosion literally blew her stern off. Seven of her eight Armed Guard gunners, who were manning the 5-inch on the poop, were killed instantly.

The *Broad Arrow* was already in her death throes when Mohr's second torpedo struck forward of the bridge. Captain Mounter and all those on the bridge with him died as the tanker burst into flames, lighting up the sea for miles around and revealing the other ships of the convoy in bold relief against the dark horizon.

With Captain Mounter and most of his deck officers lying dead on the bridge, the *Broad Arrow* was abandoned in some disarray. Several men were trapped in the accommodation by the flames, others ended up in the oil-covered water. Of her total complement of forty-seven, only twenty-six were still alive when the escort *PC-577* came to their rescue, and two of these died later.

The *Broad Arrow* was still on her way down when Johann Mohr's third torpedo found its target in the next ship in line. She was the 6,194-ton *Birmingham City*, owned by Isthmian Lines of New York and commanded by Captain Michael Barry, who had been appointed Convoy Commodore. The 23-year-old steamer, loaded with 10,000 tons of general cargo for Rio, was hit squarely amidships. The blast of the torpedo reduced her port side lifeboats to matchwood and breached the watertight bulkhead between the engine room and

No.3 hold. The sea poured through the broken bulkhead and flooded the engine spaces. She sank three minutes after being hit.

The two intact lifeboats on the starboard side were launched, and Captain Barry, his eight officers, twenty-nine ratings and eighteen Armed Guards abandoned ship. Unfortunately, one boat capsized on reaching the water and its occupants were thrown into the sea. Ten men were drowned. The remaining forty-six survivors were picked up by *PC-577*.

U-124 came back for a second attack at around 0100 on the 9th. Mohr lined up his sights on two ships which were overlapping and fired two torpedoes, then a third. His targets were the 5,101-ton *Collingsworth* of the American Mail Line and behind her the 4,554-ton *Minotaur*, registered in Mobile, Alabama. The former, under the command of Captain Barney Kirschbaum, was bound for Rio de Janeiro with 8,000 tons of coal, steel rails and bunker oil in barrels. The latter, commanded by Captain Jens Jenson, carried a similar cargo for the same port.

Mohr's first torpedo missed the *Collingsworth*'s stern by just a few yards, but the second hit home between her No.1 and No.2 holds. The third torpedo was spotted in time to swing the ship away from it, and it missed by a mere 10ft. Nevertheless, the *Collingsworth* was hit hard, and she sank within a few minutes, taking Captain Kirschbaum and eleven crew with her. Thirty-four survivors were rescued by *PC-577*, while the remaining twenty-one were later picked up by the Norwegian ship *Dalvanger*.

The third torpedo fired by U-124, which was narrowly avoided by the *Collingsworth*, went on to hit the *Minotaur* in way of her No.1 hold. The explosion blasted a huge hole in the 25-year-old steamer's hull, and she began to go down by the head. Four minutes later she had slipped beneath the waves. Her crew of sixty abandoned ship in two lifeboats, one of which was dragged under with the ship, while the other capsized. Miraculously, only six men were lost, the others swimming to three life-rafts that had floated off. *PC-577*, the convoy's unofficial rescue ship, found them a few hours later.

It had been a good night's work for Johann Mohr: six torpedoes fired and 23,567 tons of shipping and 32,000 tons of cargo sent to the bottom. The 27-year-old *Korvettenkapitän* had given the Americans a bloody nose that would help to compensate for his earlier humiliation when he tangled with *Godetia* and the US Air Force off Trinidad.

CHAPTER FOURTEEN

No Quarter Given

Günther Seibecke's devastating attack had left Convoy TM 1 in a state of turmoil. The commodore ship *Oltenia II* had gone, and the man leading the convoy, Captain Alfred Laddle, with her. *Havelock* and *Pimpernel* were astern chasing U-boats, leaving no one in overall control of the convoy. However, the remaining tankers, although in a state of shock, were maintaining their course and speed and a semblance of order.

Satisfied he had done enough damage for the time being, Seibecke had taken U-436 out of harm's way. Her place was quickly filled by another Type VIIC, U-575 under the command of 29-year-old Günther Heydemann.

U-575 was the last to join the *Delphin* pack. She had sailed from Lorient on 10 December, but had been forced to return to port when water was discovered in her periscope. Initial investigations pointed to a strong possibility of sabotage, which was becoming more common in the French Biscay ports at the time. Nothing conclusive was proved, but suspecting there might be other damage, the German authorities instituted a thorough inspection of the boat and U-575 spent another week in port, this delay being much appreciated by her crew.

Some good did come out of U-575's extended stay in Lorient. As a direct result, she was well placed to the south of the Azores when U-514's report of the sighting of TM 1 came through. Heydemann immediately increased speed and set course for the position given, arriving in contact with the convoy on the night of 8 January. Unfortunately for him, he also sailed right into the arms of the B-5 Escort Group and the vigorous counter-measures being taken following the torpedoing of the *Oltenia II* and *Albert L. Ellsworth.*

The corvette *Pimpernel* was first to detect the approach of U-575 as she came up on TM 1's starboard quarter. Lieutenant Thornton altered course to investigate suspicious hydrophone noises, and minutes late had a radar contact at 2,200yds. He fired starshell, which showed a U-boat on the surface, but *Pimpernel's* 4-inch gunners had time to get off only one round before Heydemann cleared his conning tower and crash-dived.

Pimpernel's Asdic operator was quick to lock on to the diving U-boat, and the corvette raced in to drop a pattern of ten depth charges. Contact was lost soon afterwards, and Thornton began a box search. Half an hour later, *Pimpernel* again had contact, and like a hound unleashed surged forward scattering more depth charges. Soon after the last charge went over the stern a loud underwater explosion was heard. Asdic contact was held for several more minutes, and then the echo faded. All the indications were that *Pimpernel* had sunk her U-boat, but there was no time for confirmation. Thornton was ordered to rejoin the convoy without delay to assist *Godetia*, which was then attempting to defend the tankers alone. As he approached the convoy, Thornton was given the unwelcome news that *Pimpernel's* radar was out of action, possibly as a consequence of the earlier heavy depth charging.

Pimpernel rejoined TM 1 at about 0200 on the 9th, only to find that *Havelock* was back on station and taking control. Anxious to restore order to the depleted ranks, Commander Boyle appointed Captain Joseph Miller, master of the *British Dominion*, to take Captain Laddle's place as convoy commodore. Miller, a highly competent and experienced shipmaster, accepted with enthusiasm the poisoned chalice he had been handed and lost no time in re-grouping the convoy. On a dark night, and with everyone's nerves on edge, this was no easy feat, Miller being forced to take the risk of using dimmed navigation lights. However, after several near collisions accompanied by florid megaphone exchanges, the convoy was eventually re-formed, albeit in two ragged lines, with *Vanja*, *Empire Lytton*, *British Dominion* and *Minister Wedel* leading in line abreast, while *Norvik* and *Cliona* brought up the rear. It was not the ideal formation, but for the time being it would have to do.

When everyone was in place, Miller increased the convoy speed to 9 knots, much against Commander Boyle's wishes, the SOE still being haunted by the limited bunker capacity of his corvettes. The weather remained set fair: the sky was clouded over, the wind a gentle force 2 from the south-east, the sea slight and visibility good. The world seemed at peace, until Boyle brought *Havelock* close alongside the *British Dominion* and, using a loud hailer, informed Captain Miller to the contrary. *Havelock* had received a signal from the Admiralty saying that D/F activity picked up by their listening stations ashore indicated six or seven U-boats in the vicinity of the convoy.

The *Delphin* pack was now, in fact, ten strong. It was made up of the seven Type VIICs, U-134 (Schendel), U-381 (von Puckler und Limburg), U-436 (Seibecke), U-442 (Hesse), U-571 (Möhlmann), U-575 (Heydemann) and U-620 (Stein); two Type IXCs, U-522 (Schneider) and U-511 (Scheewind); and the very-long-range Type IXD2, U-181 (Luth). This was a very formidable force and indicative of Dönitz's determination to sever the Allied oil supply line to North Africa.

Herbert Schneider in U-522 was in the van of the pack, still flushed with victory following his part in the attack on Convoy SC 107 just over a month earlier off Newfoundland. Then Schneider had been credited with sinking four ships totalling 20,000 tons gross. Twenty-eight-year-old *Kapitänleutnant* Schneider was a man of many talents. Having joined the German Navy in 1934, he served in surface vessels for two years before becoming bored with the life and transferring to the *Luftwaffe*. He flew reconnaissance sorties during the Spanish Civil War but, still unable to settle down, returned to the Navy in 1940. After several voyages in surface ships, he volunteered for service in the U-boats. Here, at last, he found his niche, and in the summer of 1942 took command of the newly-built U-522. By the end of the year he was a holder of the Iron Cross First Class and had proved himself an aggressive and successful U-boat commander.

At 0300 on the 9th Schneider had positioned U-522 about 1,400 yards off the starboard bow of TM 1 and was at periscope depth awaiting the opportunity to strike. Unfortunately for him, the ever-alert *Pimpernel* was also to starboard of the convoy, and her Asdic picked up the submerged U-boat. Lieutenant Thornton increased speed to investigate the echo, but even as the corvette surged forward the contact faded. Realizing he had been discovered, Schneider had gone deep and was creeping away.

Twenty minutes later, Schneider was back at periscope depth and closing the convoy to take up an attack position, but *Pimpernel* was still there keeping watch. Her Asdic made contact, and Thornton raised the alarm, bringing the convoy to action stations. His warning came too late. U-522 had broken through the screen, and ten minutes later the *Minister Wedel*, leading the starboard outer column, was hit by two of the three torpedoes fired by Schneider. She went up like an erupting volcano, her cargo of fuel oil catching fire and turning her into a raging inferno. Seconds later, Schneider's third torpedo found its mark in the hull of the Panamanian-flag *Norvik*, and her 13,000 tons of oil added to the roaring conflagration. Fireballs erupted from the stricken vessels, and the flames from both burning ships turned the pre-dawn sky into a backdrop for Dante's *Inferno*. As far as the eye could see, the ocean was on fire.

Aboard the *Minister Wedel*, Captain Wilhelm Wilhelmsen assessed the damage wrought by Schneider's torpedoes and, accepting the impossibility of fighting the fires, ordered his crew to abandon ship. With the weather still reasonably calm, all thirty-eight men took to the lifeboats without incident. They were picked up within minutes by HMS *Havelock*. The destroyer then rescued the *Norvik*'s crew of forty-three.

An hour later, both torpedoed tankers were still afloat, although the *Norvik*, her main deck already awash, was clearly beyond saving. The fires aboard the *Minister Wedel* appeared to have burnt themselves out, and the possibility of saving the tanker looked real. With Commander Boyle's agreement, Captain Wilhelmsen called for volunteers to re-board the ship to see if she could be salvaged. The call was answered by most of his crew, and he chose First Engineer Olaf Ellefsen, Assistant Engineer Sverre Svendsen, Radio Operator Arvid Jonassen and two engine room mechanics to go with him.

Deep loaded as she was, the *Minister Wedel* had a low freeboard, her main deck being only a few feet above the waterline, and this allowed Boyle to manoeuvre *Havelock* alongside so that Wilhelmsen and his salvage party could board their ship. What they found was a scene of utter devastation. Most of the tanker's accommodation was burnt out, and her engine room was filled with smoke. However, there seemed to be a possibility of saving her – until *Havelock*'s Asdic obtained a contact and Boyle hauled off to investigate.

While *Havelock* had been occupied with the salvage attempt, U-571 and U-575 had made a stealthy approach and were lining up to deliver the *coup de grâce* to the two crippled tankers. Möhlmann and Heydemann were in for a nasty surprise, however. *Havelock* had raised the alarm, and the corvettes *Godetia* and

Pimpernel came racing in with depth charges flying. The U-boats beat a hasty retreat.

*

It was a fine, warm morning, with a gentle south-easterly breeze and a calm sea disturbed only by the ever-present Atlantic swell. Under any other circumstances Captain John Andrews would have enjoyed pacing the bridge of the *Empire Lytton* watching the coming of dawn. But his ship was part of a convoy in a state of chaos. The four remaining tankers were zig-zagging independently, while their naval escorts anxiously hovered around them. In addition, Andrews was painfully conscious that he and the forty-seven men under his command were stranded on top of 12,500 tons of extremely inflammable high-octane aviation spirit, while an unknown number of hostile U-boats were lurking in the pre-dawn darkness. He was also aware that he had not slept for seventy-two hours, stank of stale sweat and was sprouting a three-day growth of beard. However, as the U-boats appeared to have withdrawn, he decided it was safe to go below, even if only for a quick wash. He left the bridge in the capable hands of Chief Officer Alfred de Baughn and Third Officer Parr.

Captain Andrews had not been in his cabin for more than a few minutes, not even long enough to splash cold water on his face, when Hans-Joachim Hesse manoeuvred U-442 into position and fired his torpedoes. Andrews wrote in his report:

> I felt the shock from the explosion which was not very loud, sounding like the rending of metal. No flash was seen, and I do not think any water was thrown up. The foc'sle head had a big bulge of about 5ft, there was a hole 10ft long by 4ft broad in each bow, the fore hatch was blown in and tons of fuel oil were blown over the bridge. The fore hold and cofferdam flooded rapidly as the collision bulkhead forward was shattered . . . The stem of the ship was twisted, and the deck in way of the fore hatch was corrugated. The plates on the port side were bent outwards for about 6ft from the ship's side and the windlass was cracked.

The *Empire Lytton* appeared, in fact, to have escaped with only moderate and superficial damage. Hesse's torpedo had gone home in her forward bunker tank, containing heavy fuel oil which did not ignite. Had she been hit in one of her cargo tanks, she would have flared up like a gigantic torch. As it was, she failed to catch fire at all, and her crew were able to abandon ship. All would have been saved, had it not been for an outbreak of panic, which resulted in one lifeboat capsizing. Chief Officer de Baughn and thirteen others lost their lives.

When daylight came and it was found that the *Empire Lytton* was still afloat and not on fire, Andrews took his men back on board. The tanker was intact on deck, but an inspection of the engine room revealed that she would be unable to steam at more than 6 knots. This was not fast enough for Commander Boyle, who ruled that she must be abandoned again and left to drift. Later that morning, U-442 torpedoed her again, but once more she refused to catch fire or sink. Hesse was forced to waste another of his torpedoes in finally disposing of the tanker before darkness closed in.

*

While TM 1 was being systematically destroyed, 100 miles to the north-west *Oberleutnant* Fritz Schneewind was disconsolately scanning the horizon from the conning tower of U-511. The Type IXC was stationed at the northern end of *Delphin*'s patrol line, and so far her only contact with the convoy had been through listening to radio signals sent out by the attacking U-boats. Twenty-six-year-old Fritz Schneewind, after three Atlantic patrols in U-506, assumed command of U-511 on 18 December 1942, sailing out from Lorient on the 31st of the month. His orders were to join the *Delphin* Group in the waters between the Canaries and the Azores. This he did with keen anticipation, only to find himself posted at the tail end of the patrol line set up to ambush TM 1 and with little chance of being actively involved.

Coincident with U-511's departure from Lorient, Elder Dempster's motor vessel *William Wilberforce* left Takoradi, on West Africa's Gold Coast, bound Liverpool with a cargo of ground nuts, palm kernels, timber, palm oil and rubber. The 5,000-tonner, built on the Clyde in 1930, was under the command of Captain John Andrew and had a crew of fifty, which included six naval gunners. She also carried twelve passengers, company officials and missionaries returning home on leave from West Africa.

In following the time-honoured route to the north and joining a convoy at Freetown, the *William Wilberforce* would have expected to reach Liverpool within fourteen or fifteen days. But for reasons not explained to Captain Andrew she was instructed to proceed unescorted to Hampton Roads on the American eastern seaboard to join a convoy for Halifax, Nova Scotia. There she would wait for a suitable eastbound convoy for Liverpool. This convoluted route involved an extra 4,500 miles steaming, a minimum of fifteen more days at sea and perhaps an equal amount of time lost in port waiting for convoys to form, and might seem to be exposing the ship to unnecessary risks. The only plausible explanation was that the Admiralty wished to keep the waters north of the Canary Islands clear for convoys servicing Operation Torch.

Having zig-zagged her way diagonally across the Atlantic, on 9 January the *William Wilberforce* was some 500 miles west of the Canaries when she sailed straight into the net cast by the *Delphin* Group, most of whom were busy attacking Convoy TM 1. Had the British ship been further to the west, she might have passed undetected, but she was close enough to the *Delphin* patrol line for U-511 to catch sight of her mastheads shortly before sunset.

Delighted that he had at last made contact with the tanker convoy – or so he thought – Fritz Schneewind hauled ahead of the unidentified ship and set course to intercept her. It was fully dark when he approached his target, which was clearly visible in the light of the moon. He fired a spread of two torpedoes from his bow tubes.

Eighteen-year-old Apprentice John Bradbury, on watch on the bridge of the *William Wilberforce,* later wrote:

> At about 8 pm the ship was struck by 2 torpedoes on her starboard side. I was on the bridge with the chief officer and four others when it happened and, being on the starboard side, I was knocked out by the explosion. Fortunately, the water pouring over me brought me round pretty quickly as within a few seconds the ship started to list and about ten minutes later she sank.
>
> At first I thought I had been abandoned as I was alone on the bridge. My second thought was to get to a lifeboat. The starboard lifeboats had been blown away in the explosion, so the passengers and some of the crew boarded the

two remaining lifeboats on the port side. These were low-ered into the sea and the rest of us scrambled down rope ladders and lifelines swung over the side.

The lifeboat I was in stood off the sinking vessel and the U-boat surfaced. The U-boat commander asked us the ship's name and where she was sailing from and to. He then asked where the captain was and we said we didn't know (he was under a tarpaulin so the Germans wouldn't take him). When he asked what cargo we had been car-rying one of us shouted back, 'Peanuts'. For the moment things were a bit tricky as the commander retorted, 'I have guns trained on you – don't be impertinent!' But that's what we called groundnuts. However, he gave us our position, promised to report the sinking, and submerged.

The two lifeboats were adrift 490 miles due west of the Canary Islands and just under 900 miles from the African mainland. The Admiralty's advice to those cast adrift in lifeboats in this area was to head west to take advantage of the prevailing winds and cur-rents, with the eventual certainty of ending up in the West Indies. In theory, this was all very well, but the nearest land to the west lay 3,500 miles away. Given that a heavy wooden ship's lifeboat, even under the most favourable conditions, sails like a disabled crab and is unlikely to average more than 50 miles a day, this could involve up to two months at sea. The boats being completely open to the elements and containing only limited food and water, many of their passengers might die.

After due consideration, Captain Andrew decided that if they were to have any chance of survival they must sail east to the Canaries. His decision was reinforced when it was discovered that somewhere along the way most of the emergency rations in both boats had been stolen. They were already short of food.

By pure luck, after five days' sailing and rowing eastwards the boats were sighted by the Spanish steamer *Monte Anabel*, and the survivors were taken on board. They were landed in Las Palmas, Gran Canaria where, surprisingly, they received a very cool recep-tion. Apprentice Bradbury wrote:

> The local authorities there would not allow us ashore, so we went on to Tenerife. Here we were placed under armed guard and marched through the streets which

looked pretty unfriendly to us. We were marched beneath an arch bearing the swastika, which was scary, but to our great relief, we ended up at the British Consulate. It was 8 days since the sinking.

There is a sad postscript to this story. The survivors of the *William Wilberforce* eventually arrived in Gibraltar, where a number of them, including Bradbury, boarded another of Elder Dempster's ships, the *Mary Slessor*, bound for Liverpool. Early in the evening of 7 February 1943, a few hours after sailing from Gibraltar, the *Mary Slessor* hit a mine and sank. John Bradbury survived, but thirty of the *Mary Slessor*'s crew lost their lives, and with them went Chief Officer Joseph Jones and Second Officer John of the *William Wilberforce*.

*

Back with the ravaged Convoy TM 1, Captain John Andrews watched from the deck of the corvette *Saxifrage* as his late command, the *Empire Lytton*, disappeared astern. As he turned away to go below, he saw a flash, followed by clouds of black smoke mushrooming up from the horizon astern. U-442 had returned to torpedo the *Empire Lytton* again. This time the tanker caught fire and began to sink.

When *Saxifrage* rejoined TM 1 late on the 9th, the convoy was in a desperate state. It now consisted of just three tankers, the *British Dominion*, the *Vanja* and the *Cliona*, around which Boyle's four-strong escort force hovered protectively. Beyond them was a ring of twelve hungry U-boats, hidden beneath the waves and waiting for the opportunity to strike again. Desperate to prevent the fuel reaching the Allied armies in North Africa, Admiral Dönitz had called in every available U-boat in the area. Equally determined to get through, the remaining tankers had abandoned their zig-zag and were steaming all out for the safety of British waters. With light variable airs barely ruffling the calm sea and only a slight swell running, they had worked up to 10 knots, still not fast enough but a reassuring improvement on the previous convoy crawl.

Throughout that night and much of the next day the U-boats continued to harass their prey, closing in from time to time to loose off their torpedoes at the fleeing tankers but each time repulsed by the depth charges of the escorts. No hits were scored by either side.

After dark on the 10th, in an attempt to throw off the pursuit, Commander Boyle ordered a bold alteration of course to the south-east, resuming the north-easterly course at 2130. For a while it seemed that the ruse had worked, then, at 2140, with the convoy 120 miles to the north-west of the Canaries, Herbert Schneider's U-522 again slipped through the screen and fired a spread of three torpedoes at the tankers.

It was unfortunate for *British Dominion* that she happened to be in the line of fire. The first of Schneider's torpedoes struck in her pump room, directly below the bridge, while the second and third went home simultaneously in her engine room and the adjoining No.9 cargo tank, which contained a quarter of a million gallons of high octane fuel.

Captain Miller, who was on the bridge of the tanker, was knocked unconscious by the blast, and when he came to his clothes were on fire and his ship was burning furiously around him. The only other person then remaining on the bridge was Canadian-born Third Officer Phillip Harris, who used his jacket to smother the Captain's burning clothes before jumping overboard. Miller made to follow him, but when he looked over the side he saw the sea was covered in blazing petrol. Harris had jumped to his death.

Miller then went down to the main deck, where he found First Radio Officer Norman Hooper. The two men went to the starboard side of the ship and met up with six ratings who appeared from the forecastle. With their help they tried to launch a life-raft from the rigging, but it was jammed fast. Captain Miller wrote in his report:

> On looking over the side I saw the sea along the starboard side was free from flames back as far as the mainmast, owing to the ship still having way and there appeared to be a reasonable chance of escaping from the starboard side. I saw the starboard midship lifeboat still apparently intact. We all went up to the bridge deck by way of the ladder from the fore and aft gangway and proceeded to lower this starboard boat. However, we found that the after fall had been burnt through between the reel and the lowering cleat, so I gave orders to let the forward fall go with a run at the same time the after fall was thrown off the pin, allowing the boat to fall bodily into the water.

Fortunately it fell at an angle stern-first taking the strain of the forward fall and painter, thus pulling the boat into a fore and aft position, enabling the boat to tow by the painter. The ship was still making between 4 and 5 knots so we put the scrambling net over the side and 7 of us climbed into the boat, the 8th man slid down the lifeline.

Having been towed by the ship for about fifteen minutes through a sea of flame, the survivors cast off and rowed clear of the ship. They then dropped astern to look for other survivors. Whilst they were doing this, the corvette *Godetia* arrived and came alongside the lifeboat. Miller's report continues:

Seven men got out of the boat on to the corvette and just as I was about to follow them the corvette made a contact on a submarine. The painter of the boat had been accidentally released, and thinking all the men were safely aboard the Commanding Officer went full speed ahead to attack. I was still in the boat hanging on to a breast rope and was pulled overboard, but luckily succeeded in getting my arm through the mesh of the scrambling net which was still hanging over the side. The corvette quickly gathered speed with me still hanging on the net until someone saw my plight and stopped the engines and I was hauled aboard.

Captain Miller, whose face and neck were badly burned, was in a state of complete exhaustion when he reached *Godetia's* deck, but his concern was still for his crew. He persuaded Lieutenant Pierce to go back to look for more survivors. Eventually, seven men were found in the water. Of the *British Dominion's* total complement of fifty-three, only fifteen had survived. Miller concluded his report to the Admiralty with words of praise for the men under his command:

I would like to bring to your notice the gallant actions of some of my crew. The 3rd Officer was aged about 21, a Canadian, had he not put the fire out on my clothing I should probably never have regained consciousness and would have burnt with the ship. Unfortunately this man dived into the burning sea and was not seen again. Gunlayer Hawkins behaved with magnificent cool courage in organizing and leading the party of men swimming about in the water, keeping them away from the fire and keeping up their spirits until the rescue ship arrived. This saved the lives of at least two of the crew who were in difficulties, unfortunately one of these men died.

All the crew behaved exceedingly well throughout the numerous attacks. The Chief Officer was on the bridge during the worst attacks being at all times cool, and calmly altering course as if he was carrying out a manoeuvre. 2nd Officer G.M. Jackson who was gunnery officer, kept his guns' crews alert and ready for action, seldom leaving his post and sleeping by his gun throughout the voyage. He opened fire twice with the 4" gun on submarines on his own initiative and is a thoroughly reliable man. He lost his life while still at his post of duty at the 4" gun.

Deliverance came for the battered remnants of TM 1 on the morning of the 11th with the arrival from Gibraltar of the destroyer HMS *Quentin*, accompanied by the corvettes *Penstemon* and *Samphire*. With a Catalina patrolling overhead, the U-boats were at last forced to withdraw, even though Dönitz had signalled, 'The last two tankers must also fall.' The two tankers in question, *Cliona* and *Vanja*, reached Gibraltar at 0930 on 14th January. There they expected to discharge their cargoes, but so urgent was the need for oil in North Africa that they were ordered to carry on into the Mediterranean, where they were subjected to constant attacks by U-boats and German and Italian aircraft before berthing, the *Cliona* at Algiers and *Vanja* at Oran.

The loss of seven tankers, ninety-seven men and nearly 80,000 tons of fuel was a serious blow to the Allied cause, since by this time British supplies of oil in North Africa were down to a mere 7,000 tons. So decisive had the victory been for the U-boats that General von Arnim, Commander of the Afrika Korps, sent a message of congratulation to Admiral Dönitz thanking him for the substantial contribution the *Delphin* boats had made to the battle on the African Front.

Epilogue

In the Second World War, Hitler's U-boat menace came perilously close to severing Britain's ocean supply lines. Had this happened, within a few short months the island nation would have faced starvation and, eventually, surrender. The threat was lifted only by the ferocious defence of the convoys put up by the Royal Navy's little escort ships and by the extraordinary tenacity of the merchant seamen who, despite the fearful odds they faced, came back voyage after voyage, determined to get their cargoes through. Of these dark days Winston Churchill wrote:

> Amid the torrent of violent events one anxiety reigned supreme. Battles might be won or lost, enterprises might succeed or miscarry, territories might be gained or quitted, but dominating all our power to carry on the war, or even keep ourselves alive, lay our mastery of the ocean routes and the free approach and entry to our ports.

The turning point in the North Atlantic came with the sailing of the westbound convoy ONS 5 from Liverpool in April 1943. Forty-two merchant ships were accompanied by the British Escort Group EG.B7, consisting of two destroyers, a frigate, four corvettes and two armed trawlers. Between 28 April and 6 May ONS 5 came under attack by thirty U-boats and lost thirteen ships. The U-boats also suffered grievously, with seven of their number sunk and eight so damaged that they were forced to return to base. Neither side was justified in claiming victory, but history sees the battle for ONS 5 as the beginning of the end of the domination of the sea lanes by Hitler's U-boats. After the war, Admiral Dönitz wrote in his memoirs:

> The enemy lost 12 ships with a total tonnage of 55,761 tons, but we had to mourn the loss of seven U-boats. Such high losses could not be borne. Notwithstanding the fact that 12 ships had been sunk I regarded this battle as a defeat.

Even after this serious setback, Hitler still decided to continue to send U-boats into distant waters. Operation *Monsun* (Monsoon) began at the end of June 1943, with eleven Type IX boats, accompanied by a supply boat, setting out to round the Cape of Good Hope into the Indian Ocean. By arrangement with the Japanese, they were to set up a base at Penang, from where they would operate against Allied shipping trading with India and the Persian Gulf, much of which was then sailing unescorted. The rewards promised to be great.

Only five of the twelve U-boats that had set out from Biscay reached the Indian Ocean, the rest being sunk along the way. Others followed over the next six months, but the operation proved so costly, with very few Allied ships sunk in return, that it was called off.

In the year ending 31 December 1943, the U-boats succeeded in sinking two and a half million tons of Allied shipping in all areas of operation; still very significant, but a mere third of the previous year's harvest. In this same period, Germany lost 238 U-boats and 10,000 men. The Allies had not yet won the war at sea, but the tide was on the turn.

Bibliography

Books

Bennett, Ralph, *Ultra and Mediterranean Strategy 1941–1945*, Hamish Hamilton, 1989

Blair, Clay, *Hitler's U-boat War*, Vols. 1 & 2, Weidenfeld & Nicholson, 1997 & 1998

Bryant, Arthur, *The Turn of the Tide 1939–1943*, Collins, 1957

Burn, Alan, *The Fighting Commodores*, Leo Cooper, 1999

Carruthers, Bob, *The U-boat War in the Atlantic*, Vol. 2, Pen & Sword Books, 2011

Cave Brown, Anthony, *Bodyguard of Lies*, W.H. Allen, 1986

Churchill, Winston, *The Second World War*, Vols. 2 & 3, Cassell & Co, 1950

Costello, John and Hughes, Terry, *The Battle of the Atlantic*, Collins, 1977

Falls, Cyril, *The Second World War*, Methuen & Co, 1948.

Findlay, Alexander George, *North Atlantic Memoir*, Richard Holmes Laurie, 1979

Haldane, R.A., *The Hidden War*, Robert Hale, 1978

Hampshire, A.C., *Lilliput Fleet*, William Kimber, 1957

HMSO, *The Battle of the Atlantic*, HMSO, 1946

Hoyt, Edwin P., *U-Boats*, McGraw-Hill Book Co, 1987

Kelshall, Gaylord T.M., *The U-boat War in the Caribbean*, US Naval Institute Press, 1994

Lund, Paul and Ludlam, Harry, *Atlantic Jeopardy*, Foulsham, 1990

Mallmann Showell, Jak. P., *U-boats Attack!*, Spellmount, 2011

Mallmann Showell, J.P., *U-boats Under the Swastika*, Ian Allan, 1973

Mason, David, *U-Boat*, Macdonald, 1968

Metzgen, Humphrey and Graham, John, *Caribbean Wars Untold*, University of West Indies Press, 2007

Middlebrook, Martin, *Convoy*, Quill, 1976

Middlemiss, Norman L., *The British Tankers*, Shield Publications, 1995

Nolan, Liam and Nolan, John E., *Torpedoed*, Belleview Publications/ Trafford Publications, 2007

Padfield, Peter, *Dönitz – The Last Führer*, Castle & Co, 1985

Parker, Mike, *Running the Gauntlet*, Nimbus Publishing, 1994

Poolman, Kenneth, *Focke-Wulf Condor, Scourge of the Atlantic*, Macdonald & Janes, 1974

Rohwer, Jürgen, *Axis Submarine Successes 1939–1945*, Patrick Stephens, 1983

Smith, David J.B., *Being Silent They Speak*, Stand-Easy, 2012

Stern, Robert C., *Type VII U-boats*, Caxton Publishing, 1998

Terraine, John, *Business in Great Waters*, Leo Cooper, 1989

Thomas, David A., *The Atlantic Star 1939–1945*, W.H. Allen, 1990

United States Navy Dept., *Sailing Directions for the West Coasts of Spain, Portugal, and Northwest Africa and Off-Lying Islands 1942*, Hydrographic Office, 1942

Veranov, Michael and McGeoch, Angus, *The Third Reich at War*, Siena, 1998

Waller, Allan Lansley, *Dawn Will Always Break*, Waller, 1997

Whitehouse, Arch, *Subs & Submariners*, Doubleday & Co,1961

Williams, Andrew, *The Battle of the Atlantic*, BBC Worldwide, 2002

Williamson, Gordon, *Wolf Pack*, Osprey Publishing, 2005

Other Sources

Daily Telegraph

Imperial War Museum

National Archives, Kew

Royal Navy Submarine Museum

Sydney Morning Herald

31st Anti-Submarine Group Gibraltar

www.uboatarchive.net

www.convoyweb.org.uk

www.uboat.net

www.warsailors.com

www.wikipedia.org

Index